"My one purpose in life is to help people find
a personal relationship with God, which,
I believe, comes through knowing Christ."

—BILLY GRAHAM

Billy Graham

GOD'S AMBASSADOR

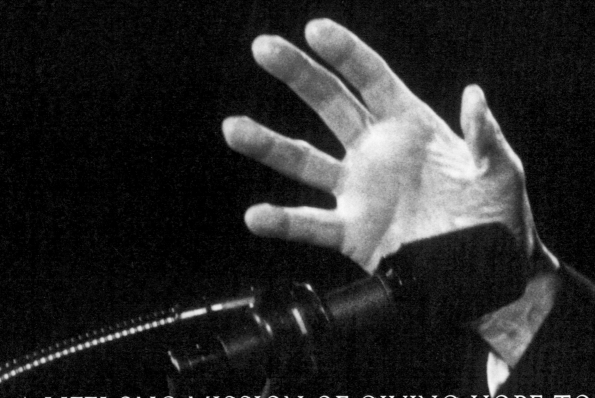

A LIFELONG MISSION OF GIVING HOPE TO THE WORLD
AS WITNESSED BY PHOTOGRAPHER RUSS BUSBY

Billy Graham
Evangelistic
Association

W PUBLISHING GROUP™
A Division of Thomas Nelson, Inc.

TEHABI BOOKS

ACKNOWLEDGMENTS

The idea to publish this book was first considered in the mid-1980s, when Billy remarked that the best record of his entire ministry was the pictures that had been taken over the years. While photographing much of his life, I had also made it a priority to obtain tapes or copies of his speeches. Even so, I realized a book could only be a glimpse into a very busy man's life, as God has opened so many doors for Billy. Although it's impossible to name the many people who helped with this project over the years, I would like to thank the late Jim Collier of World Wide Pictures; the BGEA Minneapolis office staff; the Montreat office staff, especially Evelyn Freeland, Stephanie Wills, Elsie Brookshire, and Dr. John Akers, who supplied and confirmed much of Billy's material; and my staff in BGEA's photo department—Carolyn Jones, Becky Johnson, and my assistant, Earl Davidson, who runs our office. I am especially grateful to my wife, Doris, who spent much time typing and retyping late into the night. I thank Chris Capen, Tom Lewis, and their entire staff at Tehabi Books, who have worked with me to bring excellence to this project. Most of all, I am grateful to Billy, Ruth, and the entire Graham family for so kindly granting me "just one more picture" much of their life. Thank you all. —RUSS BUSBY

W PUBLISHING GROUP™

www.wpublishinggroup.com
A Division of Thomas Nelson, Inc.
www.ThomasNelson.com

TEHABI BOOKS

Copyright © 1999 Billy Graham Evangelistic Association
Minneapolis, MN 55403

All rights reserved under International and Pan-American Copyright Conventions. No part of this publication may be reproduced, stored in a retrieval system, or transmitted in any form or by any means, electronic, mechanical, photo-copying, recording, or otherwise, without the prior written permission of the Billy Graham Evangelistic Association.

ISBN 0-8499-4365-5

CIP data available upon publication from:
Tehabi Books
4920 Carroll Canyon Road
San Diego, CA 92121

Printed and bound in Korea through
Dai Nippon Printing Company

Billy Graham: God's Ambassador was organized, designed, and prduced by Tehabi Books in conjunction with BGEA. *Tehabi*—symbolizing the spirit of teamwork—derives its name from the Hopi Indian tribe of the southwestern United States. As an award-winning book producer, Tehabi works with national and international publishers, corporations, institutions, and nonprofit groups to identify, develop, and implement comprehensive publishing programs. Tehabi Books is located in San Diego, California. www.tehabi.com

Chris Capen, President and Publisher
Tom Lewis, Senior Vice President
Sharon Lewis, Vice President, Finance and Administration
Andy Lewis, Vice President, Development
Sam Lewis, Vice President, Technology
Tim Connolly, Director, Sales and Marketing
Marty Remmell, Director, Trade Relations
Nancy Cash, Editorial Director
Sarah Morgans, Editor
Mo Latimer, Project Manager
Maria Medina, Administrative Assistant
Curt Boyer, Production Artist
Kevin Giontzeneli, Production Artist
Tiffany Smith, Executive Assistant
Clayton Carlson, Consultant
Gail Fink, Copy Editor
Laura Georgakakos, Copywriter
Laurie Gibson, Copy Proofer
Denise McIntyre, Copy Proofer
Maddy Hanes, Transcription Assistant

Tehabi Books offers special discounts for bulk purchases for sales promotions or premiums. Specific, large quantity needs can be met with special editions, including personalized covers, excerpts of existing materials, and corporate imprints. For more information, contact: Eric Pinkham, Director of Corporate Publishing and Promotions, Tehabi Books, 4920 Carroll Canyon Road, Suite 200, San Diego, CA 92121, (800) 243-7259 www.coffeetablebooks.com

PHOTOGRAPHY CREDITS

Except as noted below, the photographs used in this book were taken by Russ Busby while on assignment for the Billy Graham Evangelistic Association (BGEA).

Note: Letters refer to the position of the photo on the page, beginning from left to right and proceeding from top to bottom.

Associated Press: 82a
Austin, Ike: 251b
Bettman Archive, Ltd.: 41ab, 72, 84a, 85
BGEA Archive: back cover bc, 6–7, 42b, 43, 47a, 49abc, 50abc, 52, 53, 55, 56–57, 60ab, 61a, 63, 64b, 73abcd, 75bc, 76abc, 77, 78, 79b, 80b, 81ac, 82bc, 84cd, 87b, 92ab, 95a, 97, 110, 127b, 132c, 157g, 184b, 193def, 194e, 199b, 200f, 208a, 212a, 213ab, 223ad
Billy Graham Training Center at The Cove: 254ab
Blau, Tom: back cover d, 67a, 69a, 70b
Bruce Sifford Studio: 61b
Capa, Cornell, Magnum Photos: 86, 90, 91b, 95b
Chicago *Tribune*: 217b
CP Photo: 194d
Damadian, Dr. Raymond, courtesy of: 125c
Davidson, Earl: back cover a, 98, 117b, 122c, 135a, 164a, 229f
Glenn, June Jr.: 70c, 180a
Graham, Billy and Ruth, personal collection: 28, 29, 30abc, 31ac, 32bc, 33, 34ab, 35a, 36, 37, 38ab, 39a, 40abc, 46b, 48, 54ab, 66, 67b, 68c, 69b, 70a, 71, 74, 87a, 171, 172a, 174a, 175b, 176abc, 177ab, 178a, 183c, 186b, 200d, 234ab, 235a, 238bc, 246
Graham, Franklin: back flap, 21
Graham, Melvin, courtesy of: 31b
Gustafson, Roy: 195a
Impact Photo: 93
International News Photo: 75b
Karlson, Russell G.: 39b
Kelly, Colleen, courtesy of: 121b
Kemsley House: 83b
Keystone Press Agency, International: 64a, 79
Kregger, Paul: 222b
Lederhaus, Dick: 163d
Life magazine, Lomis Dean: 44
Life magazine, Edward Clark: 46a
Life magazine, John Dominis: 59
London *Daily Mirror*: 80
Los Angeles *Times*: 181a
Lundberg, Ake: 130b
Mari, Arturo: 199f
Munn Studio: 58b
Muse Photo Bureau: 62
New York Times: 96
News of the World: 81
Osthus, Bob: 249acd
Ray, Jean Luc: 245a, 250a
Samaritan's Purse: 276a, 276c, 277a
Scottish Sunday Press: 83a
Shirley, Clifford: 261a
Smyth, Walter: 195d
Sunday Mirror, Joseph Costa: front flap, 45, 97
Thomas Airviews: 94
U.S. Air Force: 223bc
Valdez, David (White House): 187a
Vetter, Rudy: 172d
White House: 170b, 178b, 179c, 182a, 185a, 186a, 189
Whittingham, Dick: 8–9, 47b, 51
Wilson, M. L.: 68b

> *"In 1956, as we began to set up the BGEA photo department, it was amazing to discover that good professional quality photos were already available from all major events in Billy's life prior to that time, including his Bible school days. There was no doubt in our minds that God had sent these professionals to document Billy's early ministry. Across the years other photographers have also supplemented our work. As such, we have tried to credit everyone for their labor, often of love."*
> —RUSS BUSBY

Contents

"Billy then realized more
than ever that he had
a purpose, a call.
His letters, which had always
been serious, now began to
show even more clearly
that he had but one passion:
to preach the Gospel."

—MORROW GRAHAM,
BILLY'S MOTHER

SHAPING A LIFE

When God called
Billy Graham to be
an evangelist, he
never looked back.

"I read Ephesians again and again, where it mentions that the Lord gave some to be evangelists and some to be pastors. God just did not want me to be a pastor. It was time to take up what the Lord called me to do—evangelism."

—BILLY GRAHAM

A LIFETIME MINISTRY BEGINS

The Los Angeles tent meetings in 1949 began in mid-September and saw Billy Graham preach eight weeks to more than 400,000 people.

"I have had the privilege of preaching the Gospel on every continent in most of the countries of the world. And I have found that when I present the simple message of the Gospel of Jesus Christ, with authority, quoting from the very Word of God— He takes that message and drives it supernaturally into the human heart ."

—BILLY GRAHAM

MILLIONS OF LIVES CHANGED

The 1996 Charlotte crusade in Billy's hometown attracted over 75,000 people to its closing night.

"Everywhere I go
I find that people—
both leaders and individuals—
are asking one basic question:
'Is there any hope for the future?
Is there any hope for peace,
justice, and prosperity
in our generation?'"
—BILLY GRAHAM

INSPIRING OTHERS

Billy Graham greeted President and Nancy Reagan in Washington, D.C., during the National Prayer Breakfast in February 1981.

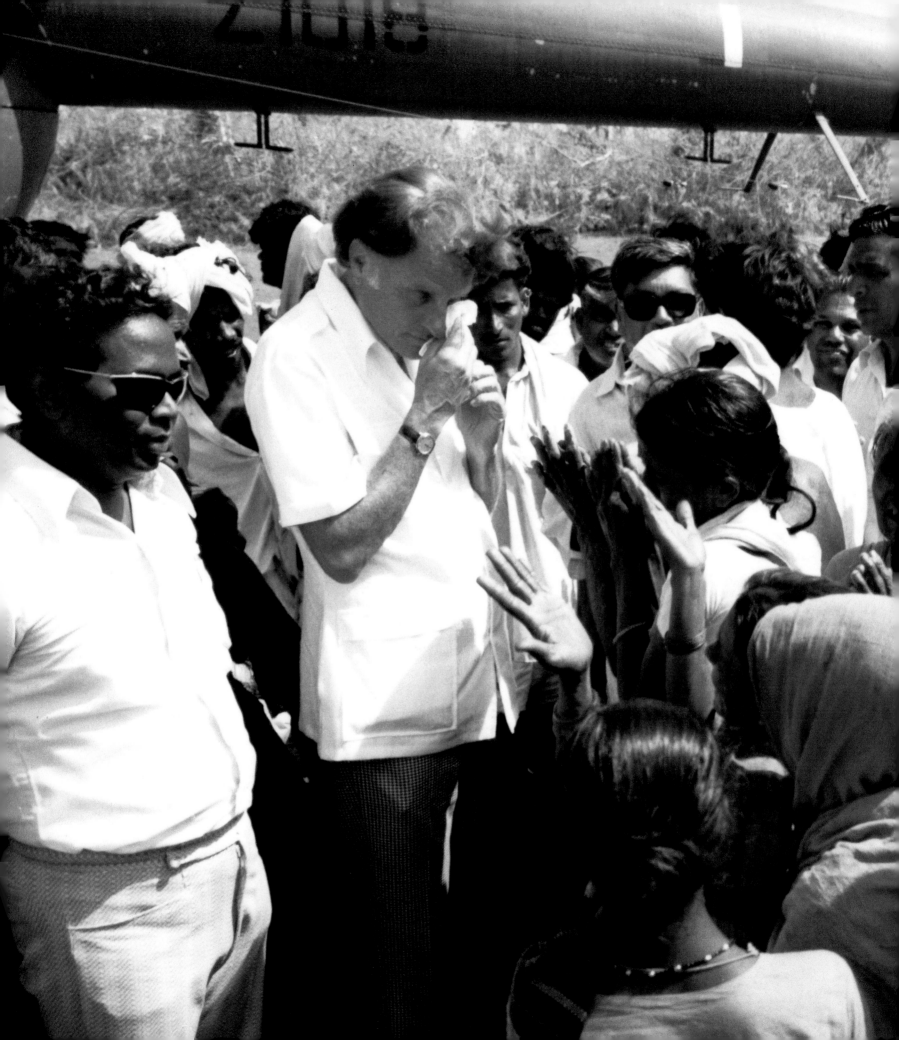

"As Christians we have a responsibility toward the poor, the oppressed, the downtrodden, and the many innocent people around the world who are caught in wars, natural disasters, and situations beyond their control."

—BILLY GRAHAM

REACHING OUT TO A BROKEN WORLD

When tidal wave survivors from various villages greeted Billy Graham in Andhra Pradesh, India, he was moved to tears—and to take action through the BGEA World Emergency Relief Fund.

*"Ruth and I were called
by God as a team.
She urged me to go, saying,
'God has given you
the gift of an evangelist.
I'll back you.
I'll rear the children
and you travel and preach.'
. . . I'd come home
and she had everything
so organized and
so calmed down
that they all seemed
to love me.
But that was because
she taught them to."*

—BILLY GRAHAM

**REFLECTIONS
FROM HOME**

Billy Graham's
struggle was to
strike a balance
between his work
and home so that
his children didn't
grow up hating
the ministry.

"I realize that my ministry would someday come to an end. I am only one in a glorious chain of men and women God has raised up through the centuries to build Christ's church and to take the Gospel everywhere."
—BILLY GRAHAM

A CONTINUING MINISTRY

Started in a single-room office in Minneapolis, Minnesota, in 1950, the Billy Graham Evangelistic Association has reached more than one billion people.

THE MAN, THE MINISTRY, AND THE MESSAGE

Through four decades, I have been privileged to document with a camera most of the events in Billy Graham's life and ministry. From my first assignment in 1956 to Billy's most recent meeting in 1999, I have witnessed and recorded the many unusual opportunities he has had to share his faith with others. I also have made a special effort to gather his messages and collect documents covering his ministry. From this unique vantage point I am convinced that there are three key reasons why God has used Billy Graham.

First, Billy is truly humble before both God and man. He is the same caring individual in private as he is in public.

Second, Billy's motives have always been right before God; they have not been self-serving.

Third, Billy spends time in God's Word—the Bible—not just to preach to others but to understand what God has to say to him and to guide his life by its truth.

I believe the only way to explain Billy's success is simply that God chose Billy Graham to represent Him at this particular time in history. Billy is one in a long line of God's servants, as we can all be in our own way if we listen to and obey Him.

—RUSS BUSBY

◄

Billy emphasized a point from the Bible at the 1962 Chicago crusade.

"He has walked with royalty and received unprecedented media attention for over four decades but is still something of a small-town boy, astonished that anyone would think him special. In a profession stained by scandal, he stands out as the clearly identified exemplar of clean-living integrity. In a society divided by divorce, he and the wife of his youth have reared five attractive and capable children, all of whom are faithful Christians. He is, in short, an authentic American hero."

—BILL MARTIN,
AUTHOR OF
A PROPHET WITH HONOR:
THE BILLY GRAHAM STORY

The Man

When Billy Graham was born, no one could ever have predicted the unique path he would one day follow. He was born to a typical American family on a farm outside a small southern town. Those who knew him then described him in the usual ways: nice kid, good boy, spirited, typical, average. Nothing special. Even at the moment—and there was a particular moment—when he heard God calling him, little seemed to change. He dated girls, played baseball, did his chores, and grew up.

How, then, did he become the Billy Graham known today around the world? Quite simply, he did what he has asked millions to do: He made a decision for Christ and began to follow Him. It was not always an easy decision. Being God's messenger has required personal sacrifice, time away from home and family, missing special moments with his wife and children. It required the help of parents, in-laws, and a whole team of dedicated people. But for Billy Graham, there was no other choice. God called and he answered:

"I have often said that the first thing I am going to do when I get to heaven is to ask, 'Why me, Lord? Why did You choose a farmboy from North Carolina to preach to so many people, to have such a wonderful team of associates, and to have a part in what You were doing in the latter half of the twentieth century?' I have thought about that question a great deal, but I know also that only God knows the answer."

. . .

"Suppose you had all the knowledge in the libraries, all the power of the world's leaders, all the gold in the world, all the sex you wanted. What would all that profit you if you lost your soul? The soul must really be worth something if it's worth more than that—and God thought it was worth sending His Son to die for."

. . .

"I'm counting totally and completely on the Lord Jesus Christ, and not on Billy Graham. I'm not going to heaven because I've read the Bible, nor because I've preached to a lot of people. I'm going to heaven because of what Christ did."

"I believe that in each generation God raises up certain people He can trust with success. I would put Billy in line with the Wesleys and Saint Augustine and Francis of Assisi. He's in that league. And what's extraordinary is that he doesn't seem to know it. He doesn't want a Graham church. He is more interested in sharing the load than in grabbing the limelight. He wants to be a servant of the Church, to challenge and spark the churches to be what they must become: the evangelizing agents of God and His Word. But there's no doubt about it: he is the most spiritually productive servant of God in our time."

—REVEREND MAURICE WOOD,
BISHOP OF NORWICH AND
MEMBER OF BRITAIN'S
HOUSE OF LORDS

TheMAN

"I am not a great preacher, and I don't claim to be a great preacher. I've heard great preaching many times and wished I was one of those great preachers. I'm an ordinary preacher, just communicating the Gospel in the best way I know how."
—BILLY GRAHAM

"*People do not come to hear what I have to say—they want to know what God has to say.*"
—BILLY GRAHAM

"I was among the friends who a decade ago urged Billy to give up strenuous crusades and spend more time writing and perhaps teaching. It's the only time I have seen the man agitated. 'No,' he said. 'My call is to preach the Gospel, and I will do that as long as God gives me the breath to preach.'"
—CHARLES (CHUCK) COLSON, FORMER COUNSEL TO PRESIDENT NIXON AND FOUNDER OF PRISON FELLOWSHIP

The Ministry

Whether he speaks to a single individual or a television camera that reaches thirty million, Billy's ministry is and always has been targeted toward one goal—calling each person to make a decision to follow Christ, and to do it today:

"The great crowds themselves are meaningless. The thing that counts is what happens in the hearts of the people. The evangelist sows the seed, and much inevitably falls upon stony ground and bears no fruit. But if only a few seeds flourish, the results are manifold. After three and a half years of preaching to the thousands of people, Christ could number only 120 followers at Pentecost. But those 120 changed the world."

• • •

"Innocent people around the world are caught in wars, natural disasters, and situations beyond their control. The Bible teaches that we have a Christian duty to help our neighbors in their time of need. We are called by God to bring the water of life for both soul and body. God created them both, and His purpose is to redeem them both."

• • •

"Jesus said, 'I am the way, the truth, and the life; no man comes to the Father but by me.' On the surface, that seems the most intolerant of statements. Think of any man on the stage of human history claiming to be the supreme embodiment of all psychological, scientific, and religious truth! He was either an egomaniac, a liar, or He was what He claimed to be. By faith I accepted Him for what He claimed to be, the Son of the Living God. That simple decision changed my life—and I have seen it change the lives of countless others across the world."

• • •

"I believe that the Bible is a living Word. And I believe that the quoted Word of God is a sword in my hand. If I stick to the Bible and preach the principles and the teachings of the Bible, and quote the Bible, it has an impact of its own."

• • •

"Martin Luther was reading his Bible when God spoke to him and it changed the course of history. You come back to the Bible. Begin to read it. Study it and God will speak to you and change you—and through you perhaps history can be changed."

"These people coming forward at a crusade were not responding to a man. They certainly were not mesmerized by the small figure of Billy Graham standing at the edge of the platform. There was no fever pitch of emotion in the crowd. Something far greater was at work. In Ruth's words, 'It isn't a culture or a personality responding to a program or a man, but the soul responding to the God who created it.'"
—JULIE NIXON EISENHOWER, FROM HER BOOK SPECIAL PEOPLE

The **MESSAGE**

"Have you ever wondered why God put you on earth, what is the purpose and meaning of life? It is to know Him, and to know His love."

—BILLY GRAHAM

The Message

For more than fifty years, Billy has preached a single, simple message: the Word of God. From turbulent war years through decades of civil unrest and assassinations to the brink of a new and uncertain millennium, Billy's message has never changed:

"God is a God of love, a God of mercy. He loves you. He has the hairs of your head numbered. He knows all about you, and He wants to come into your life and take away that loneliness. He wants to come into your life and give you new hope and new assurance, no matter what your condition."

· · ·

"On a specific day marked on the earth's calendar, and in a specific place on the earth's map, the Son of God came to the planet. It was love."

· · ·

"When we approach the Bible as history and biography, we approach the Bible in the wrong spirit. We must read the Bible, not primarily as historians seeking information, but as men and women seeking God."

· · ·

"The devil is the god of this world and he has blinded our eyes. You can be the most brilliant person in the whole world, but you will never discover God that way. You can have religion but not know Christ. It's having Christ that counts."

· · ·

"We all have a terminal disease far worse than cancer, that will kill us morally and spiritually. It's called sin."

· · ·

"Sooner or later we must leave our dream world and face up to the facts of God, sin, and judgment. The Bible says, 'All have sinned and come short of the glory of God' (Romans 3:23)."

· · ·

"I believe there is an actual, literal heaven. I believe there's an actual, literal hell. Don't ask me where and don't ask me what it's going to look like and all of that. I don't know. I only know that Jesus warned us about one and told us of the joys and the happiness of the other."

· · ·

"The greatest need in the world is the transformation of human nature. We need a new heart that will not have lust and greed and hate in it. We need a heart filled with love and peace and joy, and that is why Jesus came into the world. He died on the cross to make peace between us and God and to change us from within by His Spirit. He can change you, if you will turn to Him in repentance and faith"

"Billy Graham has no hidden agendas. He's not an emissary for any government. He's not an emissary for any organization; he's only an emissary for God."
—SIR DAVID FROST

CHAPTER ONE

SHAPING A LIFE

Deep down inside I knew something was different," Billy remembered. "I actually wanted to read my Bible. I wanted to tell others what had happened to me."

It happened at a revival meeting in Charlotte, North Carolina, near the teenager's home. The touring evangelist, Mordecai Ham, was preaching to four thousand souls in a makeshift, sawdust-floored tabernacle. As he made his appeal, and while the congregation sang "Almost Persuaded," Billy Graham went forward to register a decision that would forever direct his life.

"I didn't have any tears, I didn't have any emotion, I didn't hear any thunder, there was no lightning . . . but that's when I made my decision for Christ. It was as simple as that."

That evening, upstairs in his bedroom, by the side of the bed, Billy dropped to his knees and prayed, "Oh God, I don't understand all of this. I don't know what's happening to me. But as best as I can figure out, I have given myself to you."

Despite his new dedication, it took some time before Billy would fully understand all that was happening to him. But it didn't dull his enjoyment of life or his enthusiasm for racing his father's car along North Carolina back roads. Some even accused him of being "too worldly." Billy gave little thought to a career of preaching. "The last thing I wanted to do was be a preacher," he said later.

Yet he was fascinated by preachers. He listened to them raptly, and even imitated and practiced several pulpit styles in front of a mirror at home. But joining their ranks was not something he considered seriously.

While visiting the city jail in Monroe, North Carolina, in the company of

◀

In the late 1930s Billy stood next to a handmade sign in front of a small Florida church. The $3 sign cost more than the week's offering brought in.

"Frank was very tall and dark and had lovely wavy hair, almost black. He had a good singing voice and sang in the choir in our church. All the girls were wild about him, and when he drove his buggy down the street, he had the prettiest, high-stepping horse in Charlotte. I prayed about Frank because I wanted that man! He was something special. But at the time we were married, neither one of us could be called a dedicated Christian."
—MORROW GRAHAM,
BILLY'S MOTHER

Jimmy Johnson, a young evangelist, Billy nervously described his new faith for the first time to his captive audience. "Jesus changed my life! He gave me peace and joy. He can give you peace and joy! He will forgive your sins as he forgave mine if you will only let Him in your heart! Jesus died so that sinners might be forgiven, have their lives transformed, and find peace with God." This central theme of his preaching hasn't changed since.

For some months he struggled with God's calling for his life. Then, one night in 1938, while attending Florida Bible Institute near Tampa, Billy faced the moonlight, the breeze, and the rest of his life. On a nighttime walk around the golf course, an inner, irresistible urge caused him to sink to his knees and sob, "Oh God, if you want me to serve you, I will. I'll be what you want me to be. I'll go where you want me to go."

No sign in the heavens. No voice from above.

Yet in his spirit, Billy knew he had been called to preach and his answer was yes.

He had to preach.

"My mother was a woman who worked with her hands. You know, the day I was born she picked beans all morning and I was born about four o'clock in the afternoon. In Proverbs it says 'she . . . worketh willingly with her hands.' During the depression years she worked out on the farm as well as keeping books and answering the phone because my father and his brother Clyde had a little dairy. I remember when milk went down to five cents a quart how worried they were as to whether they could make it or not."
—BILLY GRAHAM

▼
Frank Graham, Billy's father, had the prettiest, high-stepping horse in town.

▲
William Franklin Graham, Jr. (Billy) was born in the downstairs bedroom in this frame farmhouse on November 7, 1918, three days before his father's thirtieth birthday. His parents called him Billy Frank.

◄
Billy, at age six months, posed with his mother for his first photo.

Billy, age seven (right), and his sister Catherine loved spending time with their father.

Growing Up on a Dairy Farm

On November 7, 1918, four days before World War I ended, Morrow Coffey Graham gave birth to a baby boy in a farmhouse on Park Road near Charlotte, North Carolina. She and her husband, dairy farmer William Franklin Graham, named the boy William Franklin Graham, Jr. and called him Billy Frank.

Billy Frank's roots ran deep into Southern soil. His two grandfathers, Crook Graham and Ben Coffey, had fought for the Confederacy in the Civil War. Graham carried a miniball, fired from a Yankee muzzle-loading gun, in his leg the rest of his life, and Coffey had only one leg and one eye as the result of wounds suffered during Pickett's charge at Gettysburg.

Billy grew up on the family's three-hundred-acre dairy farm and helped the hired hands milk seventy-five cows early each morning and again after school. This left him little time for foolishness. Full of energy, he became a bulldozer, a mountain goat, a tornado, and an angel in bewildering succession. A day came when Morrow Graham's heart could no longer bear the strain of his hyperactivity, and she hustled Billy Frank off to the doctor. "Billy just isn't normal," she explained. "He's got too much energy. He never runs down." "Don't worry," the doctor assured Mrs. Graham. "It's the way he's built." His diagnosis was a forecast of things to come.

Billy loved to read novels for boys. He especially loved the Tarzan books and often hung from trees in the yard, giving his version of the Tarzan yell, frightening the wits out of passing horses and drivers. "I think that yelling helped develop his voice," his father said later.

One of his school bus drivers said, "Every afternoon when Billy got off the bus with the other boys, he would reach underneath and turn the shutoff valve to the gas tank. I would go about a hundred yards and the engine would sputter out. I'd get out and shake my fist at him, but he'd only give me the laughing yah-yahs. It made him a hero to the other kids, and I couldn't really get mad at the skinny so-and-so."

Billy graduated from Sharon High, a small country school. His grades were average, nothing to boast of. His report cards reflected the fact that he worked so hard—and so early—on the farm that he sometimes fell asleep in class. He loved to read history and he had a deep, abiding love for sports, especially baseball. One of his great boyhood thrills was shaking hands with Babe Ruth. Billy dreamed of becoming a professional baseball player but he was not quite good enough at the sport.

As Billy matured, the prayers of his parents—that God would somehow direct their spirited young son—were about to be answered.

This photo of Billy's younger brother Melvin, (age three), was featured in ads for the Graham dairy.

Billy, the oldest of four children, held his younger sister, Jean.

▼

At the Graham dairy farm, Billy was up at three o'clock in the morning to help the farmhands milk the family's seventy-five cows.

▲

When Billy was nine, the dairy had so prospered that the family moved into a larger, two-story, brick Colonial house. For Billy and his younger brother and two sisters, the best thing about it was indoor plumbing. They no longer had to bathe in a washtub on the back porch.

►

Billy's yearbook expressed his hopes and plans— in his own handwriting: "My hopes and plans for the future is to serve God and do His will as a minister of the Gospel."

A Decision That Changed His Life

The Grahams attended the Associate Reformed Presbyterian Church in downtown Charlotte. "I don't ever remember not going to church," Billy said. "If I had told my parents I didn't want to go, they would have whaled the tar out of me." Billy said later, "I couldn't stand going to church until I accepted Christ as my Savior." But he did not rebel. Like it or not, he went along every Sunday.

The turning point in Billy's life came around Billy's seventeenth birthday, in the fall of 1934, when evangelist Mordecai Ham of Louisville, Kentucky, held a three-month-long revival meeting in Charlotte at the invitation of many of the city's churches.

At first Billy refused to go, but a few weeks into the meetings a friend, Albert McMakin, gathered a group of local youths and took them to the service in his pickup truck. Night after night Billy attended, becoming acquainted with Grady Wilson, and later his brother T.W., both of whom would become lifelong friends and associates. Finally one night Billy knew the time had come for him to make his personal commitment to Christ; he went forward at the evangelist's invitation on the last verse of the final hymn.

In the spring of 1936, Billy graduated from Sharon High School. During the summer, he, Grady, and T.W. Wilson got their first real experience dealing directly with the public. To earn money for college, they joined under the management of Albert McMakin to sell Fuller brushes door-to-door in South Carolina. Before summer's end, Billy was outselling all of them.

"In Billy Graham's thinking at that time, his hero was Babe Ruth. Our meeting changed his hero from Babe Ruth to Jesus Christ."
—MORDECAI HAM

REV. M. F. HAM
LOUISVILLE, KY.
Evangelist, Bible Teacher and Lecturer.

The Ham-Ramsay Evangelistic Campaigns

Bible Teaching ✦ Soul Winning
Church Enlistment

METHODS AND PURPOSE

▲

When Billy was seventeen, evangelist Mordecai Ham came to Charlotte to hold a revival.

"When my decision for Christ was made I walked slowly down and knelt in prayer. I opened my heart and knew for the first time the sweetness and joy of God, of truly being born again. If some newspaperman had asked me the next day what happened, I couldn't have told him. I didn't know, but I knew in my heart that I was somehow different and changed. That night absolutely changed the direction of my life."
—BILLY GRAHAM

Bible School and First Sermon

In January 1937 Billy Graham enrolled in the Florida Bible Institute in Temple Terrace, near Tampa. Always a lover of sunshine and the great outdoors, Billy began to blossom in Florida.

Academically, the Institute emphasized individual instruction. It aimed to give a thorough grounding in the Bible with courses in related subjects. The dean, John Minder, had an exceptional gift for encouraging students, and he zeroed in on Billy Graham. He encouraged Billy and gave him his first preaching assignment.

"Billy then realized more than ever that he had a purpose, a call," his mother said. "His letters, which had always been serious, now began to show even more clearly that he had but one passion: to preach the Gospel—the Good News."

Several events occurred at the school that left an imprint on him and helped shape his later ministry. The first was when a Christian leader whom Billy admired was accused of moral indiscretions—falsely, Billy was certain. Billy was shaken and determined that nothing would be allowed in his life to bring shame to the name of Christ. The second was a school policy of inviting many prominent Christian leaders who came to lecture and preach, people like evangelist Gipsy Smith, Homer Rodeheaver, W. B. Riley, and William Evans. Thus, Billy had early exposure to some of God's great men and women of that time.

◄

Young Billy Graham posed with two of his teachers, John Minder (left) and Cecil Underwood. On Easter Sunday evening, 1937, Minder took his young student to visit Bostwick Baptist Church, a country church near Palatka, Florida. On the way, Minder said, "Billy, you are preaching tonight." "No sir," Billy replied, "I've never preached before." "Well, you are tonight," the teacher said emphatically. "When you run out, I'll take over." Billy faced a sparse congregation of cowboys and ranchers. His attack was loud and fast. He had secretly memorized four sermons, each to last forty-five minutes. He used up all four in eight minutes and sat down.

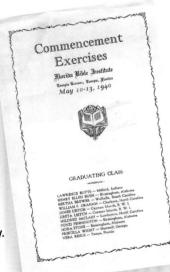

Commencement Exercises
Florida Bible Institute
Temple Terrace, Tampa, Florida
May 10-13, 1940

GRADUATING CLASS

LAWRENCE BUTTS — Milford, Indiana
HENRY ELLEN BUSH — Birmingham, Alabama
BERTHA BREWER — Walhalla, South Carolina
WILLIAM F. GRAHAM — Charlotte, North Carolina
JAMES LEITCH — Cayman Islands, B. W. I.
GRETA LEITCH — Cayman Islands, B. W. I.
MILDRED McCLAIN — Lumberton, North Carolina
FONZI PENNINGTON — Birmingham, Alabama
NORA STONE — Hartwell, Georgia
PRISCILLA WIGHT — Hartwell, Georgia
VERA REHM — Tampa, Florida

◄

Billy attended Florida Bible Institute in Temple Terrace, near Tampa, Florida,

The MAN

"Dean Minder had told me, 'You learn to preach by preaching. Go out to a mission. Stand on street corners. Be on fire for God's Word, and maybe you'll kindle a fire in your audience.' One Sunday morning, as I read the Bible text to a country audience, I came across the words Mene, Mene, Tekel, Upharsin, and mispronounced them so badly that Roy Gustafson, who had brought along his Florida Bible Institute Trio, laughed out loud. Every mistake I made drove me to correct it, but some of the most important ones I recognized only in retrospect."

—BILLY GRAHAM

Ordination to the Ministry

During Billy's time at Florida Bible Institute, God laid a heavy burden on his heart, a burden to serve Him. It was in March 1938, when Billy, returning from his nightly walk, stopped on the eighteenth green of the golf course near the school and sat on the edge of the green. There he surrendered to the call to preach. "Oh, God," he cried, "if you want me to preach, I will do it." The tears streamed down his face as he made his final commitment.

Late in 1938, when Billy was nineteen years old, he preached his first revival at East Palatka Baptist Church. A friend and teacher, Cecil Underwood, pastored the church. In the midst of the revival, Underwood casually asked Billy about his Baptist upbringing. "I'm a Presbyterian," Billy said. Presbyterian baptism meant sprinkling, not immersion. "If my deacons learn you're not a Baptist," Underwood said, "there'll be such an uproar we may have to stop these meetings."

Billy was deeply concerned. He prayed long and hard about what he should do, and when he arose from prayer in his room, God had helped him decide. He telephoned his mother and asked her to approve his changing of denominations. When she consented, he went to the meeting the next evening and told the audience that he was a Presbyterian but wanted to become a Baptist. He asked for membership in the Peniel church and requested baptism. Late in 1938, Billy and Cecil Underwood waded into Silver Lake near the Peniel church, and Underwood baptized him before a crowd of three hundred onlookers.

In 1939 Billy was ordained a Baptist minister at Peniel Baptist Church by Pastor Cecil Underwood for the St. John's River Association. In May 1940, at twenty-one, he graduated from Bible school.

Peniel Revival Begins Tonight

Services Will Be Held Each Night for Two Weeks

Billy autographed this portrait to his mother: "To the Dearest One in the World to Me—Mother."

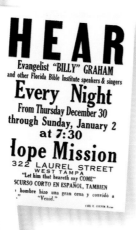

8 GREAT DAYS of REVIVAL MEETINGS

will be conducted at the **Pomona Baptist Church** by the students of **The Florida Bible Institute** of Tampa, Florida and sponsored by the Peniel Baptist Church The Young People of Peniel will sing each evening accompanied by Instrumental and Vocal Numbers by the Bible Institute Young People.

BILLY GRAHAM WILL BE THE EVANGELIST

—and—

THE SONG LEADER WILL BE **Ponzi Pennington**

Billy Graham, an outstanding 19 year old evangelist who recently conducted a wonderful revival in East Palatka is to preach each evening at 7:30.

A SPECIAL YOUNG PEOPLE'S SERVICE WILL BE CONDUCTED FROM 7:00 TILL 7:30; AND A CHILDREN'S MEETING AT 4:00.

EVERY EVENING AT 7:30

FLORIDA C.E. NEWS PRINT

HEAR Evangelist "BILLY" GRAHAM and other Florida Bible Institute speakers & singers

Every Night From Thursday December 30 through Sunday, January 2 at 7:30

Hope Mission 322 LAUREL STREET WEST TAMPA "Let him that heareth say COME" SCURSO CORTO EN ESPAÑOL, TAMBIEN hombre hizo una gran cena y convidó a "Venid."

CARL H. COFFIN, Pastor

▶ Billy preached his first revival at the East Palatka Baptist Church.

Billy Graham, the young 19-year-old evangelist and student of the Florida Bible Institute, is causing quite a sensation at the East Palatka Baptist church in the revival meeting now in progress, according to Cecil Underwood, pastor of the Peniel Baptist church whose young people are sponsoring the revival.

Young Graham does not mince words when he tells church members that they are headed for the same hell as the bootlegger and racketeer unless they get right and live right, Underwood said.

"The trouble with many churches in Florida is that they have become filled with people who care no more for God than the devil himself and that the average citizen does not go to church, because the church has nothing to offer him. What we need is a back door revival to empty our churches of the unholy element—a

College and a Wife from China

"Dear God, I prayed, all unafraid
(as we're inclined to do)
I do not need a handsome man
but let him be like you;
I do not need one big and strong
nor yet so very tall,
nor need he be some genius
or wealthy, Lord, at all;
but let his head be high, dear God,
and let his eye be clear,
his shoulders straight,
whate'er his state,
whate'er his earthly sphere;
and let his face have character,
a ruggedness of soul,
and let his whole life show,
dear God,
a singleness of goal;
then when he comes
(as he will come)
with quiet eyes aglow,
I'll understand that he's the man
I prayed for long ago."
—Ruth Bell, written in 1939
before she met Billy

While war clouds gathered on America's horizons in 1940, Billy enrolled at Wheaton College, just outside Chicago. The intellectual atmosphere of Wheaton was unlike anything Billy had known before. It stimulated him, it increased his intensity—and his opportunities multiplied.

"It was no accident that my boy chose Wheaton," Billy's mother said. "He was prayed into that place."

Billy expected to be accepted at Wheaton as a senior or, at worst, a junior. However, after examining his diploma and credits, the school's administration solemnly informed Billy that they could give him credit for only one year's work. He would have to enroll as a sophomore. Billy was disappointed, but responded, "That'll be okay."

For his major course of study at Wheaton, Billy chose anthropology.

At Wheaton, Billy met Ruth McCue Bell, who had been born in northern China. Her father, Dr. L. Nelson Bell, was a Presbyterian missionary-surgeon from Virginia who had helped build and develop a large missionary hospital in Tsingkiangpu (now part of Huaiyin). Dr. Bell described his daughter as "an interesting mixture of deep spirituality and mischievous fun."

Billy fell in love at first sight. He just could not believe anyone could be so beautiful and so sweet.

Billy wrote to his mother that this was the girl he would marry. Ruth had not fallen in love with Bill, as she calls him, yet that very first Sunday night she knelt at her bedside and "told the Lord that if I could spend the rest of my life serving Him with Bill, I would consider it the greatest privilege imaginable."

After their graduation from Wheaton, they were married on Friday, August 13, 1943, at the Presbyterian conference center in Montreat, North Carolina, where Ruth's parents had settled after leaving China. After a short honeymoon in the resort town of Blowing Rock, North Carolina, Billy and Ruth returned to Chicago.

"While in Florida, preaching in Dr. Minder's church, I got a thick letter from Ruth postmarked July 6, 1941. One of the first sentences made me ecstatic, and I took off running. 'I'll marry you,' she wrote. . . . That night I got up to the pulpit and preached. When I finished and sat down, the pastor turned to me. 'Do you know what you just said?' he asked. 'No,' I confessed. 'I'm not sure the people did either!'"
—BILLY GRAHAM

◄

Ruth's satin wedding gown was not store-bought; she made it with the help of a local seamstress. To maintain its perfect smoothness, Ruth stood as best she could in the back seat of her father's car during the drive from home to Gaither Chapel. No bride ever walked down an aisle with fewer wrinkles in her dress.

◄

Billy thought Ruth was the woman God had long been preparing to stand beside him. Her intelligence, practicality, wit, determination, and wholehearted love for Jesus Christ attracted him to her —not to mention that she was the campus beauty! Ruth could see Billy was a man who had a purpose, a dedication in life, and he was a man who knew God. She said, "He was a man in a hurry who wanted to please God more than any man I'd ever met!"

First Pastorate

Billy had offered himself as an army chaplain just after Pearl Harbor was bombed by the Japanese, December 7, 1941, pulling America into global war. But before he could be accepted, he was told to finish college, and he would have to fulfill a requirement of one year in the pastorate.

He secured his first and only pastorate at Village Baptist Church in Western Springs, Illinois, twenty miles outside Chicago, and on his first appearance there the entire congregation of thirty-five souls gathered in the church to welcome him. Because of finances only the basement had been completed, and the church (according to Ruth) was difficult to find—in summer because of weeds and in winter because of snow.

The little church in Western Springs began to grow. The church people enjoyed Billy's sermons, were amused by his loud socks and ties, and were gratified by Ruth's poise and smartness despite her limited wardrobe.

The quiet little suburban church found it had hired a whirlwind for a minister, a man who threw his extraordinary energy at all the problems relative to developing the church. Billy organized house-to-house calls on uncommitted residents, telling everyone, "Bring your neighbors. Knock on doors. Invite people to come. We'll treat them real good."

Billy was well worth the $45 per week his congregation paid him.

With Bob Van Kampen, a church elder, Billy launched the Western Suburban Professional Men's Club. He personally persuaded business executives of highest rank and tightest schedules to come and meet over dinner. Soon he had more than three hundred men coming to hear an evangelistic speaker every month.

The **MAN**

"As newlyweds in a first pastorate, Ruth and I were pretty typical lovebirds, I guess. We took hikes in the sunshine and in the rain, especially enjoying the arboretum nearby. On rare occasions, I went golfing and Ruth caddied for me."
—BILLY GRAHAM

◄

The young pastor and his wife enjoyed walking to his church.

"We followed Ruth and Billy's marriage with concern and interest. Concern because Billy's dedication was of such intensity that I, as his mother, wondered if he could maintain the pace he was carrying. By this time he was pastor of the Village Church in Western Springs, and he became the speaker on the radio program Songs in the Night.

We couldn't get the program on our house radio, so Mr. Graham and I sat in the car and tuned the radio dial until the station came in loud and clear. Then we sat back marveling and we'd say to each other, 'Imagine, that's our Billy Frank.'"

—MORROW GRAHAM

First Radio Ministry

Those nearest Billy realized that his vision was larger than a local pastorate, and they were not surprised when he agreed to become speaker on a weekly, forty-five-minute program called *Songs in the Night* on Chicago's powerful WCFL Radio. With the financial help of his church, Billy started broadcasting in January 1944. He was twenty-six.

For soloist on the radio program Billy hired thirty-seven-year-old bass baritone George Beverly Shea, a local celebrity in Christian circles. He was already a radio headliner on ABC's *Clubtime*, a program of hymns. "I'd Rather Have Jesus," a song for which Bev had written the music, was being sung by Christians everywhere.

Having fulfilled the requirements for his chaplaincy, Billy was commissioned a second lieutenant in the army and was instructed to await orders for entry to a chaplains' training course at Harvard Divinity School. However, Billy came down with a severe case of mumps that put him in bed for six weeks, during which time Ruth feared for his life as his temperature soared and he became delirious.

Because of the illness, Billy could not undertake the chaplaincy course, and the army's chief of chaplains granted him a discharge since the war's end was in sight. He then resigned as pastor of the church in Western Springs, and became the first full-time evangelist for Youth for Christ.

▼
Popular soloist George Beverly Shea became a regular performer on Billy's first radio program.

▼
The Grahams all came home to the farm to meet Billy's bride. Standing from left to right: brother Melvin, the smiling bridegroom, Sam McElroy (Catherine's husband). Seated: Ruth, Billy's father, Jean, Billy's mother, and Catherine.

Youth for Christ

A young preacher in Chicago named Torrey Johnson was forming Youth for Christ (YFC), an international evangelistic movement among young people.

Johnson heard Graham on the radio and realized that here was exactly the kind of young people's preacher he had been looking for.

To spearhead this work, Billy became YFC's first field representative. His salary would be $75 a week, plus expenses.

For those connected with YFC the priorities were twofold: first, to draw a crowd, and second, to deliver God's message. They used all the gimmicks that reason would allow: famous athletes, stunts, music. They promoted their sessions with fervor, trying to reach as many young people as possible. Invariably, the rallies outgrew the churches for which they were designed and eventually were moved into municipal auditoriums and ballparks.

Ruth settled temporarily with her parents in Montreat, North Carolina. This move was a godsend. It provided a close bond between the Bells and Billy, allowing the budding evangelist the wise counsel and friendship of Dr. Bell, and it provided a support system for Ruth and the five little Grahams who would begin arriving in short order.

In September 1945, the first bundle of joy arrived. Ruth gave birth to a baby girl whom they named Virginia Leftwich, for Ruth's mother. The Bells gave the child a loving nickname, Gigi, Chinese for little sister.

Billy dreaded leaving each time but felt God had provided a happy home for his new little family, and realizing they were secure in God's care, he was able to go with peace of mind.

Billy traveled 200,000 miles in that first year with Youth for Christ, beginning a lifetime of frequent trips that would take him away from home. He spoke in forty-seven states to rallies of up to 20,000, mostly young people, with more than 7,000 making decisions for Christ.

In his inevitable hurry to get from one place to another, Billy almost lost his life when one airliner he rode went down for a forced landing in a snowfield in the Canadian Rockies.

Crisscrossing the country for Youth for Christ, holding rally after rally, Billy eventually held one close to home, at Ben Lippen School and Conference Center in Asheville, fifteen miles from Montreat. At that rally, the song leader was absent and a young Californian on his honeymoon, Cliff Barrows, was asked to lead the singing. "When we met," Cliff said, "Billy looked at me with a smile. He grabbed both of my hands and said, 'No time to be choosy!'" It was the start of a lifelong ministry together.

INTERDENOMINATIONAL

YOUTH FOR CHRIST

EVERY SATURDAY NIGHT

FIRST BAPTIST AUDITORIUM
FOURTH & TAYLOR STS.   2,000 FREE SEATS

★ Sparkling Singspiration   ★ Timely Testimonials
★ BILLY GRAHAM, Chicago, Speaker

"Remember NOW thy Creator in the days of thy youth."
Ecc. 12:1

CHRIST FOR YOU?

ADMIT ONE
SAT. NOV. 10, 1945
7:15 P.M.

Broadcast Over KABC, 7:30-8:00

▼
Cliff and Billie Barrows were on their honeymoon when Billy asked Cliff to lead some songs.

▶
Ruth kept up with her husband's whereabouts from postcards like this one, which could be mailed anywhere in the United States for one cent.

"Leaving the church left only one thing to settle. Me. What was I going to do? It wasn't practical to start hiking all over the country with him. We broke up our Hinsdale home with no trouble. No heartache. We tossed our pots and pans into the backseat of the car and drove off. We didn't own a stick of furniture. For the first time we decided to call Montreat home. So I moved in temporarily with my parents."
—RUTH GRAHAM

▼
Ruth showed off the Grahams' first child, Gigi.

A Visit to Great Britain

Early in 1946, just after World War II, Billy made his first trip to Great Britain. He was chosen as preacher on a team that did a three-week whirlwind tour of England, Scotland, and Ireland to establish Youth for Christ in Great Britain.

Billy came home mesmerized with his first look at England. He prayed about going back, feeling a heavy burden for her people; he longed to see a revival of faith in the war-torn nation.

Youth for Christ could not sponsor another trip so quickly, so Billy set about raising money for his return trip. Soon he had enough for a frugal six months in England, and he contacted his newfound friend, Cliff Barrows, and asked if he and his wife, Billie, would join him. They accepted immediately and Ruth later joined them for part of the trip.

For six months Billy and Cliff preached all across Great Britain, speaking in twenty-seven cities and towns, at 360 meetings, between October 1946 and March 1947. A David-and-Jonathan bond was forged between the two men.

Gradually some of the flamboyance went out of their delivery. They became slightly less brash and noisy, and both realized an evolution was taking place in their thinking. About the fifth month, Billy said to Cliff, "Maybe instead of one-day rallies, God will lead us back to our country to hold some one-week meetings. Maybe even two. Pray with me about it."

▲

Post-war Britain in early 1946 was so devastated that Billy felt called to return.

▶

Billy and Ruth spent six months preaching in war-torn England with Cliff and Billie Barrows.

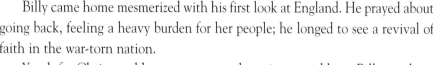

The MAN

"Britain in those days was dark and grimy. Food was still rationed. No cleaning fluids were available, so clothes were still dirty from the war. The blackouts and brownouts continued, so at night everything was pitch black. Also, it was the coldest winter in a hundred years, and little fuel was available. However, the spirit of the people was not only remarkable, it was fantastic. Their smiles, their faith, and their courage were a lesson that I will never forget."

"We started in Wales. We slept with our clothes on and ate tomatoes stuffed with bread. We had meetings in churches so filled with fog you couldn't see the balcony."

—BILLY GRAHAM

Northwestern Schools

Ruth continued to live with the Bells until the Grahams' second child, a girl named Anne Morrow, was born in May 1948, when the Grahams were able to purchase and remodel a small cottage across the road from Ruth's parents.

In December 1947, at age twenty-nine, Billy agreed to become president of Northwestern Schools in Minneapolis, Minnesota. T.W. Wilson (his boyhood friend) became vice president and George Wilson (no relation to T.W.) was the school's business manager.

During his four years as president of Northwestern Schools, the enrollment grew from eight hundred to twelve hundred students. Billy gained valuable experience he would later need in the area of finances, promotion, delegating authority, and building a team of dedicated men who desired to serve God. Billy and his friends Cliff Barrows, George Beverly Shea, and Grady Wilson, then a pastor in South Carolina, worked together on several successful citywide meetings, including one in Billy's hometown of Charlotte, which gave them a real feel for crusade work. T.W. Wilson was always left behind to handle the day-to-day business of running the school, since he was the vice president.

Billy continued to run the school, but was also eager to get the Gospel out to as many people as possible by means of evangelism. Billy and his team members turned their attention more and more to mass evangelism, with meetings in Miami, Baltimore, and Altoona (Pennsylvania). Feeling the crush of too many irons in the fire, as an administrative head of a school, vice president of Youth for Christ, and crusading evangelist, Billy confided in a friend, "I have made so many promises, I'll never be able to keep them all."

One of the promises was to Los Angeles, for a three-week campaign to begin in late September 1949.

▲

At twenty-nine, Billy became president of Northwestern Schools, in Minneapolis, Minnesota.

▶

T.W. Wilson and Billy worked closely together as the school's top administrators.

"Give him five minutes and he'll think up enough projects to keep many staffs busy for months."
—LUVERNE GUSTAVSON, BILLY'S SECRETARY AT NORTHWESTERN SCHOOLS

▶

At twenty-seven, Billy resigned his pulpit to go on the road for Youth for Christ. Little did he know that he would soon be preaching in front of hundreds of thousands of people of all ages.

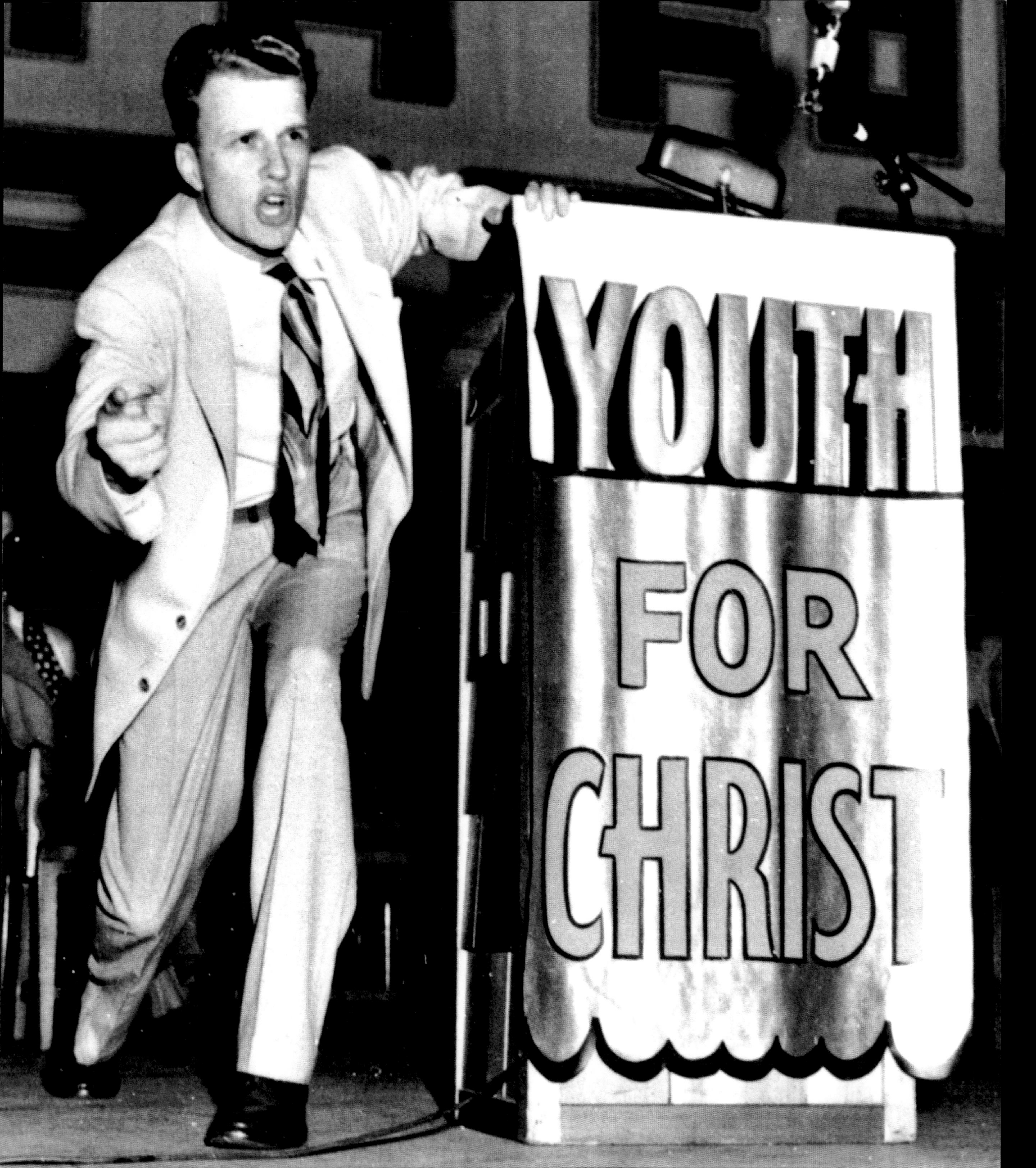
YOUTH
FOR
CHRIST

A NEW EVANGELIST ARISES

BILLY GRAHAM HOLDS A REVIVAL IN LOS ANGELES AND CONVERTS 6,000 OF HIS 300,000 LISTENERS

CHAPTER TWO

A LIFETIME MINISTRY BEGINS

In the late 1940s, Billy attended a conference in California only weeks before his largest crusade to date was to start. Some young theologians were also there, who were expressing their doubts about the authority of the Bible. "Suddenly, I wondered if the Bible could be trusted completely."

Billy began to study the subject intensively, turning to the Scriptures themselves for guidance. "The Apostle Paul," Billy said, "had written to Timothy saying, 'All Scripture is given by inspiration of God.' Jesus himself had said, 'Heaven and earth shall pass away but my Word shall not pass away.' I thought also of Christ's own attitude. He loved the Scriptures, quoted from them constantly, and never once intimated that they might be false."

Billy then recalled the moment that changed him forever. "That night, I walked out in the moonlight, my heart heavy and burdened. I dropped to my knees and opened my Bible on a tree stump. If the issue were not settled soon, I knew I could not go on. 'Oh God,' I prayed, 'there are many things in this Book I do not understand. But God, I am going to accept this Book as Your Word by faith. I'm going to allow my faith to go beyond my intellect and believe that this is Your Inspired Word.' From that moment on I have never doubted God's Word. When I quote the Bible, I believe I am quoting the very Word of God and there's an extra power in it. One month later, we began the Los Angeles crusade."

Los Angeles was Billy's most ambitious effort to date. Advance press coverage was minimal, but that changed as the weeks passed and the extraordinary conversion stories captured the public's attention. Billy was preaching with a new confidence and fervor

◄

The 1949 Los Angeles revival meetings, Billy's first major national media exposure, catapulted his message into the pages of *Life* magazine.

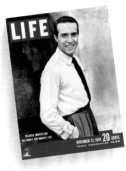

and the meetings continued night after night for eight weeks. "The Los Angeles crusade," Billy recalled, "marked a decisive turning point for our ministry."

Throughout this milestone crusade, Billy firmly believed God was at work. "Something was happening that all the media coverage in the world could not explain," he said. "And neither could I. As Ruth said, 'the credit belonged solely to God.' That was the secret of everything that had happened. God had answered prayer."

▲

Billy was thirty-one years old when the Los Angeles rally pushed him onto the national scene.

The **MAN**

"Since my experience in the mountain woods of the conference center in California, I was no longer struggling internally. There was no gap between what I said and what I knew I believed deep in my soul. I began to sense the presence and power of God that I had not felt for months, and I have not had a doubt about the Bible being God's inspired Word since that time."

—BILLY GRAHAM

◄

Los Angeles was scheduled to run for three weeks but was extended five times to a total of eight weeks.

The Road to Los Angeles

A Los Angeles committee wanted Billy to lead a citywide, old-fashioned tent revival. He told Ruth of this invitation: "That's a real big city, Ruth. Next to New York and Chicago, it's about the most important place in the country. They say they'll put up the biggest tent in the history of evangelism."

Los Angeles—the first turning point in Billy Graham's career was coming up. But first there were things to settle . . .

Billy's early citywide campaigns with Cliff Barrows and Bev Shea in Charlotte, North Carolina, and Modesto, California, in 1948 were somewhat disappointing. The crowds were small and the people coming forward were few.

Acutely aware that the ministry had its weaknesses, Billy and his new team met to discuss the most frequent criticisms of evangelism. Their list narrowed down to four main problems: finances, moral integrity, antichurch sentiments, and no follow-up for the people who made decisions for Christ. Billy determined he would change these things in his evangelistic ministry—and started immediately to do so.

▲

Billy and Grady Wilson worked closely from the start.

▼

Two combined circus tents became the Los Angeles "canvas cathedral."

Billy visited with a group from the Hollywood community, including actors Jimmy Stewart (far right) and Spencer Tracy (far left).

Los Angeles Meetings Extended

The Christ for Greater Los Angeles campaign began in late September 1949 in two old circus tents joined together in a parking lot at the corner of Washington Boulevard and Hill Street in downtown Los Angeles. The "canvas cathedral" held six thousand people.

Counselors in the separate prayer tent, which had a capacity of five hundred, answered every question of every new Christian and passed their names and addresses on to concerned ministers. Billy brought world affairs into the meetings, preaching with a Bible in one hand and a newspaper in the other.

As the three-week campaign moved to a close, some on the committee urged that it be extended one more week. The decision was left to Billy. This situation had never presented itself before and he hesitated. He asked God for clear guidance about continuing the meetings or going home.

Billy believed the sign that God gave him was the conversion of a big Texas cowboy, a local radio celebrity, heavy drinker, and racehorse owner named Stuart Hamblen.

Stuart's wife, Suzy, had taken him to the home of Henrietta Mears, a well-known figure in the Los Angeles Christian community, to meet Billy before the campaign had started. Stuart and Billy, both southerners, liked each other, and Stuart invited Billy to be a guest on his radio show. After the radio interview, Stuart urged his listeners to go down to the tent to hear Billy and blurted out, "I'll be there, too!"

Stuart sat in the front row enjoying the show. But he got uncomfortable as the preaching started, and he soon stomped out of the meeting. He was miserable, going from bar to bar, and finally dragged Suzy out of bed, calling Billy's hotel at 2:00 A.M. to have Billy pray for him.

Billy refused. He knew that Stuart had to make a definite transaction with Jesus—all or nothing—and Billy couldn't do it for him. About 5:00 A.M. Stuart gave way to Jesus Christ and made Him Lord of his life.

Later that morning, Stuart announced to his surprised listeners that he had quit smoking and drinking and would go forward at the tent meeting that night.

Convinced that Stuart's conversation was the sign he had prayed for, Billy extended the Los Angeles crusade.

▲

Stuart and Suzy Hamblen met the Grahams and began a lifelong friendship.

▼

Hollywood quickly came around. Billy and Ruth met movie stars and other prominent people. The Hollywood *Citizen-News* reported that a group of Hollywood moguls offered the thirty-one-year-old evangelist a contract to be leading man in the movies, but Billy turned the offer down, saying he would not accept it for $1 million a month.

Citizen-News

HOLLYWOOD, CALIFORNIA, FRIDAY, NOVEMBER 11, 1949

Section Page 9

'NOT FOR $1,000,000'
Graham Says 'No' to Movies

By VIRGINIA MacPHERSON
United Press Hollywood Correspondent

Dr. William (Billy) Graham, the handsome revival preacher, admitted today a group of Hollywood moguls are trying to make a leading man out of him.

"I laughed in their faces. I wouldn't do it for $1,000,000 a month," says the 31-year-old evangelist, whose tent revival meetings are taking the town by storm.

"If they'd let me make a movie short where I could preach the gospel, I might be interested."

STARS UNHAPPY

But that wasn't exactly what the gents had in mind. They were thinking along other lines. Graham is six-foot-four, with broad shoulders, blue eyes, wavy blonde hair and a beguiling southern drawl. They could see him pitching woo to some luscious movie siren.

"Movie stars are the unhappiest people in the world." Graham said. "I won't tell their names, but I had lunch at a big studio yesterday, and I talked to many of them."

He's talked to a few of the local gangsters, too. Graham particularly has his eye on Mickey Cohen, king-pin of the Hollywood under-

"I've got nothing on my mind to keep me from being social with a preacher. But about going down to his tent like he says . . . I dunno."

Dr. Graham thinks if movie stars will "unburden their hearts to him," gangsters will too.

"These stars thought fame and wealth and public adulation would be the apex of their lives," he said. "But they've found there's nothing to it.

NO MONEY APPEALS

"Now they're caught in the coils of their contracts and their publicity. They want to find the way back. But they don't know how."

Some of them have made a start, Dr. Graham said. A group of big-name stars meet secretly in Hollywood. Sometimes they gather at Jane Russell's house to pray.

Miss Russell is a regular visitor at Graham's revival meetings. Coleen Townsend has been down, too. And so have Connie Haynes, Porter Hall and John Holland.

Graham said he doesn't make any appeals for money and takes it for granted people already believe there is a God.

DR. BILLY GRAHAM
". . . not for a million dollars"

Los Angeles Examiner

Part Two   LOS ANGELES TUESDAY NOVEMBER 1, 1949   PCC

CLASSIFIE
ADVERTIS

Singer Stuart Hamblen Hits Sawdust Trail at Rev

COWBOY
QUITS

NEW YORK TIMES, NOVEMBER 2, 1949

OLD-STYLE RELIGION

Old-style religion is sweeping the city of Los Angeles . . . Graham wears garish ties, argyle socks, and an irresistible grin . . .

▼

Cliff Barrows led the choir while Billy and Bev Shea joined in.

8—3 THE DAILY TIMES HERALD, DALLAS NOV. 2, 1949 ★

Old-Style Evangelism Stirring Los Angeles

Los Angeles, Nov. 2 AP).—Old-style religion is sweeping the City of the Angels with an evangelistic show overshadowing even Billy Sunday.

Since it started six weeks ago, more than 200,000 from the city's 2,000,000 population have filed into a circus te ...

22 Part I—MONDAY, NOV. 14, 1949 *Los Angeles Times

FAITH INSPIRED—Dr. Billy Graham, youthful evangelist, delivers sermon to crowd attending revival meeting in huge tent at Washington Blvd. and Hill St. *Times* photo

Revival Attracts Throng as Eighth Week Starts

A standing room only audience was on hand yesterday as the evangelistic campaign being led by Dr. Billy Graham started its eighth week in the huge tent at Washington Blvd. and Hill St.

At the afternoon service, an estimated 1500 persons of those converted during the revival walked forward to the preacher's platform in response to the invitation. The service and sermon, "How to Lead the Christian Life," were given specifically for converts.

Dr. Graham urged them to join a "good, gospel teaching, Bible believing church" in this area and to work constantly for Christian ideals.

The revival will continue indefinitely, according to the executive committee of Christ for Greater Los Angeles because of the demand of more than 300 local clergymen plus the consistently large throngs in attendance.

Cliff Barrows, song leader who started the campaign with Dr. Graham, will remain here to lead the meetings in hymns. Plans are under way for a meeting of Los Angeles clergy to form a pattern to decentralize the revival effort when the campaign ends.

Revival Tent in Los Angeles Drawing 10,000 Each Night

Los Angeles —AP— Old-style religion is sweeping the City of the Angels with an evangelistic show overshadowing even Billy Sunday.

Since it started six weeks ago, more than 200,000 from the City's 2,000,000 population have filed into a circus tent on the fringe of downtown Los Angeles. They're still pouring in at the rate of 10,000 every night.

They come to hear the preachments of a dynamic, handsome young college president named Billy Graham. Churchmen say he's started the greatest religious revival in the history of Southern California. The revival is conducted by Youth for Christ, a nation-wide interdenominational youth rally movement. In Flint, the affiliate group is known as VCY, or Victorious Christian Youth. Graham conducted a rally at Central High School last February which attracted an overflow audience of young people.

Graham's oratory is eloquent; his doctrines are home-spun. From the singing, shouting multitudes, thousands have hit the sawdust trail and announced publicly their decision to return to Christ.

One of them was a brilliant track star at the University of Southern California before the war. His name is Lou Zamperini. An Air Force captain, he crashed in the Pacific, spent 47 days on a raft, then lived through months in a Japanese prison camp.

"It is difficult for anyone who came through the things I did to forget God, but I did," Zamperini testified.

Another convert is Stuart

Billy Graham

Hamblen, popular cowboy crooner and sportsman, son of a Methodist minister. He stepped to the pulpit to announce that he'll sell his racing stable.

"I will keep El Lobo, but only for sentimental reasons," Hamblen said. "I will never race him again." El Lobo, dubbed "the people's choice," won the $50,000 San Antonio stakes at Santa Anita in 1947.

Hamblen's sentiments are typical: "I've done practically everything everybody else has done. I've been a sinner."

Graham is 30, nephew of North Carolina's Sen. Frank Graham and president of little Northwestern Bible College in Minneapolis. He wears garish ties, argyle socks and an irresistible

▲

News of what was happening in Los Angeles was spreading across America. *Life*, *Time*, *Newsweek*, and the *New York Times* all ran stories on the new evangelist.

▶

Night after night, crowds continued to pack the tent as the momentum of the Los Angeles rally continued to build.

"I had used from twenty-five to one hundred passages of Scripture with every sermon and learned that modern man will surrender to the impact of the Word of God."
—BILLY GRAHAM

Sign of the Times

During the fourth week, as the first extension was nearing an end, Billy arrived at the tent one evening and found the place buzzing with reporters. Flashbulbs popped in his face and reporters seemed to come from every direction, hurling a barrage of questions. When Billy finally asked what was happening, a man said, "You've just been kissed by William Randolph Hearst," owner of a vast newspaper empire. The next morning, Billy Graham and the canvas cathedral were headlines in the Los Angeles papers, accompanied by many thrilling stories of changed lives.

One such story was that of Jim Vaus, an electronics expert and wire-tapper for the notorious gangster Mickey Cohen, described as the czar of the Los Angeles underworld. Another changed life was that of Louis Zamperini, the youngest long-distance runner in the 1936 Berlin Olympics.

The campaign became the topic of all Los Angeles. Many newspapers across the country carried news of the campaign and *Time, Newsweek,* and *Life* magazines all ran articles on the new evangelist.

Crowds pressed into the big tent in such numbers that, despite its enlargement to a capacity of nine thousand, the tent could not contain the people. At some meetings, more people stood outside listening to the loudspeakers than sat in the tent.

The pace took its toll on Billy. He exhausted all of his material and searched desperately for sermon topics. All he could think about was preaching. Ruth had come out to join him and was a valuable assistant in his sermon preparation.

Roy McKeown, vice president of Youth for Christ, said, "Billy was scratching for sermons every day. He was borrowing from everybody!"

▲

Billy (center) and Cliff Barrows (left) welcomed new converts Jim Vaus, Stuart Hamblen, and Louis Zamperini.

"Day after day, we were phoning churches, begging them to bring fifteen people . . . to come and see what was happening."
—REV. ROY MCKEOWN,
VICE PRESIDENT,
YOUTH FOR CHRIST

▼

Dear Billie:
I thank God my wife and I had the privilege of attending the tent meetings. We brought an old friend one night, but he won't come back. The reason he gives is that he does not like the way you kept your handkerchief hanging out of your pocket. I think Billie it would be nice if you pushed it down in your pocket. . . . I know thousands of Christians would feel the same as my old friend. And let all the people say, AMEN!

Lots of Love,
A. Scot

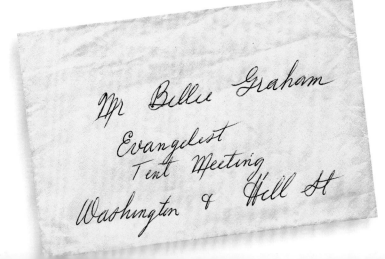

Mr Billie Graham
Evangelist
Tent Meeting
Washington & Hill St

HELD OVER BY POPULAR DEMAND!

6TH GREAT SIN-SMASHING WEEK

IN THE CANVAS CATHEDRAL WITH THE STEEPLE OF LIGHT

AT THE REQUEST OF HUNDREDS OF MINISTERS AND THOUSANDS OF FOLLOWERS THE GREATEST REVIVAL CAMPAIGN IN GREATER LOS ANGELES HISTORY CONTINUES UNTIL FURTHER NOTICE.

FOREMOST EVANGELIST IN HIS GREATER L.A. MEETINGS.

The **MINISTRY**

"Los Angeles taught us many things, among them the power of prayer, the power of the Word of God, but also the power of the press to make God's work known."
—BILLY GRAHAM

BILLY GRAHAM

AMERICA'S FOREMOST EVANGELIST IN GREATER L.A.'S GREATEST REVIVAL

Unprecedented demands by the people of Los Angeles, and definite leadings of the spirit of God have resulted in the continuance of Billy Graham's record-breaking revival meetings for at least another week. Dr. Graham, after much prayer and at great personal sacrifice has agreed. We will not announce a closing date for this great revival. The event is in the hands of Almighty God!

Clifford F. Smith
President—Christ for Greater Los Angeles

SPONSORED BY 1000 GREATER LOS ANGELES CHURCHES

6000 FREE SEATS THOSE WHO COME EARLY

BIG TENT
WASHINGTON AND HILL

His True Mission Is Confirmed

After eight weeks, on Sunday, November 20, 1949, Billy preached his sixty-fifth sermon before sixteen thousand people, and the Los Angeles campaign came to a close.

A Los Angeles minister described the aftermath of the campaign this way: "This city, with its thousands of ministers preaching every Sunday, was going lazily along and the man on the street was unimpressed. Then came Billy Graham. In eight weeks, he had more people thinking and talking about the claims of Christ than had all the city's pulpiteers in a year's time. When the crusade closed, we faced a community that was at least willing to talk about Jesus. My church got a dozen new members, but it got much more: It got new inspiration, zeal, and a spiritual uplift that can never be described."

Going to the railway station, Billy and Ruth were jostled by crowds of well-wishers and besieged by swarms of autograph seekers. At the depot, guards whisked them through gates, giving them the treatment reserved for celebrities. In the Los Angeles crusade they had forfeited their right to comfortable anonymity.

God had done more than anyone had dared to imagine. Billy was exhausted, and as he and Ruth headed to Minneapolis they were not sure whether this was the climax or just the beginning, but they had surely seen God at work.

"One day when the telephone rang it was Billy. He said, 'Mother if you only knew how the Holy Spirit is at work here, you would come.' I wanted to go very much but Mr. Graham didn't want to go up in an airplane! Los Angeles was a world away from the dairy farm."
—MORROW GRAHAM

▼

Billy's mother and father often listened to Billy on the radio at home in Charlotte.

▶

"We felt we were just spectators," Ruth said. "God was doing something, and Billy and I were just watching." Billy was careful to give all the credit to God. It had been God's work. He had only been the instrument. Clasping hands, he and Ruth sank to their knees in prayer as the train pulled away from the station.

"Physically, I wanted the campaign to close. There comes a time when the evangelist becomes physically exhausted. I had lost twenty pounds and my entire dependence had to be from God for messages and for strength. I learned that a strange spiritual law operates. Truly, God's strength is made perfect in weakness. The weaker I became, the more powerful became the preaching."
—BILLY GRAHAM

A nation that takes the risk of peace will get peace just as the nation t

The Bosto

TWENTY-TWO PAGES—FIVE CENTS

Entered as 2nd Class Matter at Boston P O
Copyright. 1950. by Post Pub. Co.

MONDAY, APRIL 24, 1

40,000 HEAR BILL
BIG RALLY ON BO

Huge Crowd Braves Rain and Chill at Greatest Prayer Meeting
Program for World Peace----Calls on President and Congress
Spiritual Regeneration Needed----Thousands Wave Handke

LARGEST THRONG IN HISTORY TO ATTEND A PRAYER MEETING ON HISTORIC BOSTON COMMON
This sweeping panorama shows part of the 40,000 men, women and children who flocked to the Boston Common to hear the Rev. Billy Graham
mon. There was a light drizzle when this picture was made, but the weather cleared shortly afterwards, though on the cool side. The crowd gave
ance Day—in which America would turn to God in repentance for sins. He urged moral and sp

4

t takes the risk of war gets war.—*Ramsay MacDonald.*

n Post | EXTRA

*****   Established 1831   TWENTY-TWO PAGES—FIVE CENTS

Y GRAHAM AT STON COMMON

Common's History as Evangelist Launches Five-Point Declare Day of Repentance for Entire Nation----Says hiefs in Thrilling Demonstration for Peace Efforts

AVES INCLEMENT WEATHER TO HEAR THE REV. BILLY GRAHAM, CRUSADING EVANGELIST
uct his final revival meeting in Boston. Despite the inclement weather the throng was the largest to attend a prayer meeting on the Com-
vangelist a tremendous ovation and he appealed with a call for President Truman and Congress to declare a national "R Day"—Repent-
regeneration to meet God's demands. (Photo by John Hurley, Post staff photographer).

Billy's first engagement after Los Angeles began as an eight-day campaign in Boston's historic Park Street Congregational Church. Billy did not believe that the revival fervor in the Far West would be repeated in staid New England. But after eighteen days, over seventy churches had caught the fire and three thousand people from all walks of life had stepped forward to declare their newfound faith in Jesus Christ!

On January 16, 1950, Boston Garden was packed to the rafters. Sixteen thousand people crammed inside while ten thousand were turned away for lack of seats. In April the team returned for a massive rally on Boston Common.

Unparalleled Opportunities

The year 1950 was significant in Billy's developing evangelistic ministry. The 1949 Los Angeles campaign had brought a swift rise to national prominence, and invitations were coming from everywhere. Beginning with Boston in late December 1949, he preached six campaigns in a year, logging twenty-four weeks of actual nightly preaching.

In swift succession, Billy preached in Columbia, South Carolina; the New England states; Portland, Oregon; Minneapolis, Minnesota; and finally Atlanta, Georgia.

Billy preached to 1.7 million people that year, including a half million each in Portland and Atlanta, with more than 43,000 decisions for Christ being made at the six crusades.

Following Boston, Henry R. Luce, the powerful owner and publisher of the *Time* and *Life* magazine empire, sent word that he was coming to the Columbia, South Carolina, campaign. Luce wanted to personally meet this young evangelist. While a guest in Governor Strom Thurmond's mansion, Billy spent an evening with Luce. The two men talked almost all night, and Luce's magazines became fair and balanced in their coverage of him.

"I knew that this man, Henry Luce, had the power at his fingertips to promote our work internationally," Billy recalled. "My interest lay not in the fact that *Time* and *Life* could give us an incredible amount of coverage, but that they could spread the word of evangelism to the ends of the world."

"I had already announced from the pulpit in Columbia that I would be preaching on judgment and hell. The temptation came very strongly to me that maybe I should switch to another subject. Mr. Luce [the publisher of Time *and* Life *magazines] was a New York sophisticate. It seemed to me to be the least likely way to win his favor. Then, the Lord laid Jeremiah 1:17 on my heart. 'Speak unto them all that I command thee: be not dismayed at their faces, lest I confound thee before them.' It was as if he was saying to me, 'If you pull your punches, I'll confound you. I'll make you look like a fool in front of men!'"*

—*BILLY GRAHAM*

LIFE MAGAZINE, MARCH 27, 1950

BILLY IN DIXIE

South Carolina gives revivalist biggest crowd he has ever pulled

Not since the great days of "Billy Sunday" twenty-seven years ago had South Carolina seen anything like it. Billy Graham, a thirty-one-year-old evangelist who rose to prominence barely six months ago in Los Angeles (*Life*, Nov. 21) was staging a spellbinding revival campaign in Columbia, South Carolina. On March 12 he hoped to fill the University of South Carolina's stadium for a bang-up final rally. When the afternoon came, more than 40,000 spectators, including Governor J. Strom Thurmond and former Secretary of State James F. Byrnes, over-flowed the stadium. It was the biggest crowd Graham had ever drawn. For almost an hour he held forth, arms waving, warning of a judgment day for all but "the righteous in sinful America." Before the meeting was over 2,000 persons had swarmed out of the stands and knelt before Graham and "made the decision for Christ."

▼ South Carolina Governor Strom Thurmond (left) joined Billy and his parents at the South Carolina crusade.

A New Organization Begins

The Portland crusade was significant, for out of it came a clear need for an organization. Needing $25,000 to go on the radio, Billy told the crowd one night in Portland of his dilemma. After the service, those in the audience came around and gave or pledged exactly $25,000, and the way was clear for Billy Graham to go on the radio.

Grady Wilson tried to deposit the money in a Portland bank. Officials informed him that if he deposited the money in his name, he would be liable for taxes; nor could the money be deposited in something like "the Billy Graham radio fund" unless it was a duly constituted organization.

Billy telephoned George Wilson (no relation to Grady or T.W. Wilson) in Minneapolis, who was then business manager of Northwestern Schools, and Wilson flew to Portland with articles of incorporation for an organization to be known as the Billy Graham Evangelistic Association (BGEA).

The money gathered in Portland in August was put to use in Atlanta. Beginning on November 5, 1950, the first weekly radio broadcast of *The Hour of Decision* was aired live on 150 stations over the ABC network.

▲

Billy had always admired George Wilson, stating, "He's got more bounce to the ounce than any Christian I know."

▶

George Wilson flew to Portland with the Billy Graham Evangelistic Association articles of incorporation.

"Billy wanted Grady to read Scripture. He wanted the choir to sing, Bev to do a solo. He wanted me to announce, and he just wanted to preach. We all had butterflies because it was going out live. We couldn't retract it. There were no tape recorders yet. Five weeks later, The Hour of Decision *had gained the highest audience rating ever accorded a religious program, and within five years 850 stations carried the program across America and around the world. Every crusade city became a studio."*
—CLIFF BARROWS

▶

Public relations specialists Walter Bennett (left) and Fred Dienert pursued Billy for months by telephone, telegram, and in person, believing he should be on national radio. Their persistence finally prevailed.

THE STATE OF MINNESOTA

DEPARTMENT OF STATE.

Be it known, that whereas

George M. Wilson
Darlene Kafka
William H. Eckholdt

Have associated themselves with the intention of forming a corporation under the name of

BILLY GRAHAM EVANGELISTIC ASSOCIATION

for the purpose of: 1. To transmit the Gospel of the Lord Jesus Christ by radio and television.

2. To spread the Gospel of the Lord Jesus Christ by tracts, books, and other publications.

3. To spread and propagate the Gospel of the Lord Jesus Christ by any and all other means.

with a capital of --without capital stock-- *and have complied with the statutes of this State in such case made and provided, as appears from the articles of incorporation.* filed in this office on the fifteenth day of September, 1950.

Now, therefore, I, Mike Holm, Secretary of State of Minnesota, do hereby certify that said above named incorporators, their associates and successors, are legally organized as, and are hereby made, an existing corporation under the name of BILLY GRAHAM EVANGELISTIC ASSOCIATION *with the powers, rights and privileges and subject to the limitations, duties and restrictions which by law appertain thereto.*

Witness my official signature hereunto subscribed and the seal of the State of Minnesota hereunto affixed this --seventeenth-- *day of* --September-- *in the year of our Lord one thousand nine hundred and* fifty.

Mike Holm
Secretary of State

After months of preparation, at exactly 2:00 p.m. on Sunday, November 5, 1950, Cliff Barrows stepped up to a microphone in crowded Ponce de León baseball park and said, "This is *The Hour of Decision* with Billy Graham!" And for the next thirty minutes, the program was on the air live over the ABC network, broadcasting coast to coast from over 150 stations.

Ruth had suggested the program be named *The Hour of Decision*, since Billy's emphasis was on people deciding for Christ.

Washington, D.C.

In the early weeks of 1952, Billy and the team began a five-week crusade in Washington, D.C. In an unprecedented act of Congress, Billy was allowed to conduct a service on the Capitol steps Sunday, February 3.

Speaker of the House Sam Rayburn gave the final authorizing decision, saying, "This country needs a revival and I believe Billy Graham is bringing it to us."

The day dawned cold and rainy, but when the team arrived at the Capitol for the service, thousands stood in the rain to hear the thirty-four-year-old evangelist.

The sergeant-at-arms of the House of Representatives estimated the crowd to be greater than at most presidential inaugurations up to that time.

On February 25, 1952, citing the "unparalleled opportunity God has given me to preach the Gospel throughout the nation," Billy resigned as president of Northwestern Schools to devote full time to evangelism. He had been president for almost four and one-half years.

During the Washington, D.C., crusade, Billy found himself in the corridors of the nation's power, and he made many friends within those circles, including Senators Richard M. Nixon and Lyndon B. Johnson.

He refused to run for United States senator in his home state of North Carolina when supporters suggested it and then applied pressure, trying to make him conform to their wishes.

▼
Billy met with Speaker of the House Sam Rayburn.

◄
The United States Capitol steps in Washington, D.C., was the scene of an unprecedented service on February 3, 1952.

The Early Team

Without proper follow-up, mass evangelism can be little more than a crowd, a wave of religious emotion that quickly evaporates. Billy prayed the Lord would send someone who knew something about this.

Dawson Trotman, the founder and leader of the Navigators ministry, arrived to help with counseling and follow-up programs in the 1951 Seattle campaign. Dawson took the lead in developing the methods that would later be refined and become such an important part of the Graham ministry. Billy, Cliff Barrows, and other members of the team were nearly exhausted from trying to do as much counseling as possible after each night's service. Dawson went to Billy and said, "Don't you believe that God has given us gifts, too? Your gift is platform preaching. Let us handle the counseling of those who come forward." This taught Billy a great lesson—to recognize the gifts God has given to others and to delegate responsibility to them.

The man who taught the team more about evangelism than probably anyone else was Willis Haymaker, who joined the group in Columbia, South Carolina. He had helped organize campaigns for Gipsy Smith, Billy Sunday, and other evangelists. Upon Willis's advice, the team changed "campaigns" to "crusades" and determined to work in close cooperation with churches wherever possible. Willis also helped lay the foundation for careful crusade preparations so that churches would be mobilized to reach their communities for Christ, and he emphasized the central role that prayer must play in evangelism.

Tedd Smith, a concert pianist from Canada, also joined Billy's growing team in Columbia to help Cliff Barrows and George Beverly Shea with the music. Being a man of many talents he also became Billy's secretary, a job that required long hours and much typing. His secretarial duties lasted many months.

▲
Dawson Trotman (left) laid out a plan of follow-up for members of the team.

▲
Willis Haymaker joined Billy in Columbia, South Carolina.

Seeking God's Way

> *"The Lord has always arranged my life so that I have to stay dependent upon Him. I just have to stay dependent because I have severe limitations."*
> —BILLY GRAHAM

At the end of the Atlanta crusade, two photographs appeared side by side in the Atlanta *Constitution*, one showing Billy waving good-bye to a crowd outside the baseball park, the other showing a box of money the ushers had collected. The inference was unmistakable, repeating the old charge that evangelism was a racket.

Billy vowed this must never happen again. But the custom of taking up a "love offering" to support their work was as old as American evangelism. How else could Billy and his team finance their work? The team must have enough to live on and enough for expenses.

Early in the 1950s, they sought the advice and counsel of older ministers. Their answer was for Billy to be paid a salary by the Billy Graham Evangelistic Association, comparable to the amount received by a pastor of a large church.

Billy summed it all up when he talked about the three things that can trap a man of God.

"First—Pride: How subtle the devil is, and how he uses pride in our lives. God says in the Bible to 'humble yourselves' (James 4:10).

"Second—Money: How many have been tripped up on money! Dwight L. Moody, the American evangelist of the 1800s, said, 'God will let thousands of dollars flow through your hands if you do not let much stick.'

"Third—Morals: Christ and Self are perfectly incompatible. To have the one, we must be prepared to surrender the other. The heart subtly schemes to hold both, but it does not deceive Christ."

▼

While Billy and the team built the foundations of their ministry program in the early 1950s, they never lost their true focus: preaching God's Word.

◄

The early team members (from left to right) Tedd Smith, Cliff Barrows, Billy, George Beverly Shea, and Grady Wilson worked together almost since the beginning.

Young Family

Billy's popularity spread like wildfire. Here was a handsome, articulate, sincere, down-to-earth man who preached the unadulterated Word of God—and lived it, too. He caught the nation's fancy, and so did the message he brought. *The Hour of Decision* gained listeners by leaps and bounds each week, and mail poured into the tiny office in Minneapolis, often seeking advice for personal problems.

"The biggest event for the children," Ruth said, "was when Daddy was home. They were mighty good about him being gone so much because they knew why he was gone."

When it was time for the inevitable good-bye, neither Ruth nor Billy displayed emotion. There was the tight hug and kiss. But in private, their individual reactions were quite different. "Many a time," Billy said, "I've driven down that driveway with tears coming down my cheeks, not wanting to leave."

"I think the one that suffered perhaps the most, and without even knowing it, was Bill because he missed all those happy times when they were growing up and all the interesting things the children said and did and just being with them."
—RUTH GRAHAM

*"We live a time
Secure
Sure
It cannot last
for long
then—
the good-byes come
again—again
like a small death,
the closing of a door."*
—A POEM BY RUTH GRAHAM
REVEALED HER EMOTIONS

◀

The sight of Billy saying good-bye to Ruth and Bunny was a familiar, if painful, one.

▲

William Franklin Graham III (Franklin) was born July 14, 1952. His father was heard to say, "I would have loved another girl, but every man needs a son."

▲

Five-year-old Virginia (Gigi) (left) and two-year-old Anne admired baby Ruth, nicknamed Bunny (1950).

▼

A sign made by
Billy's children
warned visitors about
the family's three dogs.

Inquisitive Visitors at Home

Curiosity seekers descended on the small hamlet of Montreat, tucked into a picturesque valley in the Blue Ridge Mountains. All were determined to see for themselves where the Grahams called home. They trampled through Ruth's flowerbeds and peered into the windows . . . at all hours.

By car and bus, curious tourists invaded the reserved little mountain community. They poked around the main roads and paraded up and down neat residential lanes looking for the Graham house.

They meant no harm, but their presence was disturbing, sometimes upsetting, like the time Ruth saw strange eyes peering in her bedroom window.

Ruth worked out her own classification for the "friendly intruders": If they barreled right into the yard, they were usually from the Baptist campground at nearby Ridgecrest. If they simply stopped for a quick look, they were most likely Southern Presbyterian. Only the Episcopalians drove past at a discreet pace.

Billy wrestled with the problem of having to be away from his growing family, and Ruth was deeply troubled by the fact that Billy's call to preach had somehow made the Grahams public property.

The Grahams kept the children away from the public, especially from the press, and refused to let them be put on display at crusades. They were normal kids.

"One day I noticed that Bunny had more spending money than her allowance would afford and I asked where it came from. Gigi said, 'Why don't you watch her?' So I did, and the next time a tour bus pulled up, all Bunny had to do was walk up to that busload of tourists with her little friendly face. She didn't ask for money, but the purse was quite obvious. I watched those people just automatically dropping dimes and quarters in her bag while they asked her questions. We put a stop to that in no time flat!"
—RUTH GRAHAM

▼

Anne, Gigi,
Franklin, and
Bunny shared a
bedtime story
with their mother.

◄

Billy's study had a
large window and
was on a level with
the road. He was
sometimes forced
to crawl on all fours
from his desk to the
door to escape
detection by the
many curious
tourists.

"In the early love poems I wrote: 'I could see with amusement that I was expecting too much from any human being; I was expecting Bill to be to me that which only Jesus Christ himself can be. I learned this in a happy way. It was just finding that the Lord was always with me the same time Bill was. And when Bill left, the Lord took over.'"
—RUTH GRAHAM

▼

Gigi, Anne, Bunny, Ruth, and Billy relaxed with the family dog in Montreat.

▲

Anne, Ruth, Bunny, Gigi, Franklin, and Billy enjoyed a fall day together.

A New Home in the Mountains

In 1954 the Grahams purchased two hundred acres of mountaintop land on which they could build a new home, away from the main roads and so inaccessible that at last the problem of peeking tourists would be solved.

Two years later, when the Grahams were ready to start building, Ruth's romantic sense of history surfaced. She scoured the mountains, buying old timbers from abandoned log cabins and bricks from an old schoolhouse. As the home took shape it looked to be a century old, even down to the split-rail fences. Inside Ruth designed an informal country-house atmosphere that spans all time.

Six days before the start of his New York crusade in 1957, Billy made this entry in his personal diary: "This is the first spring that I have ever spent at home. What a wonderful and thrilling few weeks this has been: to run and play with my children every day, to listen to their problems. Today, Ruth and I took our last stroll. What a wonderful companion she is. Little Franklin keeps pleading, 'Daddy don't go!' I have come to love this mountaintop and would like nothing better than for the Lord to say I should stay here for the rest of my life."

▲
The family's new home was built on a mountaintop.

▶
The Grahams' new son, Nelson, was just four days old. From left to right, Franklin, 5; Bunny, 7; Gigi, 12; and Anne, who was 9. Billy was soon to leave on an eight-country tour of Latin America.

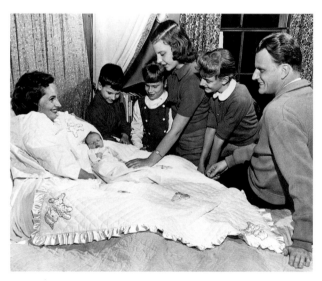

"Bill and I settled on a new house site about a mile straight up the mountain as a crow flies from Montreat. We paid $12.50 to $14 an acre for the land. The surveyors had difficulty because of the rambunctious terrain but finally agreed to call it two hundred acres."

"We built our first real home the year that Bill went to India (1956). I remember he told me that we could have two fireplaces. So as soon as he left, I told the workmen, 'Build fireplaces! Build them faster than you ever have in your life. I want five before he gets back.' They managed to pull it off and I've always felt that it is divine judgment that the fireplace in his quarters has always smoked!"
—RUTH GRAHAM

▶
Billy and Ruth enjoyed a picnic near the site of their new home.

"The day before the crusade was to open, The People newspaper hurled abuse at 'Silly Billy.' 'Must we be turned into better citizens and kinder husbands by the antics of Billy Graham's American hot Gospel circus?' But finally we began to win some as friends. Grady heard a reporter grandly announce, 'When Jesus was on earth, He rode a lowly donkey. I cannot imagine Jesus arriving in England on a great ocean liner!' Grady fired back, 'Listen, man, if you can find me a donkey that can swim the Atlantic, I'll buy it on the spot.'"

—BILLY GRAHAM

London: The Ministry Reaches Abroad

Billy wore a new conservative hat and dark coat, hoping for a good impression.

Just before they came out on deck, Billy asked Ruth not to wear any lipstick because some British clergy rated lipstick worldly and Billy wanted to please them. She refused.

Ruth wrote in her diary: "Bill stooped from being a man of God to become a meddlesome husband, so I said it doesn't seem to me to be a credit to Christ to be drab. I think it is a Christian's duty to look as nice as possible. Besides, not caring about one's appearance goes against a woman's nature. That's not going to make anybody a better Christian, either. And it's not fair to the people who have to look at you. I believe my lipstick did help."

▼

Billy faced a hostile London press conference.

Billy was facing the greatest test of his young ministry—the Greater London Crusade scheduled for three months, March through May 1954.

Billy, whose ministry was not yet well established outside the United States, was tense. He insisted that Ruth accompany him. Uneasy about leaving her four children for such a long time, she told him she would go only if she could sail home after the first month.

Her plans, however, were changed: she stayed for the duration because her husband told her he could not do without her. It was Ruth's longest separation from her children.

If the press helped establish Billy Graham's name nationally in the 1949 Los Angeles campaign, it raised its other colors at the start of the Greater London Crusade of 1954.

"It all started," Billy said, "when our Minneapolis office printed a calendar telling about our London crusade which was sent to people interested in our work. One word mysteriously got changed, which brought on me the wrath of the Labour party and the British press. After discovering what I allegedly had said, I could not blame them. The statement was, 'What Hitler's bombs could not do, socialism' (which had been substituted for my word *secularism*) 'with its accompanying evils, shortly accomplished.' The mistake was discovered and corrected before many had been printed but somehow one of the uncorrected copies got to London and into the hands of one newspaperman and a member of Parliament."

The press continued its harping into the crusade, but gradually, after interviews and press conferences, some reporters grudgingly acknowledged the American evangelist's skill and patience in answering their tricky and antagonistic questions.

"Dear folks, This is all fantastic. Last Tuesday, somewhere between the Isle of Wight and Southampton, a tug full of pressmen with twenty-five reporters and eleven photographers pulled alongside our liner. I knew they were after Bill's scalp, and there was nothing we could do but pray for wisdom and be as courteous as we could. The first question was, 'Who invited you over here, anyway?' Then such killers followed as, 'Do you think you can save England?' And, 'Don't you think you're needed more in your country?' Bill's answers were wise, really terrific. God sure helps him."

—A LETTER FROM RUTH TO HER PARENTS

Arrival in London

Londoners had converged on Waterloo Station until the platform ticket machines gave out. Post office vans and taxis were forced to a dead stop. One harassed official exclaimed, "If these are Christians, it's time we let the lions out!" It was the greatest crowd at Waterloo since the arrival of Mary Pickford and Douglas Fairbanks in 1924.

"The train from Southampton to Waterloo Station in London took about an hour, and there we stepped out into a perfect mob," Ruth remembered. "The press of the crowd was so terrific that Bill and I were instantly separated. Cheers went up, and the air was filled with 'God bless you' and 'Welcome to England.'"

Donn Moomaw, All-American UCLA football player, ran interference for the evangelist through that throng of humanity.

▲ Billy and All-American football player Donn Moomaw (center of the photo) were nearly lost in the crowd at Waterloo Station.

▶ A daily message from the visiting evangelist ran in London's *Star* newspaper.

◄ Shortly before the Grahams' arrival in Southampton, a tugboat full of journalists pulled alongside their liner and beseiged them with questions.

"Bishop . . . The repair man is here . . . !"

◄ Cartoons appeared in many papers.

▼

Billy preached before record numbers in Harringay Arena, 1954.

▼

On opening night, squads of pressmen and roving photographers did not make for an atmosphere of worship. The London dailies had sent an extraordinary array, including theater and literary critics as well as foreign and industrial correspondents.

The London Crusade

The London crusade remains one of the high spots in Billy Graham's career.

The crusade executive committee secured Harringay Arena in North London for three months, and nightly meetings were held there from March 1 until May 22. In Harringay's long history the twelve-thousand-seat arena had never been filled by any speaker for more than one night. The cost—£33,000, about $100,000. The sum seemed enormous! The executive committee had no precedent for such faith.

Landline relays (live broadcasts by telephone lines), carrying the services to a total of 405 halls and churches, were a prominent feature of the crusade from Harringay. The idea started because many people who had made long journeys across London to Harringay discovered upon arrival that the building was full and they were unable to get in. The live links from Harringay were very successful and carried the message to many parts of the British Isles.

Ruth rarely connected with her husband during those appointment-filled days. They tried to have lunch together twice a week. She missed the children terribly and daily fought the temptation to pack up and go home. Only at night in the counseling room, asking the Lord to use her to reach someone for Christ, did she feel that her time was fulfilled. The next day, she was writing letters to those whom she had counseled. They were chatty notes, full of encouragement and strength. With some, the correspondence went on for years.

► Billy preached in Harringay Arena for three months.

In some ways, March 1, 1954, was the most memorable day of Billy's ministry. The weather was foul, even worse than usual. The meeting was set for 7:00 P.M. The constant rain had turned to sleet by evening. At 6:30 P.M., just as Ruth and Billy were getting into their car for the eight-mile drive to the arena, they received a message that there were not more than two thousand people in their seats, and it looked like a handful in that big place. And more than three hundred press and camera people were watching and waiting.

"Ruth and I held hands in silence as we drove through the wet streets," Billy recalled. "I thought of the gloating stories that they would write and I thought of the thousands of prayers from around the world for that night. We just tried to prepare our hearts to face whatever God had planned. When we arrived and walked into Harringay, I could hardly believe my eyes. It seems that thousands had poured out of the Underground to fill the arena while Ruth and I were en route those long eight miles from the hotel. Tears of gratefulness to God welled up."

The **MESSAGE**

"Opening night at Harringay my theme was 'Does God Matter?' My text was 'For God so loved the world that he gave his only begotten Son, that whosoever believeth in him should not perish, but have everlasting life' (John 3:16). The same text, the same simple message, had caused Americans to respond by the thousands. 'No sin had ever escaped the eyes of God,' I explained, 'but no sinner has ever escaped the love of God.' In my closing, I said, 'There is only one way back to Him, and it is through Jesus Christ.'"

—BILLY GRAHAM

Trafalgar Square and Hyde Park

On Saturday afternoon, April 3, 1954, Trafalgar Square was packed as it had not been since VE Day.

On a warm, sunny Good Friday, April 16, an open-air rally in Hyde Park, which the police estimated at more than fifty thousand, covered half a square mile. Billy spoke on "God forbid that I should glory, save in the cross of our Lord Jesus Christ."

The final meetings were scheduled in the two largest stadiums in London—Wembley and White City—with both meetings the same afternoon.

On that final day, Billy preached to about two hundred thousand people, certainly the largest religious gathering in British history. Over a period of three months, more than two million Britishers heard Billy preach, and more than thirty-eight thousand made decisions for Christ.

"At the end of the first week our arena was jammed an hour before meeting time, and the police reported that thirty thousand had failed to get in. By the end of the first month, Londoners were almost fighting for free tickets. Socialites came to see and to hear and to be converted. Bishops were willing to sit with us on the platform. Even newspapers became friendly."

—BILLY GRAHAM

"I learned more about human nature in two hours at Harringay than I have learned in thirty-seven years. I realized the power for good . . . or for evil that can be released. Of the longing of people for a different sort of life. Of course, if I wanted to be clever I would just say man needs a God. . . . But you see that wouldn't really express what I was feeling. For all the way home I puffed at my pipe. My eyes were scalded with tears."

—WILLIAM HICKEY OF THE London DAILY EXPRESS *WROTE HIS IMPRESSION OF A* HARRINGAY *SERVICE*

▶

The crowd listened raptly as Billy preached in Trafalgar Square.

◀

At Harringay Arena, the nightly response to the invitation to come forward was overwhelming.

Daily Mail

SATURDAY, APRIL 17, 1954   THREE HALFPENCE

A multitude gathers in Hyde Park

BILLY GRAHAM SPEAKS . . . AND FIFTY THOUSAND LISTEN

THEY stretch as far, almost, as the eye can see. Fifty thousand people. They are covering half a square mile of Hyde Park.

On a platform in the middle of the multitude stands Mr. Billy Graham, the evangelist. He spoke yesterday for 20 minutes. His listeners formed London's biggest open-air religious audience since World War II.

Meeting with Cassandra

Cassandra, the waspish columnist of London's popular *Daily Mirror*, found great sport in attacking Billy and the crusade.

"Dear Mr. Graham, Will you meet a sinner first on his own ground? Will you meet someone fairly hell-bent and not averse to a little wickedness? Why should we not meet in a pub called The Baptist's Head? You could drink what you choose while I sin quietly with a little beer. Cassandra."

When Billy read the column, he said, "Now here's a fellow who knows how to use the English language." Billy wrote a letter to the columnist.

"Dear Cassandra: I should like to have the privilege of meeting you. While your articles about me were not entirely sympathetic, they were two of the most cleverly written that I have ever read. Sincerely Yours, Billy Graham."

After the evangelist and the columnist met, the columnist wrote the following:

"Billy Graham looks ill. He has lost fourteen pounds in this merciless nonstop campaign. But this fact he can carry back to North Carolina with him: it is that in this country, battered and squeezed as no victorious nation has ever been before, and disillusioned almost beyond belief, he has been welcomed with an exuberance that almost makes us blush behind our precious Anglo-Saxon reserve. I never thought friendliness had such a sharp cutting edge. I never thought simplicity could cudgel us sinners so damned hard.
We live and learn. Cassandra."

▲
Cassandra met Billy at The Baptist's Head pub.

"Dearest family: Amazing response tonight. So prompt, so quiet, and so many. Among those I talked with were a mother back-slidden for twenty years and her daughter, two little usherettes from the News Theatre on Oxford street, and a lovely young model. They called for a Spanish-speaking counselor. Monday night, a man called for someone speaking modern Greek. How these folks get enough from the message to come forward I don't know. God must be bringing them. As a Russian said, 'All my life, I've wanted to receive Christ, but I did not know what to do. As soon as I entered Harringay, I felt His presence here.' The power of God transcends all barriers, even race or language."
—RUTH GRAHAM
IN A LETTER TO HER PARENTS

A Finale in London

The strain of Billy's schedule was immense. Weeks flew by in a flurry of appointments and outside speaking engagements while, each night, people waited at the arena for another sermon. The pressure of three months of constant preaching had taken its toll. The evangelist grew thinner and thinner and the rings under his eyes deepened. A distinguished physician prescribed vitamin pills; they helped so much that Billy downed a week's supply in one gulp!

Every seat was occupied at Harringay for the eighty-eight nights of the Greater London Crusade. Some evenings there were so many people outside when the doors closed that a second service was held at 9:15 P.M.

The three months of meetings set new attendance records of over two million with nearly forty-thousand decisions for Christ.

"We held our final service in the two largest stadiums in London because of the request from so many people for tickets," Billy said. "White City Stadium was filled with 65,000 in a drizzle of rain and 2,000 responded. Then the police led the way to Wembley Stadium where 122,000 were waiting and it was still raining. I did not know how I was going to find the strength for another sermon." Billy presented a simple sermon using Joshua's words to the people of Israel: "Choose you this day whom you will serve."

Archbishop of Canterbury Geoffrey Fisher, the Lord Mayor of London, and scores of members of both houses of Parliament attended the final service.

The rise of Billy Graham as an international evangelist had been nothing short of phenomenal.

▼

Billy and Archbishop of Canterbury Geoffrey Fisher chatted on their way to the platform at Wembley Stadium.

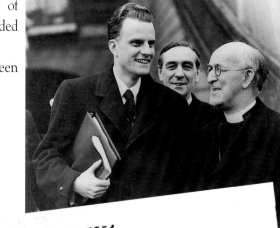

BILLY GRAHAM—AMAZING FINALE

Drama at Wembley: 10,000 converts

surge forward in the rain

By MURRAY SAYLE

ws, Thursday, May 27, 1954

Archbishop Praises The Humility Of Billy Graham

THE ARCHBISHOP OF CANTERBURY, Dr. Fishe praises the "humility" of Billy Graham, t American evangelist.

Writing in the Canterbury Diocesan Notes, he declares that the many thousands who received Dr. Graham's message did so because of "the great humility and sincerity of Dr. Graham himself, coupled with a great personal attractiveness.

"He would take or assume nothing for himself, but was clearly a seeking only to use

ALBERT HALL 'A UPHILL STRUGGLE

£10,000 TREASURY LO

LORD PENDER, presiden

Sir Winston Churchill

On Billy's scheduled day of departure, he was summoned on short notice to No. 10 Downing Street by Prime Minister Sir Winston Churchill, the man who had carried Britain through the darkest hours of World War II and was already listed in history as one of the greatest statesmen of all time.

The reports of Wembley so impressed Sir Winston that he requested to see Billy. Sir Winston motioned him to be seated and said, "Do you have any hope? What hope do you have for the world?" Billy took out his little New Testament and answered, "Mr. Prime Minister, I am filled with hope."

Sir Winston pointed at the early editions of three London evening papers lying on the table, and commented that they were filled with reports of rapes, murders, and hate. When he was a boy it was different, he told Billy. "I am an old man," he said, "and without hope for the world." Billy replied, "Life is very exciting because I know what is going to happen in the future." Then he spoke about Jesus Christ, turning from place to place in the New Testament and explaining the meaning of Christ's birth, His death, and His resurrection. Billy went on to speak of the Second Coming of Christ. The brief time that had been scheduled for their meeting was extended to forty minutes. At last Sir Winston said, "I do not see much hope for the future unless it is the hope you are talking about, young man. We must have a return to God."

"My phone rang, and a voice at the other end said that Sir Winston Churchill wanted me for lunch the following day. I was so tired, I replied, 'It's impossible. We're taking a train tonight.' Aghast, I realized that I had turned down the Prime Minister of Great Britain. Within minutes, the phone rang again, and the voice asked, 'Could you come today at twelve?' I dressed and shot over to 10 Downing Street."

—BILLY GRAHAM

◄ As Billy left his meeting with Sir Winston Churchill, he said to the press, "I feel like I have shaken hands with history."

BILLY and Sir WINSTON HAVE SECRET

'DAILY MIRROR REPORTER'

SIR Winston Churchill and the American evangelist Billy Graham shook hands yesterday—to seal a secret they vowed to keep even from their wives.

And the secret? The subject which

Scotland

Billy returned to Great Britain in 1955 for a crusade in Scotland that drew more than 2.6 million people, with over 52,000 making their decisions for Christ.

The six-week, All-Scotland Crusade was the first time Billy and his team went to a country with the official endorsement of the churches of the land. This was a united effort to reach an entire country, the evangelist's ancestral homeland.

An 18,000-seat auditorium had been built within Kelvin Exhibition Hall, plus an area for overflow seating. Billy preached to overflow crowds every night (except Sunday) for six weeks, plus many other daytime meetings. Thirty-seven relay centers in Scotland and others in Ireland and Wales were linked to Kelvin Hall for nightly services.

On April 29, a cold Friday evening, 50,000 listened at Ibrox Stadium. The following afternoon, 100,000 attended the closing service at Hampden Park Stadium.

Good Friday 1955 was the peak of the All-Scotland Crusade. The BBC assigned one hour to the service on both radio and television simultaneously. The evangelist addressed the entire United Kingdom—an audience of 30 million people. Such an event was second only to the coronation. But at least two viewers who had not seen the coronation on television were also watching: Queen Elizabeth and Prince Philip.

"If anybody had suggested, even a couple of years ago, that a young American evangelist would draw well over 150,000 to a crusade in two days in Glasgow, the response would have been incredulous!"
—GLASGOW EVENING CITIZEN

▲
100,000 Scots attended the closing service at Hampden Park Stadium on April 30, 1955.

◄
Overflow crowds filled Kelvin Hall.

Queen Elizabeth II

On Easter Sunday, 1955, Billy was accorded the privilege of preaching to the Queen and the Duke of Edinburgh in their private chapel at the Royal Lodge.

"A note from Buckingham Palace was handed to me privately during our crusade in Glasgow, Scotland, in 1955," Billy vividly recalls. "It invited me to preach at Windsor Castle and asked Ruth and me to lunch afterward with Her Majesty Queen Elizabeth and Prince Philip."

Billy's response after the meeting: "Good manners do not permit one to discuss the details of a private visit with Her Majesty, but I can say that I judge her to be a woman of rare modesty and character. I made a pledge to remember the Queen and her family every day in my prayers."

▲

Queen Elizabeth and Prince Philip invited Billy to preach in their private chapel at the Royal Lodge.

"When we filed into the Royal Chapel, I looked around to see the location of the pulpit. I was stunned to realize that the chapel had no pulpit, just a place to stand. I carried a thick sheaf of handwritten notes on extra paper and was forced to leave them behind when I got up to speak. I had prayed so much about this moment that I knew however simple and full of mistakes my sermon would be, God would overrule and use it—but I'll tell you, I could really feel my heart beating!"

—BILLY GRAHAM

THE QUEEN HEARS BILLY GRAHAM

COURT CIRCULAR. WINDSOR CASTLE. 22ND MAY, 1955.

THE QUEEN AND THE DUKE OF EDINBURGH ATTENDED DIVINE SERVICE THIS MORNING IN THE PRIVATE CHAPEL, THE ROYAL LODGE. DR. WILLIAM GRAHAM PREACHED THE SERMON.

The Queen hears Billy Graham

THE Queen and the Duke of Edinburgh yesterday attended morning service in the private chapel at Royal Lodge, Windsor, at which the preacher was Billy Graham, the American evangelist.

He preaches the sermon in Royal Lodge chapel

Express Staff Reporter

BILLY GRAHAM preached for 25 minutes yesterday to the Queen—head of the Church of England — in the private chapel, Royal Lodge, Windsor.

Prince Philip, the Queen mother, and Princess Margaret were there too. So was Mrs. Ruth Graham, the evangelist's wife.

Billy Graham has just ended a week's crusade in London, and a meeting on Thursday night's meeting was attended by the Duchess of Kent,

▲

At the Queen's request, Billy visited Windsor Castle.

▶

Billy and Ruth were dressed for one of several formal occasions in Britain.

"During the past few months we have faced many obstacles and problems. I have been on the phone to New York an average of three or four times a day. Many problems seemed to be impossible to solve, and yet somehow they have been solved."

"The past few weeks have been weeks of filling up. The more I read and studied, it seemed, the less I knew, until today I feel more inadequate and helpless as I go to New York than at any time yet. New York is such a gigantic city, the opportunities and responsibilities are overwhelming."

—BILLY GRAHAM,
SIX DAYS BEFORE THE START OF THE
NEW YORK CRUSADE

"I believe the Lord would have us go to hard places, not easy ones. Over half the people in this great metropolis of New York are completely unchurched; some sixty nationalities love and hate and labor within its boundaries. From a human viewpoint and by human evaluation the crusade may be a flop. However, I am convinced in answer to the prayers of millions that in the sight of God and by heaven's evaluation it will be no failure and Christ will receive the glory and honor. I have prayed, worried, and wept over New York more than any other place in which we have held a crusade."

—BILLY GRAHAM

The New York Milestone

In 1957, New York presented as great a challenge to Billy Graham as London had. Some reporters wrote that Billy was coming to save New York, and indeed he was coming to do his best.

With their typical thoroughness, his team was also ready to do their best. Team members were prepared with 40,000 bumper stickers, 250,000 crusade song books, 100,000 Gospels of John, a million letterheads, 35,000 window posters, and 650 billboards posted at strategic locations within the city.

The crusade was scheduled for six weeks at Madison Square Garden.

People streamed out of the deep concrete caverns of the big city to converge on the Garden in record-breaking numbers, setting a new attendance record for a single event in the arena.

Two months into the crusade, a historic meeting was held in Yankee Stadium, a rally that was intended to be the crusade's climax. More than 100,000 gathered inside the stadium on the hottest day of the summer while thousands more pushed at the gates, trying to gain entrance.

After the Yankee Stadium rally, the crusade was extended to September 1—and that final meeting was held in the open air of Times Square.

Many triumphs were scored at the New York crusade, which finally came to a close after sixteen weeks.

During that time, more than 2.3 million people heard the Word of God preached straight from the shoulder of the tall young man from the mountains of North Carolina. More than 60,000 made decisions, and another 30,000 professed by mail the decisions they had made while watching live telecasts of the services.

▲

A cartoonist for the *Charlotte Observer* saluted the hometown boy.

▼

En route to New York by train, Billy made a brief stop in Washington to visit his old friend, President Eisenhower. Billy recalled reviewing the plans for the New York crusade: "I could tell that he had already read about it. . . . He said it would be wonderful if people all over the world could love each other. I agreed, and I tried to point out that the Gospel has a vertical as well as a horizontal aspect, that men must be born again and be truly converted to Christ before they have the capacity to love. He heartily agreed."

DORTHY KILLGALLEN, SYNDICATED COLUMNIST

. . . Thrill seekers expecting hysteria would be better off at a rock and roll concert. Graham does not court hysteria. Neither does he hypnotize individuals or masses. . . . To Billy Graham heaven is just as real as Chicago.

▶

Billy had been invited to New York by the city's Protestant Council. The crusade was supported by 1,500 churches, which supplied volunteer workers to help each night. Thousands of ushers, choir members, and counselors had been trained for the event, but Billy said the most important volunteers were the thousands of people all over the world who were praying for New York.

There had been some talk about giving choice seats on the main floor to church delegations but Billy set the policy: "We are here to bring God's message to the unchurched. Let the delegations praise the Lord from the balcony." They did.

▼

Crowds lined up early to see Billy at Madison Square Garden.

"We have not come to put on a show or an entertainment. We believe that there are many people here tonight that have hungry hearts—all your life you've been searching for peace, joy, happiness, and forgiveness. I want to tell you, before you leave Madison Square Garden this night, you can find everything that you have been searching for in Christ. He can bring that inward deepest peace to your soul. He can forgive every sin you've ever committed. And he can give you the assurance that you are ready to meet your God, if you will surrender your will and your heart to Him."

—BILLY GRAHAM

The Big Town Responds

The MAN

"Billy Graham's crusade to save New York from sin apparently has clicked. Midtown bookstores report the biggest demand for the Bible in years."
—WALTER WINCHELL, RADIO COMMENTATOR

"Industry executives were puzzled by the lack of tangible sponsorship. They were familiar with the buying and staying power of big accounts like General Motors and Procter & Gamble. Graham's programs, which cost $60,000 a week, were sponsored by God."
—BURNHAM AND FISHER, THE NEW YORK CRUSADE

The crusade had been scheduled for six weeks; however, the New York executive committee had taken an option on Madison Square Garden for three months.

Almost nightly, Billy was called from the platform to address the overflow crowds spilling out into the streets when every seat was taken and the arena's doors were closed. Scheduled to end June 30, the crusade was extended.

The Big Town shook its head in wonder, and a thoughtful few began to ponder what attraction led those thousands to the Garden.

No doubt about it, New York was confounded.

The outpouring of publicity on behalf of a minister of the Gospel both startled and baffled its historians. "His show will be a cold turkey in two weeks," one critic avowed. "His voice is already gone," a bookie said. "He won't last that long. I'll lay odds on it."

Yet many more thoughtful citizens began to be deeply interested in what was going on at Madison Square Garden.

"I had some hesitancy about taking this engagement because it was a variety show. However, I remembered that Jesus ate with publicans and sinners, even though He was denounced by the Pharisees. Here was an opportunity to give my testimony to 40 million Americans over NBC Television."
—BILLY GRAHAM

Billy's powerful preaching drew crowds to Madison Square Garden and prompted favorable media coverage and editorial cartoons.

Billy was trying to divert New Yorkers from the city's mind-boggling array of entertainment and cultural events to the possibility of a personal encounter with God. He had learned by instinct and experience that no evangelist makes news sitting in his hotel room—he needed the media to reach the people—so he regularly made time for interviews and guest appearances like this one on the Steve Allen Show.

▶

An estimated 96 million people viewed one or more of the seventeen 1957 Saturday night live telecasts. Viewers sent in more than one and a half million letters during the three months of the telecast.

Telecasts Begin

The American Broadcasting Company made a prime-time hour available each Saturday night, and seventeen telecasts were made from Madison Square Garden over ABC's far-flung network. Suddenly, here was Billy Graham preaching in the nation's living rooms, and the impact was tremendous. ABC estimated the weekly Saturday night audiences at 7 million viewers, the largest single congregation to hear the Gospel up to that time.

June 1, 1957, was a turning point for the crusade ministry. On this midsummer Saturday night ABC allocated an hour of prime viewing time, and suddenly the nation was being offered front-row seats in the Garden. To pay for the initial contract of four weekly telecasts, the evangelist received from a foundation the largest single gift that had ever been made to his association—$100,000.

By the late 1950s, most Americans had heard of Billy Graham, but only a fraction had ever experienced a crusade. The team had just not been to that many places yet. Now, on those first national religious telecasts, viewers could watch from the comfort of their living rooms and find out what Billy Graham was really all about. Billy said, "We are reaching more through these telecasts than we could reach in a lifetime in Madison Square Garden."

On July 10, 1957, a lunch-hour meeting occurred amid the concrete canyons of lower Manhattan. The team had learned in London to take the crusade to the people. Secretaries, clerks, and financiers stood shoulder to shoulder in New York's financial district to hear a Gospel message.

PHYLLIS BATTELLE, INTERNATIONAL NEWS

. . . A man who refuses to quit when he's ahead, Billy Graham pits religion against show business tonight when his Madison Square Garden war with the devil makes its television debut. His opposition will be two of television's best—Perry Como and Jackie Gleason. Billy himself is all modesty. He doesn't give himself much of a chance to outdraw his two opponents and says he will be satisfied "if I get the leftovers."

THE WORLD TELEGRAM

PEOPLE ASK, "WHAT DID HE ACCOMPLISH?"

The powerful evangelist bequeathed two gifts to our polyglot town: a dedicated fellowship of more than 60,000 "spiritual babies" newly converted to Christ, commisioned to spread love and battle sin; and an all-new concept and privilege to the people of New York of discussing religion without smirking, attending church without apology, and reading the Bible without feeling vaguely like a fanatic.

ON TELEVISION

BILLY GRAHAM

and

NEW YORK

CRUSADE

direct from
Madison Square Garden

SATURDAYS June 1-8-15-22

COAST TO COAST
ABC-TV NETWORK

8:00 p.m. E.D.T.

◄ Billy preached at a noon meeting in Harlem, August 1, 1957.

"I had nothing to give. I had exhausted my material. I had exhausted my body. I had exhausted my mind. Yet the preaching had far more power. It was God taking sheer weakness—it is when I get out of the way and say, 'God, You have to do it.' I sat on the platform many nights with nothing to say, nothing. Just sat there. And I knew that in a few minutes I'd have to get up and preach, and I'd just say, 'Oh, God, I can't do it!' And yet, I would stand up and all of a sudden it would begin to come . . . just God giving it, that's all."

—BILLY GRAHAM

"*They said Yankee Stadium couldn't be filled. But it was. God did this and all the honor, credit, and glory must be to Him.*"

—BILLY GRAHAM

Yankee Stadium

The Yankee Stadium rally on July 20, 1957, was meant to be the climax of the New York crusade. Attendance reached more than one hundred thousand inside, with thousands more pushing against the gates. Vice President Nixon's mother had telephoned her son from California to make a request: "I have been watching Billy Graham on television, and he looks so thin. I want you to call and urge him to get a good rest before he ruins his health." The Vice President promised to do so. And he did.

When Billy made his entrance, walking beside him across Yankee's turf was Richard M. Nixon.

"I bring you a message from one who is a very good friend of Billy Graham," Nixon told the crowd, "and one who would have been here if his duties had allowed him, the greetings and best wishes of President Eisenhower."

At the close of his message, because there simply was not room, Billy could not ask inquirers to come forward to the platform. Instead, he asked all who would acknowledge Christ as their Savior to stand. It was impossible to estimate the response as literally thousands rose from their seats.

◄

Billy and Vice President Richard Nixon joined the audience in prayer on the platform during the Yankee Stadium rally.

◄

Historic Yankee Stadium was filled to overflowing on the hottest day of the year, 105 degrees in the shade.

▼
Retreating from a round of newspaper interviews, Ruth ironed her husband's shirts. Broadcast equipment for *The Hour of Decision* filled the corner of their hotel room.

The **MESSAGE**

"This is the spot that thousands of tourists think of as New York. Many foreign visitors judge America by Times Square. Some stare in wonderment at the blaze of lights; others hurry along streets to the theaters and places of amusement. Here in Times Square is the dope addict, the alcoholic, the harlot . . . along with the finest citizens of the world. Let us tell the whole world tonight we Americans believe in God!"

—BILLY GRAHAM,
CLOSING SERMON OF THE
NEW YORK CRUSADE,
SEPTEMBER 1, 1957

◄
People from Maine to California watched by television as Billy preached his farewell sermon to New York from Times Square. Broadway had never seen such a sight. Times Square had held huge crowds before—on New Year's Eve—but these people were praising God.

"I have lived in New York City for twenty-five years, and through my church and interdenominational contacts have had the opportunity to appraise the spiritual life of the city for a quarter of a century. I would like to testify that never in this period of time has there been anything even remotely approximating the profound spiritual impact which Billy Graham has made on New York City. For the first time there has been a definite soul-searching on the part of the people . . . I have never seen prayer take hold as it did in the days preceeding the crusade, and as it continued all the way through."
—RUTH PEALE
(MRS. NORMAN VINCENT PEALE)

▼
More than two million people listened to Billy face-to-face at either the Garden meetings or other rallies, and more than sixty thousand men, women, and young people came forward to decide for Christ.

CHAPTER THREE

MILLIONS OF LIVES CHANGED

B illy Graham has preached the Gospel face-to-face to more than 100 million people on six different continents, in 84 countries of the world, and in all of America's fifty states. His crusades across the globe—in Europe, Asia, North and South America, Australia, and Africa—have broken stadium attendance records. And with the advent of radio, television, and satellite broadcasts, Billy has reached more than 2 billion people.

News of the first crusades in Los Angeles, London, and New York traveled like lightning around the world, challenging both Christians and non-Christians to believe that the particular place in which God had put them was not beyond hope. As invitations to hold crusades began pouring in from every continent, Billy and his team evaluated each opportunity, formulating a decision-making procedure that continues to this day. Before accepting any invitation, they consider criteria ranging from community needs, local interest, and available meeting facilities, to time and even weather conditions.

One of the most important considerations has always been local church support. Early on, Billy and his team decided to accept only those invitations that come from unified ministers and laypeople of many different churches who have banded together in a common desire to spread a strong Bible-based message to their community. Ultimately, though, the final decision regarding crusade invitations has always been made by Billy himself, after much prayer.

A Billy Graham crusade leaves an unmistakable imprint on its host city. If only for a brief time, people become aware of God through the media—from radio, television, billboards,

◄

On September 22, 1991, more than 250,000 people attended New York's Central Park rally, making it the largest North American crusade event ever.

*The*MESSAGE

"I present a God who matters, and who makes claims on the human race. He is a God of love, grace, and mercy, but also a God of judgment. When we break his moral laws we suffer; when we keep them we have inward peace and joy. I am calling for a revival that will cause men and women to return to their offices and shops to live out the teaching of Christ in their daily relationships. I preach a Gospel not of despair but of hope for the individual, hope for society, and hope for the world."
—BILLY GRAHAM

and newspapers. Suddenly, Christians grow less afraid to talk to their friends and neighbors about their belief in God.

People who come forward at a crusade are given Bible-study materials and referred back to their local churches, which, as a result, receive many new members anxious to know God.

Civic leaders, church leaders, and those who have participated in the meetings at every level attest to the positive results in their communities. As individual lives are changed, these changes touch families, families touch communities, and changed communities impact cities longing for renewal.

Major Billy Graham crusades have been held in eighty-five countries on six continents.
Note: The locations on the following pages reflect the names of cities and countries in use at the time of each crusade.

During the 1970s and 1980s, Billy made historic inroads into what at the time were Communist-controlled countries. In a part of the world where atheism was officially sanctioned, tens of thousands of people gathered to hear Billy preach the Gospel. In 1992, shortly after the fall of Communism in the Soviet Union, Billy and his team conducted his first full-scale religious crusade in Russia.

Reporters typically measure a meeting's success in terms of attendance and response statistics but Billy has a different standard: "If I talk to one person and get him to say yes to Jesus Christ, I consider that to be a successful meeting."

The **MINISTRY**

"The real story of the crusades is not in the great choirs, the thousands in attendance, nor the hundreds of inquirers who are counseled. The real story is in the changes that have taken place in the hearts and lives of people."
—BILLY GRAHAM

ASIA

In June 1973, a record 1.1 million people made Yoido Plaza in Seoul, South Korea, Billy's largest meeting ever held anywhere in the world.

"I would like to say that I am just one man among many that have come for this crusade. We have a whole team of people and most of us have been together for nearly fifty years. I'm introduced as though I'm doing it all. They have far greater skills than I have, they have far greater abilities and gifts than I have. But it's the Lord using this group of people along with the local churches to make Christ known to the community."
—BILLY GRAHAM

NORTH AMERICA

The largest crowd at any event in the Los Angeles Memorial Coliseum was the 1963 Billy Graham crusade, with 134,254 inside and 20,000 more outside.

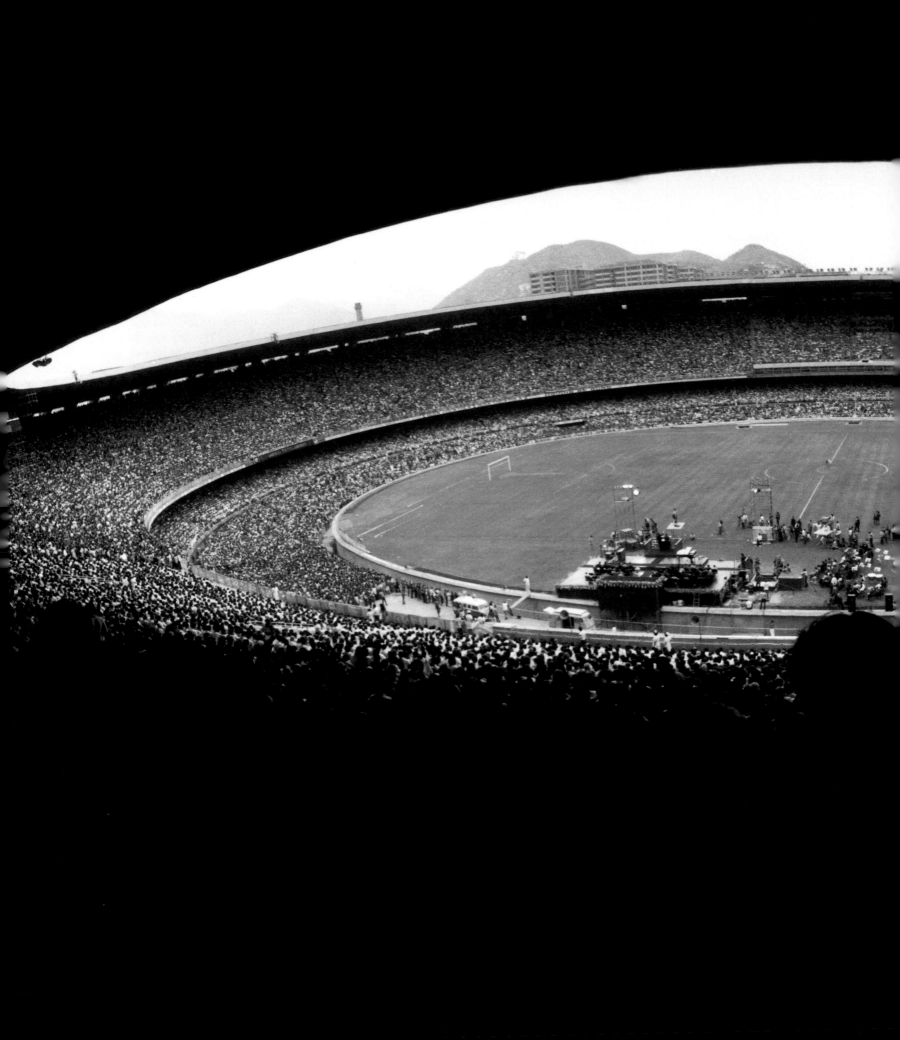

*The*MESSAGE

"*God is a God of love, a God of mercy. He has the hairs of your head numbered. . . . He wants to come into your life and give you new hope.*"
—BILLY GRAHAM

SOUTH AMERICA

In October 1974, the largest crowd to attend an evangelistic service in the western hemisphere—225,000 people—filled Rio de Janeiro's Maracana Stadium.

The **MESSAGE**

"I have had the privilege of preaching this Gospel on every continent in most of the countries of the world. And I have found that when I present the simple message of the Gospel of Jesus Christ, with authority, quoting the very Word of God—He takes that message and drives it supernaturally into the human heart."

—BILLY GRAHAM

EUROPE

In July 1966, a capacity crowd of 95,000 inside and 8,000 outside heard Billy at London's Wembley Stadium.

"*I am just a spectator watching what God is doing.*"
—BILLY GRAHAM

AUSTRALIA

The closing meeting for the 1959 Sydney, Australia, crusade filled two adjoining stadiums with 150,000 people.

"I am convinced, through my travels and experiences, that people all over the world are hungry to hear the Word of God. As the people came to a desert place to hear John the Baptist proclaim, 'Thus saith the Lord,' so modern man in his confusions, frustrations, and bewilderment will come to hear the minister who preaches with authority."

—BILLY GRAHAM

AFRICA

In March 1973, Johannesburg's Wanderers Stadium held 60,000 people, making it the largest multiracial gathering ever held in South Africa to that time.

Changed Lives: The Objective

The MESSAGE

"They've come to make life's most important commitment. I feel terribly unworthy at that moment. I feel terribly inadequate to help them. I know it has to be of God, that I can't do anything. No matter what they do for the rest of their lives, for one moment they've stood before God."
—BILLY GRAHAM

All ages, all nationalities, all races, all religions, rich and poor, educated and uneducated—thousands of people from all walks of life testify to the change Christ brings in their lives as they come forward at Billy Graham crusades.

"Time alone is the great judge of the genuineness of people's decisions," Billy says. But for hundreds of thousands over a period of half a century, his message has marked a turning point from doubt to faith, from unbelief to trust, and from nominal assent to full commitment.

Billy issues the invitation to come forward with these words: "I'm going to ask hundreds of you to get up out of your seats and come and stand here and say by coming, 'I am willing to acknowledge that I have sinned—I have broken God's laws. I am ready to change my way of living and receive Christ and follow Him, no matter what the cost.' I am asking you to make that commitment right now. You can say yes to Christ, and a great transformation can take place inside of you. You can become a new person. You may be Catholic, Protestant, Jewish; you may not have any religion, but God is speaking to you and you know you need Christ.

"All I am is a messenger to tell you that God loves you, Christ died for you, and He will forgive you when you receive Him into your heart. You are not coming to me; you are coming to Christ. I have no supernatural power; I cannot save you.

"The night that I came to Christ, the evangelist extended the invitation for quite a long time. And I was the last to come. And I'm glad that he waited. If God is speaking to you, this is your moment with God—you come."

The **MESSAGE**

"I am going to ask you
to bow your heads and
I want you to pray this
prayer after me.
Pray it out loud.
Oh God, I am a sinner.
I am sorry for my sins.
I am willing to turn
from my sins.
I receive Christ
as Savior.
I confess Him as Lord.
From this moment on,
I want to follow Him
and serve Him
in the fellowship
of His church.
In Christ's name.
Amen."
—Billy Graham

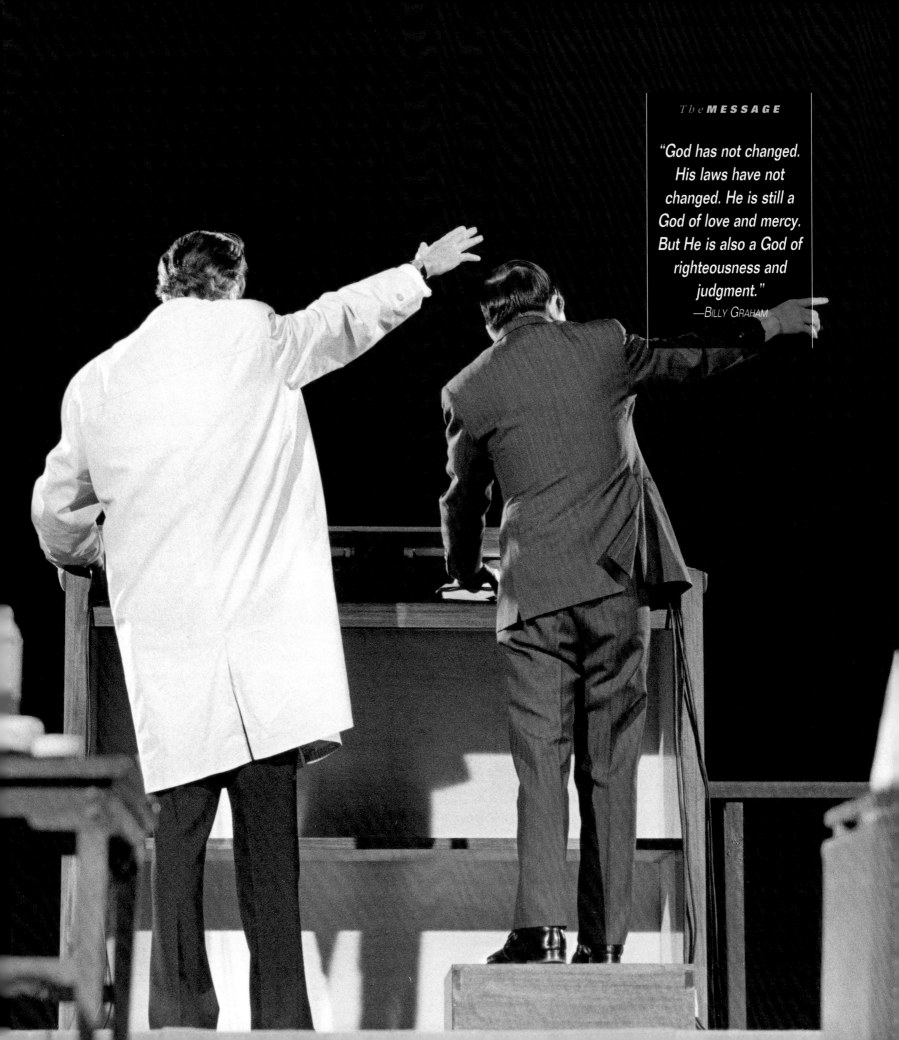

"God has not changed. His laws have not changed. He is still a God of love and mercy. But He is also a God of righteousness and judgment."
—BILLY GRAHAM

"I faced many challenges in life. But the greatest challenge was not earning a place on the Olympic team; it wasn't crashing in a bomber in the Pacific; it wasn't even spending two and a half years in a Japanese concentration camp. The greatest challenge of my life took place at the Billy Graham tent meeting in Los Angeles in 1949. At a time when our marriage was under great strain, my wife accepted the invitation of neighbors to attend. She came home speaking of a peace and joy in her heart that she had never known before. This put us a little further apart than we already were, but now she and her new Christian friends began to pray for me. I went to the tent meeting and was impressed, but was not going to return. Finally, my wife persuaded me to do so, after agreeing to my condition, that when this fellah says, 'Every head bowed, and every eye closed,' we're getting out! But we didn't because that night I faced the all-important questions of what I thought of Jesus Christ, and if I would receive Him as my Savior. I thank God that I made the correct decision and accepted Him. Now, after nearly half a century, I'm still carrying a torch for Jesus."
—LOUIS ZAMPERINI, OLYMPIC RUNNER AND WORLD WAR II HERO

◄

In Seoul, South Korea, 1973, translator Billy Kim interpreted every word and gesture.

"There are four things that are very important to help you as a new believer:
First, read the Bible. It is God's Word, written to you.
Second, pray. Take everything to God in prayer, because He loves you and you are now His child. Talk to God like you would your best friend.
Third, witness for Christ. Tell someone about your decision for Christ. Then witness by your smile and by your love and concern for others.
Fourth, get into a church where Christ is proclaimed and where you can serve Him."
—BILLY GRAHAM

"I went to hear what Billy Graham had to spout about. Our divorce was almost through and our son was due in court; I went to the meeting in anger thinking my husband was stupid. But Jesus cracked me that night. My heart was broken before Him. I gave my life to Him and was born again."
—LONDON

Crusades Across Asia

Asia is a continent ruled by many religions. Billy's invitations to Asian countries came from small minorities of Christian believers who wanted to share their faith with their friends and neighbors.

All of Billy's meetings in Asia have been attended by large crowds. In fact, the largest meeting Billy has ever held anywhere in the world was in Seoul, South Korea, where 1.1 million people sat on an old, unused runway and listened through thousands of loudspeakers stretched for almost a mile.

HONG KONG		JAPAN		ISRAEL		REPUBLIC OF CHINA	
Hong Kong	1956	Fukuoka	1980	Jerusalem	1960	Taipei, Formosa	
	1975	Okinawa	1980				1956
	1990	Osaka	1980	SOUTH KOREA		Taipei, Taiwan	1975
INDIA		Tokyo	1956	Seoul	1956		
Bombay	1956		1967		1973	SINGAPORE	
Calcutta	1977		1980		1984	Singapore	1978
Kohima, Nagaland			1994				
	1972			PHILIPPINES			
Kottayam	1956			Manila	1956		
Madras	1956				1977		
New Delhi	1956						
	1977						
Palamcottah	1956						

"There are so many gods in Japan. I was at a loss as to how to get to heaven. This is the first time that I learned I get to heaven through Jesus Christ."
—TOKYO

▼
Thousands turned out to hear Billy preach in Madras, India, 1977.

▶
During the 1994 crusade, many left their seats at the Tokyo Dome when Billy called them forward.

Crusades Across Africa

Billy made his first trip to Africa in January 1960, preaching for three months across the continent. He traveled more than fourteen thousand miles, speaking to capacity crowds in large stadiums and small groups out in the bush.

Life magazine covered part of his trip and reported that "Billy talked to a third of a million Africans. . . . Some of Africa's enthusiasm and Graham's accomplishments stemmed from his insistence on nonsegregated meetings." He deliberately bypassed the Union of South Africa in 1960 because of its apartheid policy of total segregation. Thirteen years later he returned, once the government allowed integrated meetings in both Johannesburg and Durban.

EGYPT		KENYA		Ibadan	1960	RWANDA-URUNDI	
Cairo	1960	Kisumu	1960	Jos	1960	Usumbura	1960
		Nairobi	1960	Kaduna	1960		
ETHIOPIA			1976	Lagos	1960	SOUTH AFRICA	
Addis Ababa	1960					Durban	1973
		LIBERIA		NORTH RHODESIA		Johannesburg	1973
GHANA		Monrovia	1960	Kitwe	1960		
Accra	1960					SOUTH RHODESIA	
Kumasi	1960	NIGERIA		RHODESIA		Bulawayo	1960
		Enugu	1960	Salisbury	1960		
						TANGANYIKA	
						Moshi	1960

Billy visited Uhuru Park in Nairobi, Kenya, in 1976.

Integrated crowds filled King's Park Rugby Stadium in Durban, South Africa, 1973.

"The crusade has touched hundreds of people from every corner of our community and across the spectrum of belief and denomination. I am especially pleased that so many Roman Catholics found it an opportunity to deepen their relationship with Christ. I see the possibility of faith and practice being enriched in lasting ways."

—A BISHOP OF THE ROMAN CATHOLIC DIOCESE OF NEW YORK

▼

Toronto's Skydome in Ontario, Canada, held a record 68,500 when Billy preached in 1995.

Crusades Across North America

Billy has preached in most of the countries of North America, from Canada and all fifty states in the United States, to Mexico and several Central American countries.

BAHAMAS		Toronto	1955	**UNITED STATES**		CALIFORNIA	
Nassau	1982		1967			Anaheim	1969
			1978	ALABAMA			1985
BARBADOS	1958		1995	Auburn University		Fresno	1958
					1965		1962
CANADA		COSTA RICA		Birmingham	1964	Hollywood	1951
			1958		1972	Los Angeles	1949
ALBERTA				Dothan	1965		1958
Calgary	1981	GUATEMALA		Montgomery	1965		1963
Edmonton	1980		1958	Redstone Arsenal		(25th Anniversary	
					1962	Celebration)	1974
BRITISH COLUMBIA		JAMAICA	1958	Tuscaloosa	1965	Modesto	1948
Vancouver	1965			(University of Alabama)		Oakland	1971
	1984	MEXICO		Tuskegee	1965		1997
		Mexico City	1958	(Tuskegee Institute)		Sacramento	1958
MANITOBA			1981				1983
Winnipeg	1967	Villahermosa	1981	ALASKA			1995
				Anchorage	1984	San Diego	1958
NOVA SCOTIA		PANAMA	1958				1964
Halifax	1979			ARIZONA			1976
		TRINIDAD	1958	Phoenix	1964	San Francisco	1958
ONTARIO					1974		1997
Hamilton	1988			ARKANSAS		San Jose	1981
Ottawa	1998			Little Rock	1959		1997
					1989	Santa Barbara	1958

▲

A record-breaking crowd of 90,000 filled Philadelphia Stadium in Philadelphia, Pennsylvania, in 1961.

▲

Another record crowd—30,000—filled the 27th of February Stadium in Villahermosa, Mexico in 1981.

◀ War Memorial Stadium in Little Rock, Arkansas, has been the scene of more than one crusade, including this one in 1989.

"I used to think Jesus was for the birds. To be frank, I hated Him. I had tried everything, including Buddhism and an Indian guru, vegetarianism and LSD, political rallies and marches, rock concerts, and grass. Then one evening I flipped on the TV and your crusade was being telecast. Then I knew what I had been searching for. That night Jesus came to live in me. He filled me with happiness and peace. He surrounded me with love. He took away my tears."
—PHOENIX, ARIZONA

▼ California's Anaheim Stadium held a record number of people— 80,600—in 1985.

▶ 116,000 sweltered in 110-degree heat at Soldier Field in Chicago, Illinois, 1962.

COLORADO	
Denver	1965
	1987

CONNECTICUT	
Hartford	1982
	1985
New Haven	1982
(Yale University)	

FLORIDA	
Boca Raton	1961
	1981
Bradenton-Sarasota	
	1961
Cape Canaveral	
	1961
Clearwater	1961
Ft. Lauderdale	1961
	1985
Gainesville	1961
Jacksonville	1961
Miami	1949
	1961
Orlando	1961
	1983
St. Petersburg	1961
Tallahassee	1961
	1986
Tampa	1961
	1979
	1998
Vero Beach	1961
West Palm Beach	
	1961

GEORGIA	
Atlanta	1950
	1973
	1994
Augusta	1948

HAWAII	
Hilo	1965
Honolulu, Oahu	
	1965
Kahului, Maui	1965
Lihue, Kauai	1965

IDAHO	
Boise	1982

ILLINOIS	
Chicago	1962
	1971
Wheaton	1959
	1980

INDIANA	
Indianapolis	1959
	1980
	1999
South Bend	1977

IOWA	
Des Moines	1948

KANSAS	
Manhattan	1974
(Kansas State	
University)	

▲
More than 75,000 stood in the Boston Common for a 1964 crusade.

▲
William Franklin Graham IV attended his first crusade with his mother, Jane Austin Graham.

"I was complaining because your telecast was on instead of my favorite program. But I began to listen, and finally I called the number on the screen. Now Jesus has changed my life."
—DALLAS, TEXAS

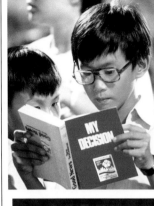

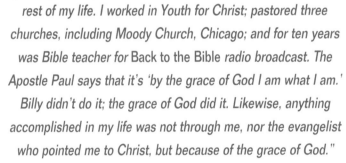

"Back in 1945, I went to a Youth for Christ rally held in my high school auditorium. The speaker was a young evangelist. His name was Billy Graham. That night, I experienced saving grace. The grace of God not only changed me as a teenager, but gave me a vision and purpose for the rest of my life. I worked in Youth for Christ; pastored three churches, including Moody Church, Chicago; and for ten years was Bible teacher for Back to the Bible radio broadcast. The Apostle Paul says that it's 'by the grace of God I am what I am.' Billy didn't do it; the grace of God did it. Likewise, anything accomplished in my life was not through me, nor the evangelist who pointed me to Christ, but because of the grace of God."
—DR. WARREN W. WEIRSBE, PASTOR, BIBLE TEACHER, AND AUTHOR OF MORE THAN ONE HUNDRED BOOKS

◄
A record 52,000 filled Jackson's Mississippi Memorial Stadium in 1975.

"...[when] my first child was born. I was unmarried. At eighteen I was married, but the marriage lasted only six months. I became involved in drugs and prostitution and eventually ended up in a mental hospital. Discharged without medical permission, I shot myself and ended up once again in a psychiatric facility. The next time I saw a television program with Billy Graham, I telephoned for some counseling, and it was then that I finally received the assurance of my salvation."

—CHICAGO, ILLINOIS

"In 1973, I was assigned to investigate Billy Graham. I took a week, attempting to find the real story: the evangelist gone bad. But as I spent time with Billy Graham, I began trusting him and came to respect him. He talked to me about commitment but, at that time in my life, I was sure of myself and confident in my career. I had my life under control and didn't see any need to give it over to Christ. I had heard of people surrendering their lives to God, and I always took it as a sign of weakness. It was after my marriage ended, more than two decades later, that I located the Living Bible Billy Graham gave me. . . . [He] had written in the front of the Bible, 'May this book become a part of your life—Philippians 1:6.' Flipping through the pages to the verse reference, I read: 'I'm sure that the God who began the good work within you will keep right on helping you grow in His grace until his task within you is finally finished on that day when Jesus Christ returns.' Now I was ready to make my commitment to Christ . . . My assignment to investigate the evangelist finally resulted in me uncovering the truth about God."

—COLLEEN KELLY, FORMER RELIGION EDITOR OF THE ATLANTA JOURNAL

▲
In 1996 the Metrodome in Minneapolis, Minnesota, held 70,000 while an overflow crowd of 25,000 watched on big screens outside.

"For five years I was in a private hell. I was on two different anti-depressants and two different tranquilizers. During the Las Vegas crusade telecast I accepted Jesus as my personal Savior. Many times I had wished I could start all over again, and now I have."
—PROVIDENCE, RHODE ISLAND

◀

Crowds filled Indianapolis, Indiana's coliseum in 1959.

"I've been in church all my life, but this is the first time I have made a personal commitment to Jesus."
—KANSAS CITY, MISSOURI

"I would like to thank Dr. Graham for coming to Pittsburgh to serve in this crusade. He's here because he was invited by business leaders, community leaders, and church leaders and he's really here to serve us. This is a Pittsburgh crusade where Billy Graham brings his skills. Some ask, 'Did his crusade in '53 and '68 make a difference?' I can say from personal experience that I have met countless people here in Pittsburgh and all over the country who really had their life changed either at a Billy Graham crusade or the seeds were planted, and so I don't think we will ever know how many leaders in this county, both religious and otherwise, have been impacted by a Billy Graham crusade, and it's certainly true of so many leaders here in Pittsburgh. And many times it isn't felt for ten to twenty years later.

Billy Graham is truly a man sent by God to deliver the message of Jesus Christ, a fairly simple message. A man supportive of our churches, he doesn't have his own agenda. A man who is supportive of our leaders, he's not trying to take over a massive leadership role."
—C. FRED FETTEROLF, FORMER PRESIDENT AND CHIEF OPERATING OFFICER, ALCOA; CRUSADE CHAIRMAN, 1993 PITTSBURGH BILLY GRAHAM CRUSADE

KENTUCKY
Lexington 1971
Louisville 1956
1964

LOUISIANNA
Baton Rouge 1970
New Orleans 1954
Shreveport 1951

MAINE
Bangor 1964
Portland 1964
1982

MARYLAND
Baltimore 1949
1981

MASSACHUSETTS
Amherst 1982
(University of
Massachusetts)
Boston 1950
1964
1982
(Northeastern University)
Cambridge 1982
(Harvard University,
Massachusetts Institute
of Technology)
Newton 1982
(Boston College)
South Hamilton 1982
(Gordon-Conwell Seminary)
Springfield 1982

MICHIGAN
Detroit 1953
1976
Grand Rapids 1947

MINNESOTA
Minneapolis–St. Paul
1950
1961
1973
1996

MISSISSIPPI
Jackson 1952
1975

MISSOURI
Kansas City 1967
1978
St. Louis 1953
1973
1999

MONTANA
Billings 1987

NEBRASKA
Omaha 1964

NEVADA
Las Vegas 1978
1980
Reno 1980

NEW HAMPSHIRE
Hanover 1982
(Dartmouth)
Manchester 1964
1982

NEW JERSEY
East Rutherford 1991

NEW MEXICO
Albuquerque 1952
1975
1998

NEW YORK
Albany 1990
Buffalo 1988
New York 1957
(Spanish) 1960
1969
1970
1991
Rochester 1988
Syracuse 1953
1989
Uniondale 1990

▲
Billy preached in
the Las Vegas
Convention Center
in 1980.

"In 1984 I was getting ready to go out one night and party. My TV was turned on and a Billy Graham crusade was on. For an hour I sat down and watched this program. This was the man my mom and dad watched when I was a kid. There I sat on my bed, dressed up, ready to go out and party, and there came Billy Graham speaking God's Word. He wasn't making it easy. The Word of God pierced my heart, convicted me of my sin, and at the end of the program I called that phone number on the screen. A lady talked and prayed for me—like she knew me. And that changed my life. She prayed that I would have favor with God and man. And after that prayer— my life changed and I started writing songs that were popular. I got rid of all the drugs and the alcohol. It proved to me that if we follow God's laws we will be the best we can be. That's what God did for me. I was living way below the level God wanted for me and I was missing out on all of His blessings."
—PAUL OVERSTREET, COUNTRY-WESTERN SONGWRITER

◄
A large TV screen in the parking lot
was provided for the overflow crowd
at the Meadowlands Sports Complex
in East Rutherford, New Jersey.

NORTH CAROLINA		
Asheville	1953	
	1977	
Chapel Hill	1982	
Charlotte	1947	
	1958	
	1972	
	1996	
Greensboro	1951	
Jacksonville	1962	
Raleigh	1951	
	1962	
	1973	

NORTH DAKOTA	
Fargo	1987

OHIO	
Cincinnati	1977
Cleveland	1972
	1994
Columbus	1964
	1993

OKLAHOMA	
Oklahoma City	
	1956
	1983

OREGON	
Portland	1950
	1968
	1992

PENNSYLVANIA	
Altoona	1949
Philadelphia	1961
	1992
Pittsburgh	1952
	1968
	1993

PUERTO RICO	
Ponce	1958
	1967
San Juan	1958
	1967
	1995

RHODE ISLAND	
Providence	1964
	1982

SOUTH CAROLINA	
Columbia	1950
	1987
Greenville	1966

SOUTH DAKOTA	
Sioux Falls	1987

TENNESSEE	
Chattanooga	1953
Knoxville	1970
Memphis	1951
	1978
Nashville	1954
	1979

TEXAS	
Dallas	1953
Dallas–Fort Worth	
	1971
El Paso	1962
Fort Worth	1951
Houston	1952
	1965
	1981
Lubbock	1975
San Antonio	1958
	1968
	1997

VERMONT	
Burlington	1982

VIRGINIA	
Norfolk-Hampton	
	1974
Richmond	1956
Williamsburg	1976

WASHINGTON	
Seattle	1951
	1962
	1965
	1976
	1991
Spokane	1982
Tacoma	1983
	1991

WASHINGTON, D.C.	
	1952
	1960
	1986

WEST VIRGINIA	
Huntington	1964

WISCONSIN	
Milwaukee	1979

WYOMING	
Cheyenne	1987

"I'm grateful to Dr. Graham and his organization for bringing the Gospel of Jesus Christ to Columbus and to Ohio. With the breakdown of religious, moral, and family values, Dr. Graham's evangelism is needed more today than ever before in our nation's history. Thank you, Dr. Graham, for spending one week in your life with us so that one day we will be able to share eternal life with our Father in heaven. Your witness and words have brought about a spiritual awakening— a new beginning for the 150,000 Central Ohio souls who have attended this crusade."

—GEORGE VOINOVICH, FORMER GOVERNOR OF OHIO

In 1987, Howard Wood Field in Sioux Falls, South Dakota, held 25,000, the largest crowd to attend any event in the state's history.
◄

▼
A counselor used sign language to communicate with a blind and deaf inquirer.

A record crowd of 74,000 heard Billy at the Seattle, Washington, Kingdome in 1976.

"*As a twenty-one-year-old student, in my first year of medical school, I discovered it is possible to have a personal relationship with God through Jesus Christ. This was at the 1957 Billy Graham crusade in Madison Square Garden, New York. An act of faith was what it took . . . for me to walk forward and accept Jesus Christ. Today I understand that faith was not only saving my soul but expanding my scientific mind. That same faith has led me through my life as a research scientist. People think that science is science and faith is faith. That simply is not true. No scientific discovery is ever made without the scientist himself making a leap of faith. In 1980, we built and sold our first MRI machine. Today they are used worldwide to detect not only cancer but a long and growing list of other diseases hidden inside the human body. I try never to forget that it was God who gave me the ability to invent in the first place . . . and, in this regard, I'm reminded of the decision I made in Madison Square Garden. That was the greatest discovery of my life—greater than MRI—namely, that the greatest purpose a man can find for his life is to serve God.*"

—DR. RAYMOND DAMADIAN,
RESEARCH SCIENTIST AND INVENTOR OF THE MRI MACHINE

▶
Billy preached to a record crowd of 55,300 at Denver, Colorado's Mile High Stadium in 1987.

▶
The Washington Convention Center in Washington, D.C., hosted a crusade in 1986.

Crusades Across Europe

Billy was invited to hold a crusade in London in 1954 that lasted three months. Since that time he has preached to packed crowds in most of the countries in Europe. Billy has always felt a special burden for Europe, where many of the great cathedrals stand empty today.

BELGIUM		FINLAND		NORWAY		SWITZERLAND	
Brussels	1975	Helsinki	1954	Oslo	1955	Basel	1960
			1987		1978	Bern	1960
DENMARK						Geneva	1955
Arhus	1955	FRANCE		RUSSIA		Lausanne	1960
Copenhagen	1954	Lyon	1963	Moscow	1992	Zurich	1955
	1965	Montauban	1963				1960
		Mulhouse	1963	SCOTLAND			
ENGLAND		Nancy	1963	Aberdeen	1991	WEST GERMANY	
Birmingham	1948	Paris	1954	Edinburgh	1991	West Berlin	1954
	1984		1955	Glasgow	1955		1960
Blackpool	1982		1963		1961		1966
Bristol	1984		1986		1991		1990
Cambridge	1980	Toulouse	1963			Dortmund	1955
Ipswich	1984						1970
Liverpool	1984	ITALY		SWEDEN		Dusseldorf	1954
London	1954	Turin	1967	Gothenburg	1955	Essen	1960
	1955				1977		1993
	1966	NETHERLANDS		Stockholm	1954	Frankfurt	1954
	1967	Amsterdam	1954		1978		1955
	1989	Rotterdam	1955			Hamburg	1960
Manchester	1961					Mannheim	1955
Norwich	1984	NORTHERN				Nurnberg	1955
Oxford	1980	IRELAND					1963
Sheffield	1985	Belfast	1961			Stuttgart	1955
Sunderland	1984						1963

▼
More than 18,500 came to Bercy Sports Stadium in Paris, France, to hear Billy in 1986.

▼
In 1960, Billy preached to 100,000 at the Reichstag in West Berlin, Germany. One week after the meetings ended, access from East Berlin was stopped; less than a year later, the Berlin Wall was built.

Billy's 1987 Finland crusade was witnessed by 42,500 at Helsinki's Olympic Stadium.

▼

An overflow crowd watched on a large TV screen outside packed Villa Park in Birmingham, England, 1984.

◄

Stadium lights over Anfield in Liverpool, England, illuminated the 1984 crusade.

◄ In 1984, Billy preached in a chill wind and below-freezing temperatures in Sunderland, England, near the North Sea.

◄ Houston businessman and longtime BGEA board member Carloss Morris counseled a young, physically disabled inquirer.

► Temperatures on the platform registered 106 degrees Fahrenheit at the Cincinnati crusade in 1972.

► Torrential rain did not dampen the response to the Gospel message at London's Wembley Stadium in 1984.

◄ Moscow's Olympic Stadium in 1992 held 50,000 while an overflow crowd of 20,000 more listened outside.

The **MAN**

"I am convinced the greatest act of love we can ever perform for people is to tell them about God's love for them in Christ."

—Billy Graham

▼
More than 3,000
filled Waldensian
Church in Turin,
Italy, in 1967.

▲
Billy brought God's
message to the
Swedish people in
Stockholm, 1978.

*"For thirty-seven years my
life was miserable. I
went through two broken
marriages, and for many
years suffered terrible
depressions . . . I didn't feel
that life was worth living,
and sometimes I wished
that I were dead. . . . I saw a
leaflet announcing that Billy
Graham would be coming
. . . I knew nothing about
him but decided that I would
go to hear him. That night I
asked Jesus Christ into my
heart. I handed my whole
life over to Him, and can't
begin to describe the
wonderful peace, joy, and
love that flowed into my life
from that moment."*
—BLACKPOOL, ENGLAND

Crusades Across South America

Billy's first trip to South America was to address the Baptist World Conference of 1960 in Rio de Janeiro, Brazil. He spoke to 143,000 in a large stadium and met many pastors from across South America who invited him to come to their countries.

In January and February 1962, Billy and his team spent six weeks preaching up and down South America's west coast; they returned in September and October for five more weeks of preaching on the east coast. Billy preached in every large city and all of the countries except Bolivia. Because La Paz, Bolivia, is located at an altitude of over 12,000 feet, Billy was advised that unless he spent considerable time becoming acclimated to the altitude, preaching could prove very difficult because of shortness of breath.

▼

When preaching, Billy refers to the Bible and to outline-style notes he prepares in advance, like these from his sermon on John 3:16.

ARGENTINA		BRAZIL		COLOMBIA		PERU	
Buenos Aires	1962	Rio de Janeiro	1974	Barranquilla	1962	Lima	1962
	1991	Sao Paulo	1962	Bogata	1962		
Cordoba	1962		1979	Cali	1962	URUGUAY	
Rosario	1962					Montevideo	1962
		CHILE		ECUADOR			
		Santiago	1962	Quito	1962	VENEZUELA	
						Caracas	1962
				PARAGUAY		Maracaibo	1962
				Asuncion	1962		

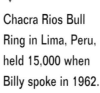

— John 1:12 "But as many as received him, to them gave he power to become the sons of God, even to them that believe on his name."

— Romans 4:5 "To him that worketh not, but believeth on him that justifieth the ungodly, his faith is counted for righteousness."

— Ephesians 2:8: "For by grace are ye saved through faith."

▼

River Plate Stadium in Buenos Aires, Argentina, in 1991.

▼

Chacra Rios Bull Ring in Lima, Peru, held 15,000 when Billy spoke in 1962.

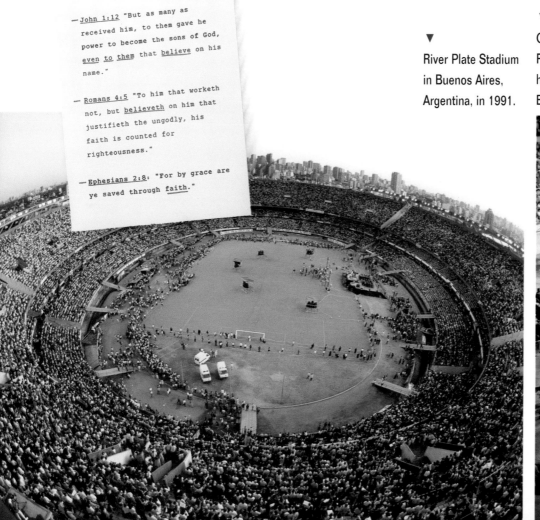

Crusades Across Australia/New Zealand

In 1959, Billy visited Australia and New Zealand for the first time, spending nearly six months preaching in both countries. An estimated 50 percent of Australia's total population heard Billy in person or by landline relays.

Billy and his team returned in 1968, 1969, and again in 1979 to preach the love of God. Each time, they met hundreds in every city who had made decisions for Christ in earlier meetings, many of whom had become pastors and leaders in their communities.

AUSTRALIA					NEW ZEALAND	
Adelaide	1959	Melbourne	1959		Auckland	1959
Brisbane	1959		1969			1969
	1968	Perth	1959		Christchurch	1959
		Sydney	1959		Dunedin	1969
			1968		Wellington	1959
			1979			

THE SYDNEY MORNING HERALD,
MAY 4, 1979

BEHIND THE 'MAGIC' OF BILLY GRAHAM

Sir, Your paper's report on Monday night's Billy Graham crusade meeting referred to the crowds response to "the old Billy Graham mysterious magic."

There is no magic. What your reporter saw, and possibly did not understand was God at work. God could evoke the same response without Billy Graham but He choses instead to work through people. Billy Graham is just one of those people. —K. A. Wilson

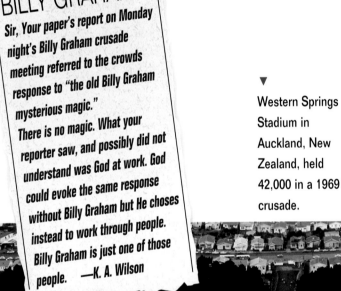

▼
Western Springs Stadium in Auckland, New Zealand, held 42,000 in a 1969 crusade.

▲
More than 65,000 attended the 1959 Wayville Showground crusade in Adelaide, Australia.

"My prayer is that God will accomplish what He wants to accomplish in this crusade. When Jesus Christ had finished His whole life, He hadn't fed everybody, He hadn't healed everybody, He hadn't solved the problems of the world or of His own country. But He said, 'I have finished the work that You gave me to do.' And I believe that God has sent us here at this particular time. I believe that He has a work for us to do here. I believe there are people who are going to be reached in this crusade that could not be reached for Christ and the church in any other way, or at any other time."

—BILLY GRAHAM

Volunteers Are the Key

A Billy Graham crusade simply could not be held without the assistance of thousands of volunteers who work, pray for, and help with the events in each city. A typical crusade involves anywhere from 500 to 1,200 churches representing 70 to 90 different religious groups and beliefs. All told, local churches provide thousands of volunteers for a typical crusade.

Guided by a small number of staff members from the Billy Graham Evangelistic Association who act as advisers, volunteers fulfill a wide range of duties. A team of about 50 local leaders form the executive committee. They are assisted by an office staff of another 100 volunteers, who together plan and organize the crusade by performing such tasks as securing funding and arranging for the facility.

An additional 10,000 serve as members of prayer groups. Before the crusade begins, they pray for the crusade team and for the thousands of people who will attend and come forward. During the typical crusade, more than 5,000 volunteers serve as counselors. Meeting one-on-one, they talk and pray with every person who responds to the invitation to come forward.

Music, a central part of each crusade, is provided by a 4,000-voice choir—again, all volunteers from the local community. Another 1,000 men and women fill the role of ushers. During the crusade, a 300-person co-labor corps keeps track of all who come forward, so that each may be sent information about nearby churches. And after the crusade, literally thousands of volunteers serve as visitation workers, following up with a personal visit or telephone call to those who came forward making decisions for Christ.

Operation Andrew

BILLY GRAHAM CRUSADE

◄

Taking to heart the biblical story of Andrew who "went to find his brother . . . and he brought him to meet Jesus" (John 1:40–42), members of area churches are urged to reach out to their neighbors and relatives, praying for them and bringing them to crusade meetings.

"As one who has become a full-time volunteer in the crusade, I have been especially impressed with the high degree of professionalism in the Graham organization—even better than I found in the White House. Also, the ethical and spiritual integrity of the Graham team has served to further reinforce my previous opinion as to the character and reputation of Dr. Graham and his organization. All of this has increased the measure of my faith in our Lord and biblical Christianity."
—HARRY S. DENT,
SOUTH CAROLINA BILLY GRAHAM
CRUSADE VOLUNTEER AND
FORMER WHITE HOUSE
STAFF MEMBER

"Because of Billy Graham's visit, a new generation of leadership will emerge which will have a significant impact on the life of this city and even worldwide. My coming to Christ at the Billy Graham crusade in London in 1954 is a living example. I've given over twenty years of my life to the Christian ministry."
—REVEREND JOHN GUEST

"I am a member of the human race. I am a world citizen. I have a responsibility to my fellow humans, whatever their religion. And I am convinced that only Christ can meet the deepest needs of our world and our hearts. Christ alone can bring lasting peace—peace with God, peace among men and nations, and peace within our hearts. He transcends the political and social boundaries of our world."
—BILLY GRAHAM

PREACHING IN COMMUNIST LANDS

A crowd estimated at 150,000 greeted Billy in the public square outside the Orthodox cathedral in Timisoara, Romania.

*The*MESSAGE

"Nowhere in Mark 16:15—'Go ye into all the world, and preach the Gospel to every creature'—nor in any similar Scripture did Christ command us to go only into the western or capitalist world. Nowhere did He say to exclude the Communist world."

—BILLY GRAHAM

From Moscow's Red Square to the farthest corners of Russia, people longed for God's Word.

▼

The Communist World

While thousands of people yearned to get out from behind Eastern Europe's Iron Curtain, Billy was looking for a way to get in.

Billy had prayed and planned since 1959, when he and his associate Grady Wilson sat in Moscow's Lenin Stadium, praying that someday God would open the door and allow them to preach the Gospel in the Soviet Union. Billy said, "I knew that the Soviet Christians had been praying for years for me to come and preach. But our visas did not permit public speaking in 1959."

In July 1967, Billy preached for the first time inside a Communist country, Yugoslavia. Technically it was not part of the Soviet bloc, yet these were Eastern Europe's first open-air evangelistic meetings since World War II.

Dr. Alexander Haraszti, a Hungarian-born surgeon, had left Hungary in 1956 with his wife and family of four and was practicing medicine in Atlanta, Georgia. He had an obsession, which he called a burden from the Lord, to get Billy into Eastern Europe to preach. His qualifications were unique: besides his medical degrees he held degrees in theology and linguistics, spoke several languages, and had been a Baptist minister before leaving Hungary. Having grown up under Communist rule, he'd been trained in Marxist-Leninist philosophy and had personally experienced religious and church policies under the Communists. Still, it took him five years and fifteen trips to negotiate Billy's first visit to Hungary. The government first had to be assured that Billy would not issue political statements hostile to the Communist government and would preach only the Good News of Jesus Christ. The first Hungarian meetings finally took place in 1977.

After the visit to Hungary, other Communist-bloc nations began opening their doors to Billy as well. Governments were cautious and often permitted no publicity or advertising of any type. Under Communist rule, atheism was the official government policy, thus religious belief in every Communist country was not encouraged. News of his coming was often spread by word of mouth only. Even Billy and his team were sometimes kept in the dark about each day's scheduled meeting times, because officials feared the crowds and believed every event might turn into an antigovernment demonstration.

"Are you aware that the Soviet government has used you for their propaganda?" a New York reporter asked Billy after his return from Moscow. "Yes, I am aware of this," Billy answered, "but I have been using them for my propaganda, and my propaganda is more powerful. We are using them to preach the Gospel of Jesus Christ to their people."

▶

In Arad, Romania, people crowded an apartment building next to a church to hear Billy's message by loudspeakers.

Yugoslavia

When Billy visited Yugoslavia for two days in July 1967, his first preaching venture in a Communist country took place in pouring rain at a soccer field owned by Roman Catholics—because the government had barred the meetings from the public stadium.

Despite the foul weather, more than 3,500 attended the Sunday morning service. When Billy stood to preach he said, "I will make my message brief because it is raining so hard." Dr. Josip Horak, his interpreter, turned to Billy and said, "Oh, no, please don't—that is why we have come—to hear your message."

Although the rain worsened as the 70-minute service progressed, no one left. In total, more than 10,000 heard Billy speak during his two days in Yugoslavia.

Hungary

After five years of shuttle diplomacy by Dr. Alexander Haraszti, Billy received a long-awaited invitation to visit Hungary in September 1977. The invitation came from the Council of Free Churches and the Ecumenical Council of Churches in Hungary.

With only three weeks advance notice, Billy and his team embarked on a whirlwind tour of three cities: Budapest, Debrecen, and Pecs. He had lengthy dialogues with pastors and church leaders, delivered a personal greeting to government officials from President Jimmy Carter, visited a 46,000-acre collective farm and a Budapest factory, and was a guest of honor at a U.S. Embassy reception hosted by Ambassador Philip Kaiser. All of this plus preaching at a theological seminary and giving five evangelistic messages—in just eight days.

▲
More than 3,500 heard Billy speak at a rainy Roman Catholic soccer field outside Zagreb, Yugoslavia's second-largest city,

▶
With Dr. Haraszti interpreting, Billy spoke to 30,000 at the Tahi Baptist Youth Camp in Hungary.

Poland

Billy's invitation to visit Poland came one year after his successful first visit to Hungary. During negotiations Tadeusz Dusik, director of the State Office for Religious Affairs in Warsaw, said, "If it is in the interest of Poland, we will invite Billy Graham. I have to report to my superiors. But as soon as I have an approval, we will send an invitation."

Poland is more than 90 percent Roman Catholic. The invitation for the six-city, ten-day preaching tour came from the Polish Baptist Union and the Polish Ecumenical Council, and with the support of the Catholic church.

In October 1978, Billy preached to overflow crowds in Baptist, Reformed, Lutheran, Orthodox, and Catholic churches, including Poland's largest church, Christ the King, a Catholic church in Katowice, a coal-mining city.

In Cracow Billy preached in Saint Ann's, a seven-hundred-year-old Catholic church. He was scheduled to have tea with Cardinal Karol Wojtyla but the Cardinal had rushed to Rome, where he was elected Pope John Paul II a few days later. (They did meet just over two years later in Rome.)

▲

Saint Ann's church in Cracow, Poland, the church of Pope John Paul II, welcomed Billy.

◄

In Katowice, a crowd of 10,000— all standing— heard Billy preach at Poland's largest church, Christ the King Roman Catholic church.

East Germany

During a ten-day visit to Germany in July 1982, Billy preached his first sermon in East Germany from Martin Luther's pulpit in the city church of Wittenberg, birthplace of the Reformation.

In honor of the occasion, he chose Luther's favorite Bible verse, "The just shall live by faith" (Rom. 1:17), saying, "Just as spiritual renewal came five hundred years ago in Martin Luther's day and changed the course of history, I pray that today spiritual renewal might once again sweep the GDR [German Democratic Republic] and the world."

Billy preached to packed churches in every city, often with young people making up 65 to 80 percent of the congregations. Aisles, doorways, and even windows were clogged. To handle the overflow crowds, loudspeakers were placed in basements and closed-circuit televisions were set up in nearby churches.

▲ In East Germany, Billy preached from Martin Luther's pulpit.

Czechoslovakia

Czechoslovakian churches existed under tighter restrictions than those in Hungary, Poland, or East Germany. Yet the believers were strong in spirit.

During his eight-day visit to three cities in September 1982, Billy preached to large crowds in small churches. In the town of Bratislava, 1,200 people squeezed into a 450-seat Brethren (Evangelical Free) church by sitting or standing in the aisles, the steps, and the platform.

Billy preached on familiar Bible verses and told his listeners, "No problem is too difficult for God, and no one is too far away for Christ to reach."

▲ This little child may have had the best view in the crowded church.

▼ Crowds filled every available space in the Brethren Church of Bratislava, Czechoslovakia.

An Invitation to the Soviet Union

In October 1978, PepsiCo CEO Don Kendall, a friend of Billy Graham and also a personal friend of Leonid Brezhnev, head of the Communist Party in the USSR, arranged a meeting in Washington between Billy and Soviet Ambassador Anatoly Dobrynin. Billy told the ambassador he wanted to visit the Soviet Union to preach the Gospel, just as he had done in Hungary and Poland.

Dobrynin asked why his country should allow such a preacher to visit. Billy reminded him of growing anti-Soviet feelings in the U.S. and said that he hoped his visit might help build bridges and lessen tensions between the two nations.

By the early 1980s, the cold war had heated up and tensions were running high between East and West—especially the Soviet Union and the United States.

In 1982, an invitation to speak and preach in the Soviet Union finally arrived. Billy was asked to address an international religious leadership conference on the perils of nuclear war.

Billy agonized over the invitation. It was common knowledge that the Soviet government orchestrated these so-called peace conferences for propaganda purposes, and Billy feared being used as one of their tools. "I asked several people's advice, including Henry Kissinger and Richard Nixon. Nixon said, 'This is a big risk, but I believe that in the long run it will be for the benefit of the Gospel that you preach. You'll be criticized, but take the long view. It is very important to reach over the heads of the leaders to the people.'"

But many opposed the trip—even some of Billy's own board members. After much prayer, Billy made his decision based on I Corinthians 9, in which Paul had said we are to become all things to all men so that we might win some to God.

The Sunday before Billy left, he had lunch with Vice President Bush. President Reagan joined them later and told him, "You know what's been in the press about you going to Russia. I believe that God works in mysterious ways. I'll be praying for you every mile of the way."

▼ Patriarch Pimen (seated, left) listened as Billy preached in Moscow's Russian Orthodox cathedral of the Epiphany, 1982.

▲ Billy met with Ambassador Dobrynin and Don Kendall.

▼ Crowds filled every available space to hear Billy preach in Moscow's Baptist church, 1982.

"Bill had always said that his life was not his own. His name had been lifted from obscurity by God. As he prayed about this decision, I knew that it was a simple matter. Regardless of his advisors, if Bill believed that God wanted him to preach in Soviet Russia, he would go."
—RUTH GRAHAM

> "I'm glad I went because it opened many doors in the Communist world that I never dreamed would be opened. In our negotiations, Dr. Haraszti, my Hungarian representative had said, 'Billy Graham will not come to the peace conference unless you give him permission to come again later and preach the Gospel (Good News) in various parts of Russia.' The Russians kept their word and we were invited back two years after to preach in four cities."
>
> —BILLY GRAHAM

Opening Doors

At the Moscow peace conference in 1982, Billy delivered his address to an attentive audience of more than six hundred world religious leaders. As agreed in advance, his seven-day visit also included the opportunity for him to preach in the Moscow Baptist Church and the Russian Orthodox Cathedral of the Epiphany. He met with Soviet Jewish leaders in their synagogue and paid a pastoral visit to the Siberian Seven, religious refugees who had been living in the basement of the U.S. Embassy for four years. Billy insisted on meeting with them alone, without press coverage. "We discussed the Bible and had prayer," he said.

◄ In the Kremlin, Billy met with Politburo member Boris Ponomarev.

Billy also had long visits with several high-ranking government officials, including Georgi Arbatov, a member of the Central Committee of the Communist Party, and Boris Ponomarev, a member of the Politburo (the ten-to-fifteen-member board that controlled the government in the USSR). "Most things we discussed were private," Billy said, "but we did discuss many issues concerning human rights and international relations, and I shared my faith with everyone I met. I also handed Mr. Ponomarev a list of 150 names of believers who were thought to be in prison at the time. I told him, 'There are many believers in America, and as long as they feel their fellow believers are being oppressed by the Soviet government, the chance for better relations between our countries is very slim.' Mr. Ponomarev was very cordial and listened intently throughout my visit." Billy may have been the first foreign clergyman to meet privately with a member of the Politburo.

Billy's 1982 trip to Russia engendered much controversy. The western press wanted Billy to speak out publicly about religious repression in the Soviet Union. Billy refused, however, convinced it was more important to speak privately with Communist Party leaders, who had the authority to effect change.

> "Billy Graham was saying, 'Spirituality is alive in the Marxist, Leninist, Stalinist states . . . it's there and I know it's there.' Frankly, there were all those years when I thought he was wrong or that he didn't know what he was talking about, but it turns out he was right."
>
> —DAN RATHER, BROADCAST JOURNALIST

◄ In May 1982, Billy delivered a major address in Moscow at a peace conference titled "Religious Workers for Saving the Sacred Gift of Life from Nuclear Catastrophe."

Leningrad, Tallinn, Novosibirsk, Moscow

As agreed in 1982, Billy received an invitation to conduct a four-city, twelve-day preaching mission in September 1984. During those days Billy gave fifty addresses, preaching in churches, a seminary, and a university, and he spoke to citizens' groups and conferred with government and church officials. Billy said, "There were no restrictions on my message, which is the same message I have preached throughout my ministry."

Billy's preaching tour began in Leningrad (now Saint Petersburg), where he preached to both Baptist and Russian Orthodox congregations, a pattern repeated in the other cities he visited. He also visited the Leningrad War Memorial and the Piskaryovskoye Memorial Cemetery, site of the mass graves of more than 400,000 of the one million citizens who lost their lives during a 900-day siege by Hitler's Nazi forces.

In Tallinn, the Estonian capital that dates back to the Middle Ages, Billy met with members of Estonia's Presidium of the Supreme Soviet, who asked him if he loved Communists. Billy answered, "Yes, every one of them, and Jesus Christ also loves them."

He then flew eastward to Novosibirsk, in the heart of Siberia. There Billy visited the 80,000-student Academic City (or university) and had dialogues with several professors. He also preached in two churches where hundreds outside listened by loudspeakers.

The 1984 mission concluded with several speaking and preaching meetings in Moscow.

▲

In Tallinn, Metropolitian Alexei (left), now Patriarch of the Russian Orthodox Church, listened to Billy's message at the Orthodox Cathedral of Alexander Nevsky.

"Dr. Graham, are you aware of the fact that in the Moscow Baptist church one-third of the audience was KGB agents?"
—REPORTER AT A PRESS INTERVIEW

. . .

"No, I was not aware of this at the time of my preaching in the Baptist church. But I am glad to hear it. I always wanted to preach to KGB agents. They also need Jesus Christ for their salvation."
—BILLY GRAHAM

MESSAGE

"How marvelous it was to stand in a place like the Soviet Union and talk about the coming Kingdom and to tell them that Communism will not win. I told them capitalism would not win either; it's the Kingdom of God that is going to win."
—BILLY GRAHAM

Crowds swarmed around Billy as he left the Orthodox church in Novosibirsk.
▼

"Russia offers some measure of church freedom. But freedom is relative. I don't have freedom in the United States to go into a public school to preach the Gospel, nor is a student free in a public school to pray, or a teacher free to read the Bible publicly to the students. At the same time, we have a great deal of freedom for which I am grateful."

—Billy Graham

▲

Five thousand heard Billy's message at the Patriarchal Cathedral of the Epiphany in Moscow.

A scene repeated everywhere: dozens of tape recorders captured Billy's message.

▼

"Shortly after my 1984 visit, I received a letter from Georgi Arbatov— the first correspondence I ever received from a ranking Communist official. He was quite upbeat about our visit . . . and he regretted that we hadn't had more time to talk. For the time being—as a substitute, he wrote, 'I am reading some of your books. I couldn't agree with you more when you say that life is a glorious opportunity if it is used to condition us for eternity.' He added that his wife had read one of my books 'with great interest.'"

—Billy Graham

▲

Billy met with Georgi Arbatov, a ranking Communist official.

Romania

In Bucharest, Billy preached in the Jewish Choral Synagogue.
▼

Billy's September 1985 Romanian journey proved to be one of the most remarkable preaching experiences of his entire ministry. Massive crowds lined the streets, packed churches, and overflowed onto rooftops to hear him preach the Word of God during his seven-city, eleven-day tour.

Romania is largely rural and mountainous, a land the size of Oregon. Billy and his team traveled twelve hundred miles by car and Tarom (Romania's domestic airlines), to preach in Orthodox and Reformed cathedrals; Roman Catholic, Baptist, and Pentecostal churches; a Jewish synagogue; and in the open air at an Orthodox monastery.

Hours before the services began, people of all ages started packing the churches and filling nearby streets, hoping for a glimpse of the American preacher or the sound of his voice over loudspeakers.

Some churches had strung loudspeakers on poles, treetops, and nearby apartments so the thousands on the streets could hear Billy's message. As one church worker in Oradea hung loudspeakers in a tree, a *securitate* (secret police) officer ordered him to take the speakers down. The man replied, "You take them down. They'll kill me if I do." The speakers stayed up.

The Ceausescu government was embarrassed by the large turnout for Billy's visit. They were not prepared to let the world see the spiritual hunger that existed in Romania. As a result, a hoped-for meeting with President Ceausescu was abruptly cancelled.

The Second Baptist Church in Oradea removed most of the pews to squeeze 4,000 standing people into the small L-shaped church.
▼

▼
Crowds lined the streets in Sibiu, Romania.

Hungary: A New Day in Eastern Europe

The MAN

"My visits to Hungary over the past twelve years absolutely fixed my conviction that God's Holy Spirit was releasing a spiritual force in that part of the world that was bound to challenge the atheistic philosophy that had dominated nations in that region for decades."

—BILLY GRAHAM

Billy's September 1985 services in the Hungarian cities of Pecs and Budapest hinted at the dramatic changes that were about to take place in Eastern Europe. They marked the first time religious services were held on public property since World War II.

Religious leaders representing every denomination supported the meetings, and government officials provided strong assistance by making available the Budapest indoor sports arena and an outdoor public square.

Billy's visit in July 1989 marked the largest known religious gathering in Hungary's history and the largest evangelistic service ever held in Eastern Europe. Services were held in People's Stadium and, although the facililty seated only 75,000, a total of 110,000 filled every seat and spilled over to the playing field, sitting on the grass.

"Months in advance we were permitted to send one of our crusade preparation teams to help organize the details of the meeting," Billy recalled. "The government permitted us to translate and publish our counseling materials and to advertise the meeting on radio, television, and the news media, just like our crusades in the States."

Hungarian state radio broadcast the two-hour services live, and the following weekend Hungarian state television aired a ninety-minute special of the meeting at prime time on its national network.

Only months later, by the end of December 1989, the Communist Party was dissolved in Hungary, Poland, East Germany, Czechoslovakia, and Romania, ending more than forty years of Communist rule in most of Eastern Europe.

▼

Using a Diamond Vision screen driven from England and loudspeakers to reach the crowd, Billy preached to more than 20,000 in the public square outside the medieval Roman Catholic church in Pécs.

► Budapest's People's Stadium held 110,000 when Billy visited in 1989.

The **MAN**

"I have stood in the places where history was made. I have seen with my own eyes the part that men and women of faith have played in these earthshaking events, and I have heard with my own ears their cries for freedom."
—BILLY GRAHAM

New Beginnings in Russia

Following the dissolution of the Communist Party in other Eastern European countries, the USSR's seventy-year domination halted abruptly on August 24, 1991, when the world's most powerful Communist Party ceased to exist. Later that year, on December 25, 1991, the U.S.S.R. came to an end, with all fifteen republics becoming independent states.

No individual could take credit for all the changes that took place with the fall of Communism in Eastern Europe and the Soviet Union. The courageous Romanian pastor, Reverend Lazio Tokes, noted, "The scenario was written by God." Billy Graham said, "Any history of the political events of our time which does not also include a discussion of the Bible, the impact of Christianity, and the role of faith in changing the hearts and minds of people all over the world is an incomplete and invalid study. For what is taking place in the world today is not just a protest, but a revolution in the sphere of the human heart."

▼
Toppled statutes of Stalin and other leaders graphically illustrated the end of Communist rule.

"Americans are drifting away from spiritual values as they become richer. Sooner or later they will have to go back to their fundamental values, back to God, the truth, the truth which is in God. We look to America, and we expect from you a spiritual richness to meet the aspirations of the twentieth century."
—LECH WALESA,
FIRST-ELECTED
PRESIDENT OF POLAND

"You know, eight years ago one of the Lord's great ambassadors, the Reverend Billy Graham, went to Eastern Europe and the Soviet Union, and upon returning, spoke of a movement there toward more religious freedom, and perhaps he saw it before many of us because it takes a man of God to sense the early movement of the hand of God."
—PRESIDENT
GEORGE H. W. BUSH

A billboard at the Kremlin Wall advertised Billy's 1992 meetings in Moscow.
▼

The **MINISTRY**

"As a servant of Jesus Christ, I must say again and again how unworthy I felt to minister to the people of these lands. I was reaping where I did not sow, and it was a humbling experience. Any honor or any credit for what has happened through this ministry belongs only to the Lord Jesus Christ, whom I serve, and the many people—my team and others—who helped make these journeys possible."

—BILLY GRAHAM

Moscow Renewal

Preparations for Billy's three-day Moscow crusade in October 1992 presented a unique set of challenges for the team. Russian church leaders had almost no experience in organizing any type of public outreach. Most Moscow buildings were still under government ownership, so renting office space and finding housing for the American crusade staff was a complex process. Office supplies and printed materials had to be obtained mostly from Finland because of short supplies in Moscow.

The largest nongovernment advertising campaign permitted in Moscow since the 1920s made the crusade known to Moscow's millions. The postal system delivered more than 3.2 million leaflets to every home in Moscow, while radio, television, newspapers, buses, metro cars, and fifteen hundred large billboards invited people to the meetings.

Billy said, "I've never seen such a hunger in people for spiritual things. . . . People realize the past is gone, the future is uncertain, and the present seems to be hopeless. As a result, many were open to God."

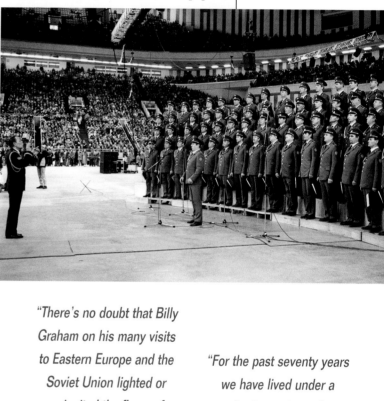

▶

The Russian Red Army chorus sang a favorite American hymn, "Battle Hymn of the Republic," at the 1992 Moscow crusade: "Christ was born across the sea. As he died to make men holy, let us live to make men free, while God is marching on. Glory! Glory! Hallelujah!"

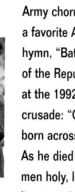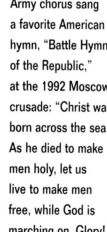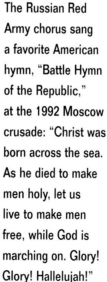

◀

On the final Sunday afternoon at Olympic Stadium, 50,000 were jammed inside the 35,000-seat auditorium while here, outside in frigid weather, 20,000 more watched on a large-screen television.

"There's no doubt that Billy Graham on his many visits to Eastern Europe and the Soviet Union lighted or re-ignited the flame of religious belief and conviction. And that, in turn, had a political impact on what took place in these Communist-dominated nations . . . and was helpful in bringing about the change from what it was sixty or seventy years ago."

—PRESIDENT GERALD FORD

"For the past seventy years we have lived under a totalitarian regime where we were given recipes for complete and absolute happiness. Now instead of quoting Marx and Lenin, we are able to quote the Bible. Instead of Party meetings, we are able to hold religious services."

—A CHURCH LEADER

"You have made many friends and your visit will have much influence and we are grateful for your sincere messages."
—ZHANG WENJIN
FORMER CHINESE AMBASSADOR
TO THE UNITED STATES

China: New Horizons

When the invitation to visit China came from the Chinese Christian Council and the Chinese People's Association for Friendship with Foreign Countries, a lifelong dream of Ruth's was finally realized. Billy remembered, "All our married life, Ruth had talked about China—and with good reason. China was where she was born and where she spent the first seventeen years of her life. Growing up in China gave Ruth a love for the Chinese people and their culture that has never left her."

During his April 1988 visit to China, Billy visited five cities, traveling two thousand miles in fifteen days. He preached in three large churches and also at a house church. He spoke at the university, meeting with scholars and students, and visited political and government leaders in several cities. Both Billy and Ruth met with Premier Li Peng in his office, discussing religion's place in China's future.

Chinese Ambassador Zhang Wenjin gave a welcome banquet in Beijing's Great Hall of the People. In his introductory remarks, he called Billy "a man of peace" and Ruth "a daughter of China."

Ruth and her family had been forced to flee China in 1937, after the Japanese bombed Shanghai and foreigners were ordered out of the country. She looked forward to heading "home" to show Billy and their son, Franklin, the home where she grew up.

As their motorcade drove for several hours through little villages with mud farmhouses, thatched roofs, water buffalo, and a few chickens, Ruth commented, "I felt at home. I'm sure I have peasant blood in my veins."

Ruth showed Billy and Franklin her favorite room, an alcove under the eaves. "This was my bedroom," Ruth said. "I spent a lot of time looking out the small window, reading my books and my Bible—I loved it here." Then a big surprise greeted her as they walked outside: several childhood friends had come to see Ruth.

"Most of the older Christians have gone on to heaven," one of them told her, "but the younger Christians are carrying on."

▲
Billy met with Premier Li Peng at the Pavilion of Lavender Light (China's White House).

Billy visited a house church in Guangzhou (Canton).
▼

In Shanghai's Muen Church and an adjoining building, Billy preached to 3,000 Chinese.

◄
Childhood friends greeted Ruth in Huaiyin.

◄
Ruth showed Billy an alcove in the home where she grew up.

▼

A huge statue of Kim Il Sung greets visitors to Pyongyang.

North Korea

The Democratic People's Republic of Korea (North Korea), the country that had once banned all religious activity and proclaimed itself "the first atheistic nation on earth," was the last place Billy ever expected to visit. Although the United States and North Korea were technically still at war (the conflict had ended in 1953, but only with a cease-fire, not a peace treaty), the Korean Christian Federation and the Korean Catholics Association invited Billy for a seven-day visit in April 1992.

During that first trip, Billy addressed more than four hundred students at Kim Il Sung University, the nation's leading educational institution and alma mater to many of North Korea's top leaders. He preached in two recently built churches (one Protestant and the other Catholic) in the capital city of Pyongyang, met with a small gathering of pastors and seminary students from various parts of the nation, and participated in high-level meetings with many officials, including Vice Premier and Minister of Foreign Affairs Kim Yong Nam.

"The highlight of our trip was our meeting with [President] Kim Il Sung," Billy said. It was President Kim who invited him for a second visit.

During the five-day February 1994 trip, Billy preached in a newly built church, lectured again at the university, was interviewed by several reporters on North Korean national television, and spoke at the Great People's Study House (equivalent to America's Library of Congress). Again Billy met with President Kim, who embraced him and said, "I consider it a great honor to have a friend like you in the United States." During private conversations with the President, Billy delivered a verbal message from President Clinton, just as he had delivered one from President Bush in 1992.

At a luncheon hosted by President Kim, Billy spoke about his own faith—a faith, he reminded the North Korean leader, that President Kim's own mother had professed. "He acknowledged that she had taken him to church sometimes when he was a boy," Billy recalled, "although he admitted with a smile that he had always wanted to go fishing instead. He listened respectfully to what I said but made little comment."

▼

A thousand people listened to Billy at the Great People's Study House.

▼

President Kim Il Sung greeted Billy on his second visit, in 1994.

▲

Billy preached at the new Chilgol Church when he visited in 1994. At left is Ned Graham, who accompanied his father on his trips to North Korea.

The Power of the Media

The **MAN**

"I always face the press and television with fear, anxiety, and complete dependence on the Lord. I think I pray as much about a press conference as I do about my sermons. It is so easy to be misquoted and misinterpreted. I have never believed that the success of our work depends on, or is the result of, publicity. However, I am convinced that God has used the press and TV coverage in our work, and it has been one of the most effective factors in sustaining public interest through the years."
—BILLY GRAHAM

When Billy first attracted media attention in the late 1940s, the secular journalists sent to cover his crusades were on unfamiliar territory: they were not used to covering evangelism. Even the language was different. While a reporter might think of the word *justified* in typographical terms, in a Christian context it means "declared as being in a right relationship with God." Reporters needed some clear explanations, so the Graham team provided a glossary of religious terms:

Grace—the undeserved favor of God
Heart—the real self; the inner man with his emotions
Faith—taking God at His word; believing what God says is true
Born Again—being given spiritual life by God

To help reporters further, the team arranged for press conferences in which the reporters' direct questions allowed Billy to provide a better understanding of his ministry.

Religion was still not a major theme of secular journalism when the Associated Press assigned George Cornell to cover Billy's 1957 New York crusade. Cornell was one of the first to specialize in a subject now covered by many full-time religion writers for American newspapers.

Billy has always made full use of the media in extending the outreach of his message. In his many opportunities to share the Gospel in newspaper, radio and TV interviews, as well as through the Internet, he has constantly been alert to the need for simplicity of presentation.

"It is good to have Billy Graham around, for things start happening much for the better in ordinary people's lives."
—JOHN KNIGHT,
SUNDAY MIRROR,
LONDON, ENGLAND

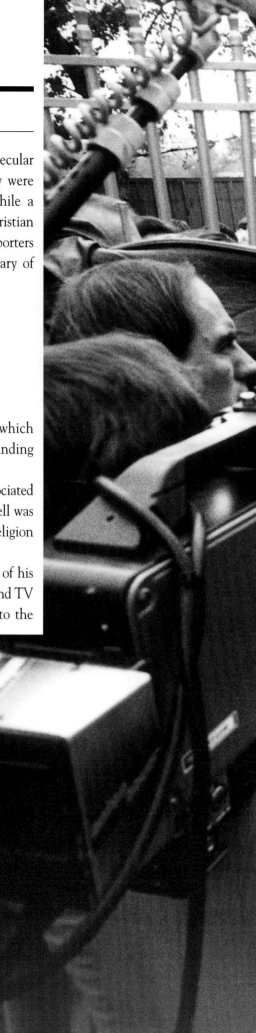

▶
In 1984, Billy met with the Russian media following a sermon in Moscow.

"It is strange how one has become used to publicity. I used to strongly resent the invasion of our privacy; now I have learned to live with it and have dedicated it to the Lord."

—*BILLY GRAHAM*

"No man could be so continually surrounded for so many years with so much adulation and criticism, and still remain the plainly decent, good-humored, thoughtfully kind man he is, without being of quality timber."
—GEORGE CORNELL, ASSOCIATED PRESS

▲

Billy has answered questions at press conferences all over the world, including this one in a smoke-filled room, at the Birmingham, Alabama, crusade in 1972.

"Everything he does is compelling. He is made of the stuff that molds men's minds, stuff that has destroyed nations when activated by a Hitler or a Mussolini, that has saved nations when embodied in an Abraham Lincoln or a Winston Churchill."
—DWIGHT NEWTON, SAN FRANCISCO JOURNALIST

"What's so special about you?"
—REPORTER AT A PRESS CONFERENCE, COPENHAGEN, DENMARK
. . .
"I'm not sure there is anything special about me. In fact, I don't think there is at all. The message I am preaching is the message the Church has been proclaiming for centuries. I believe God gave me the gift of an evangelist. And there are many evangelists being raised up all over the world."
—BILLY GRAHAM

"What is the secret of your success?"
—INTERVIEWER, SYDNEY, AUSTRALIA
. . .
"The secret is not me. So many people think that somehow I carry a revival around in a suitcase, and they just announce me and something happens—but that's not true. This is the work of God, and the Bible warns that God will not share His glory with another. All the publicity that we receive sometimes frightens me because I feel that therein lies a great danger. If God should take His hand off me, I would have no more spiritual power. The whole secret of the success of our meetings is spiritual—it's God answering prayer. I cannot take credit for any of it. "
—BILLY GRAHAM

▲

Billy extended a warm greeting to George Cornell of the Associated Press.

"Do you spend too much money on mass evangelism?"
—REPORTER AT A PRESS CONFERENCE, SYDNEY, AUSTRALIA
. . .
"We don't spend enough. We need to start asking ourselves: What is the value of a human soul before God?"
—BILLY GRAHAM

◄

Billy spoke at a New York City press conference in 1969.

►

Following his return from the USSR, Billy faced reporters at a 1984 press conference in New York City.

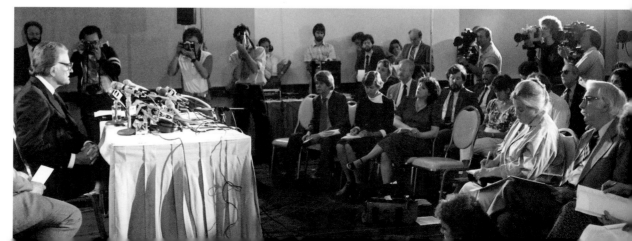

"My challenge to the press of America would be: Let's work for the reversal of the runaway trend toward moral degeneracy that has destroyed so many nations in the past. Let's seek an emphasis on positive virtues. And let's communicate the fact that fundamental moral values have the same power to heal minds, hearts, and souls of people as they've always had."
—BILLY GRAHAM, ADDRESSING THE NATIONAL PRESS CLUB

"Dr. Graham, is there really a God in heaven?"
—JOURNALIST FOR U.S. News & World Report, APRIL 25, 1966

. . .

"Yes sir, there is a God. God is not 'dead.' There are many evidences pointing to the fact that there is a God, but I don't think that we can draw a scientific conclusion. We can't go to a laboratory and demonstrate Him. However, there are many evidences that there is a God. Of course, the ultimate step, it seems to me, has to be by faith that there is a God."
—BILLY GRAHAM

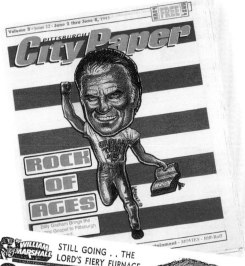

"For two years in the mid-fifties, more newspaper and magazine copy was devoted to Billy Graham than to any other person in the United States, including President Eisenhower."
—WILLIAM MARTIN,
TEXAS MONTHLY

The MAN

"God has not promised to bless my thoughts, but He has promised to bless His Word."
—BILLY GRAHAM

"I joined in to try and find out just what special magic it is that keeps the crowds pouring in. There was no Bible thumping or fanatical evangelism to drive people wild. Just a senior-looking man in a crisp blue suit saying his piece for those who wanted to hear."
—BRITISH REPORT ON MEDIA
COVERAGE OF MISSION '89

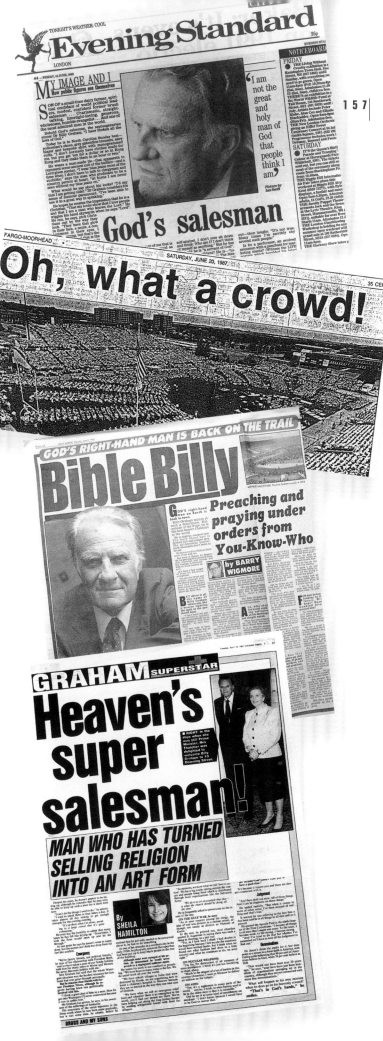

Russian media interviewed Billy aboard an Aeroflot flight in 1984.

▶ Merv Griffin, 1983

"Billy Graham has no hidden agendas. He's not an emissary for any government. He's not an emissary for any organization; he's only an emissary for God."
—SIR DAVID FROST

▲ Barbara Walters, Hugh Downs, and Joe Garagiola, 1968

▶ Bryant Gumbel in Moscow, Russia, 1984

▶ Jane Pauley, Tom Brokaw, and Willard Scott, 1981

▶ Dan Rather, 1979

▼ Tokyo, Japan, 1967

▶ Johnny Carson, 1972

"In this day of publicity and media exposure, people have a tendency to feel that you are larger than life. Many people put me on a pedestal where I do not belong. I am not the holy, righteous prophet of God that many people think I am. I share with Wesley the feeling of my own inadequacy and sinfulness constantly. I am often amazed that God can use me at all."
—BILLY GRAHAM

◄
Billy prayed before his CNN interview in 1993.

▶

Dick Cavett, 1972

◄
Sir David Frost, Sydney, Australia, 1979

▶
Paul Harvey interviewed Billy at his home in Montreat, North Carolina, in 1979.

▼
Peter Jennings, 1996

▲
London, England, 1984

◄
Diane Sawyer, 1992

▶
Larry King, 1994

Hour of Decision and "My Answer"

The Hour of Decision radio program began broadcasting November 5, 1950, from Atlanta, Georgia, over the American Broadcasting Company (ABC) network. The first broadcast was carried live by 150 stations coast to coast. The thirty-minute weekly program was hosted by Cliff Barrows, with Bible reading and a message from Billy.

Broadcasting weekly required Billy to study the Bible all the more. He tailored his messages in response to contemporary events in our nation and around the world.

Forty-eight years later *The Hour of Decision* has changed very little and is heard on hundreds of radio stations worldwide. The weekly program is translated into several languages for foreign broadcast.

Listeners from almost every country and in every conceivable circumstance have written to Billy to tell him how God changed their lives while they listened to one of the broadcasts.

At the insistence of his friends Walter Bennett and Fred Dienert, Billy started a daily advice column called "My Answer" in December 1952. Within one year, "My Answer" was syndicated in seventy-three daily newspapers across America. Today "My Answer" reaches 5 million readers through several hundred newspapers.

People were looking for biblical answers to their questions about everything from religious, social, and ethical situations to marital problems and child raising.

Billy said, "In more than fifty years of ministry and after much research and conversation with psychiatrists and psychologists, I have yet to discover a source of practical advice and hope that compares to the wisdom found in the Bible."

January 7, 1994

ead and understand ible as God's word

Billy Graham
My Answer

the Bible is God's word, you may be surprised at the way God answers that simple prayer.

Let me suggest you begin in the New Testament with one of the four Gospels (each of which tells details of the life and ministry of Jesus), for they will acquaint you with Christ. I often suggest that people who are unfamiliar with the Bible...

As you read through the Gospel of John (or any other book in the Bible), stop and meditate on what you read. Ask questions about each event or passage — questions like "What happened on this occasion? How did people react to Jesus? What was he teaching here?" In addition, ask how it applies to your life, and what difference it should make in the way you think...

MY ANSWER
What happens if we ignore God?

Dear Rev. Graham: You wrote once, I think, that sin always has consequences, but I wonder about that. I see a lot of people who live any way they want to, and the only result they seem to have is lots of fun out of life. What do you mean when you say we will pay a price if we ignore God and break His laws? – Mrs. B.H.

Dear Mrs. B.H.: One of Satan's greatest lies is to deceive us into believing that we can sin and get by with it. But it simply isn't true.

It goes back to the very beginning of the human race, when God told Adam and Eve they would die if they disobeyed Him and ate...

▶
During his 1962 South American visit, Billy broadcast *The Hour of Decision* from missionary station HCJB in Quito, Ecuador.

"I am a life-termer in this state penitentiary, and for ten years I have been dreaming and planning for the day when I could escape this horrible place. My plans for escape were almost complete when last Sunday a man in the cell next to me turned his radio to The Hour of Decision. I could not help but listen. My soul was stirred with memories of Mother and home. I began to realize how far I had wandered from Mother's teachings. I remembered the little Baptist church we used to attend. . . . At the close of your sermon, I knelt in my cell and sobbed my confessions to God. My heart was strangely warmed, and for the first time in my life I felt the presence of God. . . . I have discarded my plans for escape because I realize that God can use me right here in this prison to help others find the wonderful peace that I have in Christ."
—*C.J., AT A SOUTHERN STATE PENITENTIARY*

Books

"I wrote my first book," Billy said, "out of a burning conviction that a book presenting the Gospel in a simple but comprehensive way was what people who had little or no religious background needed. It was one of those times when I sensed the direction of God in my life in an extraordinary way."

A New York publishing company had approached Billy about writing a book. Billy asked the publisher to provide editorial assistance and proceeded to send an outline and a mass of sermon material. As the first chapters reached Billy, he said, "I can remember yet, looking at them appalled. I tossed the whole thing in the wastebasket and Ruth and I wrote the book, *Peace with God*. We sent the manuscript to several friends, wrote and rewrote—and prayed often—but the final book contains the thoughts God gave Ruth and me."

Peace with God, Billy's first book, was published in 1953. Today more than 3 million copies in fifty languages have been circulated around the globe.

Billy has written twenty-one books. Many have sold well over one million copies and have been on best-seller lists for weeks at a time. *Angels*, written in 1975, sold one million copies in its first ninety days. After fifteen months of publication, more copies had been sold in hardback than any book in American history—except the Bible. Well over 30 million books by Billy Graham have been printed and distributed worldwide.

Billy has donated royalties from almost every book to various Christian organizations and ministries. The royalties from *Angels* went to Wheaton College, his alma mater. A small portion was set aside for his children and grandchildren's educations. Royalties from *Just as I Am*, Billy's autobiography, which has sold more than 1.5 million copies, went to the Billy Graham Evangelistic Association. It was the largest single contribution ever received by the organization.

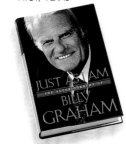

"Thank you for your book, Hope for the Troubled Heart. *Living in a nursing home, I visit some of the other residents who are not so fortunate as I am in my ninety-eighth year. Being able to get around with my walker, I take your book with me and read to the patients. The helpful readings reach each of us in a different way.*"
—R.S., TEXAS

Your book, Peace with God, *transformed my life. This happened more than a year ago when I was going through a tough time emotionally and physically. I was involved in the occult but, praise God, when I gave my life to the Lord Jesus Christ, He gave me what nothing else in the world could ever give me: abundant life, abundant peace and joy. I am eighteen years of age and am in my last year of high school.*"
—B.C., MAURITIUS ISLAND

Christianity Today

About two o'clock one morning in 1953, an idea raced through Billy's mind. "Trying not to disturb Ruth, I slipped out of bed and into my study upstairs to write. A couple of hours later, the concept of a magazine was complete. I thought its name should be *Christianity Today*."

Billy's idea that night was for a magazine aimed primarily at ministers, one that would restore intellectual respectability and spiritual impact to evangelical Christianity and reaffirm the power of the Word of God to redeem and transform men and women.

"The idea also came to me that night that we should raise enough money in the beginning to send free subscriptions to every pastor, seminary student, and seminary professor in the United States and a stack to every seminary, Bible school, and Christian college in the country," Billy said. "Such a magazine would require spiritual and intellectual leadership and professional skill I didn't have."

That expertise came from three key contributors. *Christianity Today*'s first issue was published in November 1956, with Carl Henry, a respected theologian, as editor. Billy's vision was also shared with his father-in-law, Dr. L. Nelson Bell, who had a similiar idea and whose wisdom "served as a compass," according to Billy. And the generous support for many years of J. Howard Pew, chairman of the board of directors of the Sun Oil Company, made Billy's vision a reality. A separate independent board was constituted to oversee the magazine, with Billy, its founder, as chairman.

There have been many changes in the world and in the magazine since it began in 1956. But as Billy wrote in the first issue, "The answer to the theological confusion existing in the world today is found in Christ and the Scriptures." That was the original goal and it is still the same today.

"Many of the articles in Decision magazine have helped me and have made an impact on my life. Your sermons have given me boldness to face the giants, and I finally started to obey the words and commands of God regardless of the cost. My neighbors and relatives have noticed the peace, joy, and happiness I now have."
—C.I., NIGERIA

"I was saved years ago while reading Decision magazine; I was led to the Lord by some woman's testimony. I wish I had kept that issue of Decision. I am still taking part in service to the Lord. What a wonderful Savior we serve—He is so kind and patient with us."
—E.B., KENTUCKY

Decision Magazine

"I felt we needed two publications," Billy said, "one on the theological level and a more popular magazine to help ordinary Christians in their witness and daily walk. We would also include news of our past crusades and a calendar of planned crusades across the U.S. and around the world to promote prayer support for our scheduled meetings."

Decision magazine began publication in November 1960. By the time it celebrated its tenth anniversary, circulation had passed 4 million.

Decision is published monthly in several languages (including Braille) and is distributed in 163 countries. In addition to individual recipients, bulk mailings are sent to prisons, hospitals, and overseas mission groups.

"My husband, Terry, and
I became Christians when
your film, The Restless
Ones, was shown at the
University Theatre in
Thunder Bay. Since then
we have been active in
church, and God has led
us to Bible school as
well as into a ministry
to native people."
—T. AND N.C.,
ONTARIO, CANADA

World Wide Pictures

Billy often said, "Thousands will come to see a film who would never come to hear a preacher." With that philosophy in mind, he started World Wide Pictures, a nonprofit film company that was incorporated in 1951, to produce and distribute full-length films with a spiritual message.

The first film produced by the new company was *Mr. Texas*, a western starring country-western singers Redd Harper and Cindy Walker, and featuring Billy Graham as himself. The film premiered at the Hollywood Bowl.

Since then, World Wide Pictures has produced more than two hundred dramatic and documentary films using locations in many foreign countries. Films have been dubbed or subtitled into numerous foreign languages.

The first films were shown in churches, schools, prisons, and military camps, but later films were made for theater showings.

A special 70-mm, wide-screen, Todd-AO film called *Man in the Fifth Dimension* was made for the 1964–65 New York World's Fair. The film was shown hourly from 10 A.M. to 10 P.M. in a special four-hundred-seat theater that offered viewers earphones at each seat in a choice of five languages. More than one million people saw the film, and many thousands more from every state and fifty-five nations were counseled by a volunteer staff supplied by New York area churches.

Someone recently calculated that a World Wide Pictures film is shown somewhere in the world every hour around the clock.

▲
Billy attended the premier of *The Hiding Place*.

▲
Billy Graham Pavilion was a towering presence at the 1964–65 New York World's Fair.

"Fifteen years ago I saw the film, Time to Run. Your message in it changed my life, for I made a decision for Jesus Christ that night."
—G.J., NORTH CAROLINA

►
Billy talked with Dick Ross, former president of World Wide Pictures, during the filming of a movie.

"I am an elementary school teacher and will be starting my doctoral program in the fall. As a child, I was mentally, physically, and sexually abused. I have been extremely angry at God. I tried to commit suicide twice. During one of my suicide attempts, the television was on and you were there. I called your number and received an hour-long conversation with a counselor. I thank God for the grace He has supplied, as it is beyond my scope of thinking. I want you to know that you have been an instrumental tool whom God has used. I feel as if I have been reborn and been given a new life. Today I am excited about living."
—J.G., IOWA

Telecasts

Billy's first national telecast began on June 1, 1957, from the New York crusade at Madison Square Garden. The meetings were telecast live for one hour at prime time each Saturday night for seventeen weeks on the ABC television network, which went from coast to coast. At the conclusion of the seventeen telecasts, more than thirty thousand people across the nation wrote to tell of their decisions to accept and follow Christ.

Realizing that television was a powerful vehicle for shaping character and influencing people for good or for evil, Billy started telecasting his crusades and other special programs via two hundred stations for one hour, twelve times each year in the United States, while forty foreign countries carried selected telecasts at prime time in their countries.

Since March 1981, ten regional phone centers have been set up across America, Canada, Hawaii, and the Bahamas for each telecast. The centers were staffed for each crusade telecast by thirty-five hundred trained volunteers who answer the calls for spiritual help in response to Billy's crusade message. To date, more than 750,000 callers have received biblical answers to their many questions, and more than 25 percent of the callers prayed to receive Jesus Christ as their personal Lord and Savior.

◄ The first regional telephone counseling centers were set up in 1982.

▲ Technological advancements have allowed Billy to reach more people than anyone ever dreamed possible.

"As an undergraduate student, I acknowledged Jesus Christ as a historical figure, but beyond that I gave little or no thought to who He was. I vacillated between atheism and agnosticism. I didn't believe God was real. Here I was, a rational, logical person; a trained scientist. That evening, when I turned on the television, a Billy Graham crusade came on. I didn't want to see anything religious, but I listened. Billy Graham made a persuasive argument that Jesus Christ is much more than I had ever realized. At the end of his message I was intellectually convinced that God had come to earth in the person of Jesus Christ. I walked into the bathroom and closed the door; I bowed my head and said to God, 'It's over! You win! Do whatever You want with me.' I became a believing Christian. I couldn't get enough of the Bible."
—R.G., NEW JERSEY

Satellite Crusades

Satellite technology has given new meaning to Billy's crusade ministry. Today millions of people can hear him by satellite in any part of the world, almost as if they were hearing him in person.

During the Euro '70 crusade in Dortmund, Germany, the meetings were carried live by television relays (cable and microwave) to 36 cities across Europe and shown in rented theaters, halls, and churches. In 1985 from the Sheffield, England, crusade, satellites were used for the first time to telecast the services live in 230 rented auditoriums all over Great Britain.

As satellite technology improved and became less expensive, requests began coming from churches in every part of the world to broadcast a Billy Graham crusade in their town. Thousands of churches in each area began preparing as if Billy were coming in person. Various international conferences on evangelism, especially the two held in Amsterdam in 1983 and 1986, gave the Billy Graham Evangelistic Association contact with 12,000 evangelists from every part of the world who could help prepare for a satellite-transmitted Billy Graham crusade. Churches cooperated by providing counselors, renting halls, printing tickets, advertising the event, and inviting their friends, neighbors, and guests to hear Billy preach about God's love for them on a large screen in their community. The Billy Graham Evangelistic Association sent volunteers to train church leaders who in turn trained their own people to evangelize in their communities, with the help of the satellite crusades.

Satellite crusades have made it possible to preach the Good News of God's love to all people—literally to every part of our world—in their own language, through simultaneous translation.

▲

Translation booths for many languages enabled the Word to be spread across the globe.

◄

Global Mission in 1995 was transmitted from 17 satellite pathways to 30 satellites across all 29 time zones for a total of 300 hours of transmission over three days.

▲

Crowds watched Billy's simulcast at one of the 1,400 satellite crusade locations during Mission World Europe.

1989—Mission World Africa
Telecast in 6 languages
from the London crusade
to 33 countries in Africa

1990—Mission World Asia
Telecast in 48 languages
from the Hong Kong crusade
to 33 countries in Asia

1991—Mission World Latin America
Telecast in 6 languages
from the Buenos Aires crusade
to 20 countries in Latin America

1993—Mission World Europe
Telecast in 45 languages
from the Essen, Germany Mission
to 1,400 crusade locations
in 55 countries

1995—Global Mission
Telecast in 117 languages
from the San Juan, Puerto Rico crusade
to 3,000 crusade locations
in 185 countries and territories

The **MESSAGE**

"I present a God who matters, and who makes claims on the human race. He is a God of love, grace, and mercy, but also a God of judgment. When we break his moral laws we suffer; when we keep them we have inward peace and joy. I am calling for a revival that will cause men and women to return to their offices and shops to live out the teaching of Christ in their daily relationships. I preach a Gospel not of despair but of hope for the individual, hope for society, and hope for the world."

—*Billy Graham*

Thousands responded to Billy's invitation at the Georgia Dome in Atlanta, 1994.

CHAPTER FOUR

INSPIRING OTHERS

Billy has often said, "Whether the story of Christ is told in a huge stadium, across the desk of a powerful leader, or shared with a golfing companion, it satisfies a common hunger. All over the world, whenever I meet people face-to-face, I am made aware of this personal need among the famous and successful, as well as the lonely and obscure."

Billy's ministry has been played out on a large and visible stage during five decades of tremendous social change and upheaval, including the civil rights movement, political assassinations, and terrorist attacks. But his personal desire has been to lead one individual at a time to a new way of life.

Every U.S. President since World War II has found occasion and reason to call on Billy, who readily responded. Both Johnson and Nixon, the two with whom he was probably closest, offered him high positions in the government—which he quickly and politely refused. Billy has also shared the friendship of many well-known figures in the fields of sports and entertainment. Most of his time, however, is spent with ordinary people from all walks of life.

But Billy has found that all people, famous or not, share the basic questions of life: "Who am I? Where did I come from? Where am I going? Is there meaning in my life? Only God can give us the ultimate answer to those questions."

◄

Billy offered a warm heart, a listening ear, and encouraging comments to President Lyndon Johnson at the 1966 National Prayer Breakfast in Washington, D.C.

"We sometimes forget that some of the loneliest people in the world are those who are constantly in the public eye. They have spiritual needs just like everyone else. Also, I have found many world leaders who sense that our problems today are so complex that they defy solution. They know that the only answer is to be found in God."

—BILLY GRAHAM

▲
Billy has been a frequent visitor to the White House.

▼
Billy and President Lyndon Johnson shared a warm moment at the White House in the 1960s.

"Billy and I were riding in a car to a private luncheon with two high-ranking U.S. government officials. As we passed security and drove toward the house, Billy said he felt it would be better if we did not take any pictures. I explained that we had obtained permission, but Billy repeated his wish. He was afraid his hosts might think he was only interested in being photographed with them and that it might also interfere if he had an opportunity to talk about spiritual issues. Naturally, I waited in the car with the driver. I have gladly missed several good photos because I too believe that the spiritual opportunity is more important than the photograph."

—RUSS BUSBY

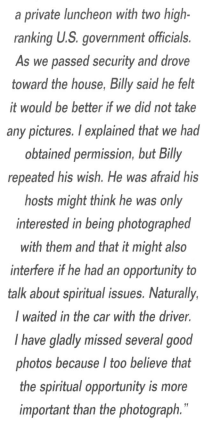

▶
Billy and President Eisenhower met privately in the late 1950s, and on occasion read together a Bible that Billy had given him.

National Prayer Breakfasts

It was the vision of Christian leader Abraham Vereide to have an annual national prayer breakfast. He repeatedly urged Billy to help him.

In the spring of 1953 Billy held a crusade in Washington, D.C., and made many contacts among government leaders. Vereide approached Billy and Senator Frank Carlson of Kansas about asking President Eisenhower if he would attend a national prayer breakfast. The first breakfast was held at the Mayflower Hotel, paid for by Conrad Hilton.

President Eisenhower not only attended but also spoke, saying: "As Benjamin Franklin at one time during the course of the stormy consultation at the Constitutional Convention said, because he sensed that the convention was at the point of breaking up, 'Gentlemen, I suggest that we have a word of prayer.' And strangely enough, after a bit of prayer the problems began to smooth out and the convention moved to the great triumph that we enjoy today, the writing of our Constitution."

President Ronald Reagan spoke at the 1987 National Prayer Breakfast: "Fellowships have begun to spring up through all three branches of the government, and they have spread throughout the capitals of the world to parliaments and congresses far away.

"I wish I could say more about it, but it's working precisely because it is private. In some of the most troubled parts of the world, political figures who are old enemies are meeting with each other in a spirit of peace and brotherhood. And some who've been involved in such meetings are here today.

"There are such diversities in the world, such terrible and passionate divisions between men, but prayer and fellowship among the great universe of God's believers are the beginning of understanding and reconciliation."

Since the first one in 1953, National Prayer Breakfasts have been attended by every U.S. President.

▲ Abraham Vereide (left) urged Senator Frank Carlson and Billy to help him start the National Prayer Breakfasts.

▶ President Kennedy (left) and Vice President Johnson (right) listened intently as Billy addressed the 1963 breakfast, less than a year before the President's tragic death.

The **MAN**

"All of the Presidents I have known (except Truman), I knew long before they ever became President."
—BILLY GRAHAM

▼ President Nixon, 1969

▼ President Ford, 1975

▼ President Carter, 1979

President Reagan,
1987

President Bush,
1989

President Clinton,
1993

Harry S. Truman

In 1950 a congressman called Billy and asked, "Would you like to meet the President?" Billy said yes and flew to Washington. Without any briefing on protocol, he went in with three colleagues and spoke with President Truman, who told Billy he lived by the Sermon on the Mount. Before leaving, Billy recalled, "I put my arm around him and I said, 'Could we pray?' And of course that was taking advantage of the President's graciousness in receiving us. He replied, 'Well I don't see any harm.' And so I prayed with him."

When Billy got outside, the press surrounded him and said, "Now we weren't in there, we didn't get any pictures; would you pose for a picture and . . . answer some questions?" So Billy told them what he had said and then posed on the White House lawn, "kneeling in prayer, like a fool," as he later recounted. "But God was planning all that because He taught me a great lesson." A few days later, a columnist reported that President Truman had called Billy "persona non grata at the White House" because he had shared their conversation with the press. "It was a terrible mistake on my part and from then on I knew that you do not quote famous people."

Years later, Truman warmly received Billy at his Independence, Missouri, home and they laughed together over the evangelist's youthful indiscretion.

▶

Billy met with President Truman in 1967 at Truman's home in Independence, Missouri.

Dwight D. Eisenhower

"This is what I have found out about religion: it gives you courage to make the decisions you must make in a crisis and then the confidence to leave the results to a Higher Power. Only by trusting God can a man carrying responsibility find peace and repose."

—DWIGHT EISENHOWER

"Billy Graham is one of the best ambassadors our country has but he told me 'I'm an ambassador of heaven.'"

—DWIGHT EISENHOWER

During Mr. Eisenhower's presidential campaign, Billy recommended that the candidate and his wife join a church. Eisenhower said, "If I join a church now, people will think I'm doing it to get votes, but I promise I will join a church whether I win or lose."

After his inauguration, Eisenhower kept his word and joined the National Presbyterian Church pastored by Dr. Ed Elson, one of his former chaplains in Europe. During his tenure at the White House, the President attended church almost every Sunday.

"Eisenhower was the first President that really asked my counsel in depth when he was sending troops into Little Rock," Billy said. "He called me one morning in New York, where I was preaching in Madison Square Garden, and said he was thinking about sending troops down there to enforce the law [against segregation]. He said, 'What do you think?' I said 'I don't think you have an alternative, this is a terrible thing.' Within an hour [Vice President] Nixon called to ask the same question . . . I told him the same thing."

Just before Eisenhower died, Billy was invited to see him at Walter Reed Hospital. When Billy entered the room, he noticed that "Eisenhower had his normal, big smile. He knew he didn't have long to live. He said, 'Billy, I want you to tell me once again how I can be sure my sins are forgiven and that I'm going to heaven, because nothing else matters now.'" Billy took out his Testament and read several Scriptures. He pointed out that we are not going to heaven because of our good works, we are going to heaven totally and completely on the merits of what Christ did on the Cross, and that Eisenhower could rest in the confidence that Jesus had paid it all. Eisenhower said, "Well, let's pray," and Billy prayed for him and held his hand. When Billy had finished praying, Eisenhower looked up. And he had that marvelous smile, and said, "Thank you. I'm ready."

Mamie and President Eisenhower talked with Billy and Dr. Ed Elson at National Presbyterian Church in Washington, D.C., in 1953.

▼

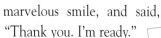

ONLY NUDIST CAN TOP BILLY—

Evangelist Graham Meets Ike And Nixon Clad Only in Towel

INDIANAPOLIS — (P) — Evangelist Billy Graham Wednesday staked claim to a curious clerical "first" that's not likely to be topped very soon.

Graham thinks he's the only minister ever to conduct an audience with the president and vice president of the United States while splendidly, if not decorously, clad in a bath towel.

"It happened last Monday at Burning Tree Country club in Washington," Graham said,

grinning as he told of the incident in an impromptu hotel room news conference.

"Mr. Nixon and I had just finished a round of golf, and I was taking a shower. The vice president came in and said Mr. Eisenhower had just entered the clubhouse after playing, and he wanted to talk to me.

"I just grabbed a towel and came out— guess I didn't think anything about it being unusual. Later Mr. Nixon told me that I probably was the first minister ever to talk with the president and vice president under just those conditions."

For Billy Graham — from his friend with warm regard — Dwight D. Eisenhower

John F. Kennedy

Four days before he was inaugurated as President, John Kennedy invited Billy to spend the day with him in Palm Beach. When Billy arrived, Kennedy yelled out the window, "I'll be out in a minute. Go out to the pool and talk to my father. He wants to tell you something." Billy had never met Ambassador Joseph Kennedy before. "You were invited here because I was in Stuttgart, Germany, with the president of Notre Dame University," the ambassador said. "We saw signs all over town where you were speaking at the football stadium. We decided to go out and see what it was like. We saw sixty thousand people there. We told the Pope about it a few days later. The Pope said, 'Yes, I wish we had a hundred Billy Grahams!' I came back and told Jack, 'One of the first things you have got to do is get in touch with Billy Graham, because you had this religion problem during the campaign between the Catholic and Protestant and I believe he can help heal it.'"

"We drove around in JFK's white Lincoln convertible. During our conversations, I became aware that he was concerned about the moral and spiritual condition of the nation. He was especially concerned about the scars that might have been left by the intense religious issue during the presidential campaign. He asked me a number of questions about the Bible. I remember he asked, 'Where do you think history is going and what is the objective of history?' I told him that the Bible teaches that history would someday come to a dramatic conclusion with the Second Coming of Jesus Christ. He responded, 'I'm interested in that.' That was the beginning of a friendship."

During Kennedy's funeral service in the Capitol rotunda, Billy stood about thirty feet from Mrs. Kennedy and the family. He watched the faces of America's leaders. Many of them asked, "How could it happen in America?" A senator grasped Billy's hand and said, "We must get back to God." Billy recalled, "I could not help but think of the brevity of life. I am convinced that we need a new awareness of the fact that death is rapidly approaching for each of us and that the Bible has many warnings for us to prepare to meet God."

▲

As Vice President Johnson, Billy, and Lady Bird Johnson listened, President Kennedy spoke at a "ladies' luncheon" held in connection with the National Prayer Breakfast.

"Hearing from you who has accomplished so much good for so many people around the world is greatly appreciated. The President greatly admired you and what you are doing."
—ROBERT KENNEDY, IN A HANDWRITTEN NOTE TO BILLY AFTER PRESIDENT KENNEDY'S FUNERAL

The MAN

"President Kennedy invited me to the White House on four or five occasions, once during the Cuban missle crisis. Another time, before his trip to South America, he asked me to demonstrate how I spoke through an interpreter at my crusades abroad."
—BILLY GRAHAM

▲

Bobby Kennedy (left) escorted Caroline, Jackie, and John Jr. from the Capitol rotunda where JFK's body lay in state.

◀

President Kennedy took Billy, Robert McNair (left), and Senator George Smathers (right) for a ride in Palm Beach.

▲
Billy and President
Kennedy enjoyed a
light-hearted
moment at a
National Prayer
Breakfast.

▶
President
Kennedy's body
lay in state in the
Capitol rotunda.

Lyndon B. Johnson

"My mind went back to those lonely occasions at the White House when your friendship helped to sustain a President in an hour of trial. . . . No one will ever know how you helped to lighten my load or how much warmth you brought into our house. But I know."

—LYNDON JOHNSON,
IN A PERSONAL LETTER TO BILLY
SHORTLY AFTER LEAVING OFFICE

There was a religious side to Lyndon Johnson that people did not know. Often he proudly showed visitors to the Oval Office a faded letter on the wall from General Sam Houston. It was addressed to Johnson's great-grandfather, an evangelist who had led Houston to faith in Christ. "You could be converted by reading that letter," recalled Billy. Johnson's grandfather had taught Bible at Baylor University.

Billy was probably closer to Lyndon Johnson than to any other President. He was invited to the family ranch several times and spent more than twenty nights at the White House during Johnson's administration. "I saw the working of the presidency and the White House through him more than any other President," Billy said.

Presidents have a lot of advisers. President Johnson once told Billy he had over a thousand people who were supposed to report directly to him. He said, "The problem in this job is not making decisions but knowing what decisions to make, since each decision affects everyone differently."

Ruth and Billy were dining alone one evening with President and Mrs. Johnson the weekend before the Democratic convention of 1964. The President read a list of fourteen names as possible vice presidential candidates. Then he looked at Billy and said, "Billy, which one would you choose?" When he asked that question, Ruth kicked Billy under the table. They'd known President and Mrs. Johnson for many years, so Billy just looked at her and said, "Ruth, why did you kick

me?" And the President looked at her and he said, "Ruth, what did you kick Billy for?" And she said, "Mr. President, I think that he ought to give you only spiritual counsel, and not political counsel." And he said, "Ruth, you're right." Later, when Ruth and Mrs. Johnson went out to the private living room, the President closed the door and said to Billy, "All right, tell me who you really think." Billy suggested Hubert Humphrey. "I think he'd already made up his mind, but he did choose Hubert Humphrey."

▲
Billy often visited President Johnson at the White House.

Lyndon liked to talk in his bedroom late at night. Every time Billy would say to him, "Let's have prayer," the President would get out of bed and get on his knees to pray.

Billy was deeply honored to have President Johnson attend his 1965 Houston crusade in the Astrodome. This was the first time that a sitting President had attended a Graham crusade.

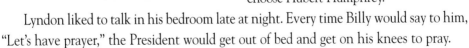

The MAN

"President Johnson was an outgoing sort of person. When I went to Washington and stayed in a hotel, if he found out about it, he'd call right up and say, '[There will] be a car there in fifteen minutes. Your hotel is over here.' And I'd move over to the White House."

—BILLY GRAHAM

▼

Billy enjoyed many moments with President Johnson at the LBJ ranch. He described his good friend as "a very rough and very tough man with his staff and other people. On occasion he would use pretty rough language, even in front of a clergyman, though he would always say, 'Pardon me, Reverend.' He really did love people, especially minorities and the poor. He wanted to do something for them."

▲

Ruth, Billy, President Johnson, Lady Bird, and Lynda Johnson entered the First Christian Church in Washington where Billy preached at Johnson's inaugural prayer service.

▲

One day at his Texas ranch President Johnson took Billy out under the oak tree where he was going to be buried and said, "Now Billy, you're going to preach my funeral here. Preach the Gospel, tell them how to get to heaven and all that, but tell them a little bit about me. Tell them a little bit about what I tried to do." And they both smiled. On Thursday, January 25, 1973, Billy spoke these words at the funeral of his good friend: "Lyndon Johnson was a mountain of a man with a whirlwind for a heart. He will stand tall in history. To him the Great Society was not a wild dream but a realistic hope. The thing nearest to his heart was to harness the wealth and knowledge of a mighty nation to assist the plight of the poor and underprivileged. . . . For the believer the brutal fact of death has been conquered by the historical resurrection of Jesus Christ. For the person who has turned from sin and has received Christ as Lord and Savior, death is not the end. For the believer there is hope beyond the grave. There is a future life! The Bible says in John 11:25–26, 'I am the resurrection, and the life: he that believeth in me, though he were dead, yet shall he live: And whosoever liveth and believeth in me shall never die.'"

Richard M. Nixon

▲

Richard Nixon visited Billy and Ruth at their home in the 1960s.

▼

Ruth, Pat Nixon, Billy, and President Nixon joined the singing at the 1970 Knoxville crusade.

President Nixon and Billy had been personal friends since 1950. From the very beginning of their friendship Billy said, "I realized he had one of the most brilliant minds I was ever to know."

Nixon was a private and complex person, but beneath the surface Billy found him to be warm and compassionate, quite different from the popular caricatures of him. He often answered letters from friends with a handwritten reply. "He was a strong family man," Billy remembered, "and I have never known anyone who was more devoted to his wife or his children and their families."

Nixon was a man of genuine faith, rooted simply in the teachings and prayers of his devout Quaker mother. Often he had Billy pray with him and read the Bible to him when they would visit.

Billy remembered the year Watergate was just beginning: "Nixon wanted me to come to the White House. Before I left, I put my arm around him, and I said, 'Mr. President, let us have a prayer.' He said, 'Billy, I would like to say something first. We have been here now four years. I thought some of my enemies would have had me by now. You know I am a hated man.' We had a prayer. And when I finished praying, I looked up at him and tears were coming down both sides of his checks. I will never forget that night.

As the Watergate scandal unfolded, Billy urged the President to reveal all the facts, no matter the cost: "I am a pastor and a minister; when a person needs you, that's when the call is the strongest. But I would be neither his friend nor God's servant if I did not point out what the righteousness of God demands at such a time as this."

In the last year of Nixon's presidency, Billy never got to see him. He couldn't even get an answer from a secretary or anybody he knew at the White House. Later someone told Billy that Nixon had said to the entire White House staff, "Don't let Billy Graham near me, I don't want him tarred with Watergate."

The MESSAGE

"O God, our new President needs Thee as no man has ever needed Thee in leading a people! There will be times when he will be overwhelmed by the problems at home and abroad that have been building up to the breaking point for many years. Give him supernatural wisdom, courage, and strength for these four years. Protect him from physical danger. And in the lonely moments of decision grant him an uncompromising courage to do what is morally right . . ."
—BILLY GRAHAM
INAUGURAL PRAYER,
JANUARY 20, 1969

"I could tell Billy Graham anything in confidence and it would never make the public print . . . and he could speak to me in confidence. We were two people who could, in effect, let our hair down."
—RICHARD NIXON

▲
Presidents Clinton, Bush, Reagan, Carter, and Ford (with their wives) attended the memorial service for Richard Nixon, who will always be remembered for his boldness in ushering in a new era of history by opening the door to China. In later years he had become America's senior statesman, for many felt he had no peer in the area of foreign affairs.

◄
Billy spoke at Nixon's funeral in 1994.

The MESSAGE

"There comes a moment when we all must realize that life is short, and in the end the only thing that really counts is not how others see us, but how God sees us. For the believer there is hope beyond the grave, because Jesus Christ has opened the door to heaven for us by His death and resurrection."
—BILLY GRAHAM
SPEAKING AT
RICHARD NIXON'S FUNERAL

Gerald R. Ford

Gerald Ford had served in the House of Representatives since the Truman days. When he took the oath of office as President of the United States he said to the American people, in his inaugural address, "I am acutely aware that you have not elected me as your President by your ballots, so I ask you to confirm me as your President with your prayers . . . Let us restore the Golden Rule to our political process. And let brotherly love purge our hearts of suspicion and of hate . . ."

To critics of his relationship with Billy, Ford said, "I've heard the comments from some sources that Billy mixes politics with religion. I never felt that and I don't think that thousands and thousands of people who listen to him felt that.

"Billy dropped by the Oval Office on several occasions while I was President. They were get-togethers of old friends. They had no political or other significance. It was simply an expression, or an extension, of our long-standing friendship."

The **MAN**

"I agreed with the presidential pardon because I believe that the trial of a former President would be destructive and not in the best interests of the nation. A one-or-two-year trial would tear America apart."
—BILLY GRAHAM

▼

Billy joined President Ford for a round of golf at a pro-am tournament in Charlotte, North Carolina, 1974.

▲

Billy visited President Ford at the White House in the mid-1970s.

Jimmy Carter

"To me, God is real. To me, the relationship with God is a very personal thing. God is ever present in my life. He gives me guidance when I turn to Him. . . . "We ought constantly to search our national and individual consciousness and strive to do better, which doesn't mean to be more powerful and auto-cratic, but more filled with love and understanding and compassion and humility."
—JIMMY CARTER

In 1966, staff members from the Billy Graham Evangelistic Association went to Americus, Georgia, to hold a film crusade. Billy needed a chairman who would hold integrated meetings, which he demanded for all of his work. "Jimmy Carter was the only man who had the courage to be the chairman," Billy said. "That was before Carter ever ran for any political office. Then when Jimmy was governor of Georgia he was the honorary chairman of our Atlanta crusade."

Carter remembered, "When I was asked to head up a Billy Graham evangelical program in Sumter County, in strict segregation days . . . I told the planning groups they would have to be integrated . . . blacks and whites together. And when I went to the major churches, none of them would let us come in. So we went to the basement of an abandoned school building and that's where we had our integrated planning meetings. And then the Billy Graham films were shown in our local theater."

▲

Billy and former President Carter met privately during the 1994 Atlanta crusade.

◄

Governor and Rosalynn Carter attended the 1973 Atlanta crusade in Atlanta Stadium.

"Billy and Ruth Graham have been to visit us both in the governor's mansion in Georgia and in the White House. His reputation is above reproach or suspicion. He's been a Christlike figure with a global beneficial impact in evangelism."
—JIMMY CARTER

To our good friends Ruth & Billy Graham
Jimmy Carter   Rosalynn Carter   11-2-79

▲

Following a White House visit, Billy and Ruth received this memento.

Ronald W. Reagan

Billy met Ronald Reagan a year after he married Nancy. Mrs. Davis, Reagan's mother-in-law, introduced them, saying, "I want you to get to know my new son-in-law, Ronald Reagan." Billy said, "You mean the film star?" She said, "Yes." Reagan and Billy have been close friends ever since. "I remember when Reagan was president of the Screen Actors Guild, a union leader, and a very strong Democrat."

On March 30, 1981, after the assassination attempt on President Reagan's life, Billy flew immediately to Washington, D.C., to comfort and pray with Mrs. Reagan and do anything he could for the President. Billy later contacted the father of John Hinckley, Jr., the President's assailant, and prayed with him over the telephone.

In an address during the National Prayer Service at the Washington Cathedral, January 20, 1985, Billy reminded Reagan, "During the next four years, many of you here today will have to make decisions of state perhaps greater than any of those made by your predecessors. Because of modern technology, you will hold in your hands the destiny not only of America but of the entire world. Christ, whom the Bible speaks of as the source of all wisdom, said, 'What shall it profit a man if he shall gain the whole world, and lose his own soul?' (Mark 8:36). I believe that applies to nations as well as individuals, for a nation that loses its spiritual courage will grow old before its time."

▲

Nancy and Governor Reagan joined Billy at the 1969 Anaheim crusade.

"I'm sure there will be those who will question my participation here tonight. People have become so concerned with church-state separation that we have interpreted freedom of religion into freedom from religion. There is no greater need in our land today than to rediscover our spiritual heritage."
—RONALD REAGAN,
THEN GOVERNOR OF CALIFORNIA,
AT 1969 ANAHEIM CRUSADE

"I appreciated Billy Graham being on hand at a time that was rather difficult. I remember that I wanted him to know that I had called on the Almighty for help and if He did not have some other plan, then I would recover and regain my health. But I didn't think I could call on God for help without saying that whatever life was left for me belonged to Him. I also asked the Lord to make well the young man that had shot me. I didn't feel that I could ask that I'd be saved . . . unless I had a prayer for the other person also."
—RONALD REAGAN,
REFLECTING ON THE 1981
ASSASSINATION ATTEMPT

◄

Billy and the Reagans go back a long way. This photo was taken shortly after they met.

Billy and Ruth enjoyed a visit to the White House with Nancy and President Reagan.

"It was through Billy Graham that I found myself praying even more than on a daily basis . . . and that in the position I held (of President), that my prayers more and more were to give me the wisdom to make decisions that would serve God and be pleasing to Him."
—RONALD REAGAN

President and Nancy Reagan and Vice President and Barbara Bush attended the National Prayer Service in 1985.

George H. W. Bush

> *"Billy Graham has been an inspiration in my life. It is my firm belief that no one can be President without a belief in God, without understanding the power of prayer, without faith. And Billy Graham helped me understand that. Billy has been in our home many times and he's answered all the tough questions that children and adults can ask . . . And he answered all these questions so children understood. I thank God for bringing Billy Graham into the lives of my family. He gave us great strength and through him we better know God's Son, Jesus Christ."*
> —GEORGE BUSH

▶ Billy and Ruth visited President and Barbara Bush and President Bush's mother, Dorothy, at Kennebunkport, Maine, in the early 1990s.

Billy and Ruth have been friends with the Bushes for many years. Billy knew President Bush's mother and father, and Billy and Ruth have taken vacations with President Bush and his family at Kennebunkport. "We love the whole family and we know them all and they are an incredible family," Billy said. "Ruth has often said that it's worth having George Bush as President to get Barbara as First Lady.

"We don't go to counsel him on public affairs. He's never asked me a question about how any particular thing should be run in the country," Billy said.

Billy found Bush easy to talk to about spiritual issues, "easier than other Presidents I have met. He says straight out that he has received Christ as his Savior, that he is a born-again believer, and that he reads the Bible daily. He has the highest moral standards of almost anybody whom I have known. He and his wife have such a relationship, it is just unbelievable. If you are with them in private, you know, they are just like lovers."

Billy was called to the White House January 16, 1991. When he arrived, Mrs. Bush invited him to the Blue Room to watch television.

As they watched, suddenly a CNN reporter said, "It looks like anti-aircraft fire over Baghdad." Billy turned to Barbara and said, "Is this the beginning of the war?" She looked over at him and, without saying a word, the look on her face told him that it was.

About thirty minutes later the President came in. He was a little somber, but seemed totally relaxed because he said, "I know I have done the right thing." Billy knew President Bush had spent a great deal of time in prayer and meditation over this decision. "We had prayer and talked a long time. During our conversation he said, 'Would you do something for me?' I said yes. He said, 'I would like to call Mr. Cheney, General Powell, and the leadership of our top military together tomorrow morning and have you speak to them.'" Billy readily agreed, praying for all sides in the conflict.

To the Grahams from the Kennebunkport Bushes with love— *Geo Bush & Barbara*

▼ Billy visited President and Barbara Bush at the White House in January 1991, the night the Gulf War began.

> *"Almighty God has answered the prayers of millions of people with the liberation of Kuwait and the end of offensive operations in the Persian Gulf region. We prayed for a swift and decisive victory and for the safety of our troops. Clearly, the United States and our coalition partners have been blessed with both. We thank the Lord for His favor, and we are profoundly grateful for the relatively low number of allied casualties."*
> —PRESIDENT BUSH
> IN A PROCLAMATION DECLARING
> APRIL 5, 1991, A NATIONAL
> DAY OF THANKSGIVING

"In thy sovereignty Thou has permitted George Bush to lead us at this momentous hour of history . . . give him the wisdom, integrity, and courage to help this become a nation that is gentle and kind. Protect him from physical danger, and in the lonely moments of decision, grant him Thy wisdom to know what is morally right and an uncompromising courage to do it. Give him a cool head and a warm heart."

—BILLY GRAHAM,
EXCERPTS FROM INAUGURAL PRAYER

▲

Billy and President Bush enjoyed fishing together off the coast of Maine.

▶

Billy delivered the prayer at President Bush's inauguration, January 20, 1989, in Washington, D.C.

William J. Clinton

President Clinton once recalled, "When I was a small boy, about twelve years old, Billy Graham came to Little Rock, Arkansas, to preach a crusade. Our town was torn apart by racial conflict. Our high schools were closed, and there were those who asked Billy Graham to segregate his audience in War Memorial Stadium, so as not to roil the waters.

"I'll never forget what he said—that if he had to speak the Word of God to a segregated audience he would violate his ministry, and he would not do it. And at the most intense time in the modern history of my state, everybody caved, and blacks and whites together poured into the football stadium. And when the invitation was given, they poured down the aisles together, and they forgot they were supposed to be mad at each other, and angry at each other, that one was supposed to consider the other somehow less than equal.

"He never preached a word about integrating the schools. He preached the Word of God, and he lived it by the power of his example. And one young boy from a modest family for a long time thereafter took just a little money out of his allowance every month and sent it to the Billy Graham crusade."

At a National Prayer Breakfast, President Clinton said, "I have always been touched by the living example of Jesus Christ. All the religious leaders of his day were suspicious of him and always tried to trap him because he was so at ease with the hurting, the hungry, the lonely and, yes, the sinners. In one of the attempts to trick Christ, he was asked what is the greatest commandment. And he answered, quoting Moses, 'You shall love the Lord your God with all your heart and with all your soul and with all your mind.' And then he added, as we should add, 'this is the great and foremost commandment, and the second is like it, you shall love your neighbor as yourself.'"

▲

Governor Bill Clinton joined Billy at the Little Rock Billy Graham crusade, September 1989.

"Billy and Ruth Graham have practiced the ministry of . . . being friends with Presidents of both parties, counseling them in countless ways, always completely private, always completely genuine. . . . We sat in the Oval Office reminiscing and talking about current circumstances, and I asked for Billy Graham's prayers for the wisdom and guidance of God."
—BILL CLINTON

▶

Tipper Gore, Vice President Gore, Ruth, Billy, President Clinton, and Hillary Clinton were photographed together during the 1993 National Prayer Breakfast.

▶

Billy and President Clinton shared a private moment in the Oval Office.

Political Temptations

"During these times of change and tumult in the world, we especially value Reverend Graham's wisdom and vision and his efforts to promote peace and understanding among different peoples. By sharing the teachings of the Gospel with individuals, he has made a difference in the lives of nations."
—GEORGE BUSH

Shortly after the 1949 Los Angeles crusade, the governor of North Carolina called and asked Billy if he'd be interested in being appointed to the U.S. Senate. One of the senators had died. Billy did think about it overnight and talked to his father-in-law, Dr. Bell, but he concluded, "No, the Lord called me to preach."

Presidents have offered Billy top positions. President Johnson asked him to serve in several different positions, but he said no to all of them. While swimming together at Camp David one day, the President said in front of a group of people, "Billy, you ought to be President of the United States. If you do run, I'd like to be your campaign manager." Billy laughed and said, "You're joking." Johnson replied, "No, I'm serious. I mean it."

Johnson also offered Billy the ambassadorship to Israel. Later on, sitting beside Golda Meir at a dinner at the White House, Billy said, "I am not the man. God called me to preach." And Golda Meir reached and grabbed his hand. Billy told Johnson, "The Middle East would blow up if I went over there."

Nixon once half-jokingly asked if Billy would be willing to be his running mate for Vice President, and after his election he asked Billy which administration job he would like. Billy looked him in the eye and said, "God called me to preach the Gospel, and I consider that the highest calling in the world."

When Billy was urged by a group of Republicans from the Southwest and Southeast to run for President in 1964, he told them absolutely not. When it made the newspapers and television, Ruth called up and said: "They'll never elect a divorced man because I would leave you if you run for any political office." Billy said, "Darling, you don't have to worry." She said, "Call a press conference as soon as you can because reporters are really badgering me." Billy had barely heard about it. The Republicans had contacted him just once, and by the time the night was over delegates were being pledged to him.

Billy never gave these offers serious thought. "They really haven't been temptations because the call of Christ and of the Kingdom of God was so strong, and always has been," he said.

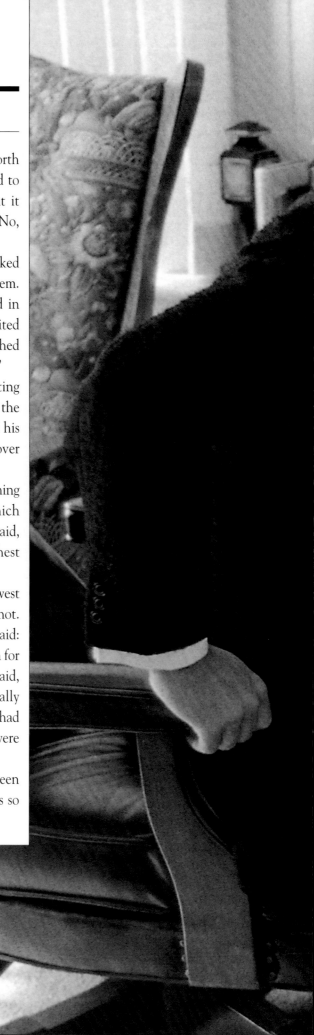

▶

Billy often worked in his personal study in Montreat.

The **MINISTRY**

"You could not offer me a job as an ambassador or a cabinet post that I would give a second thought to. When God called me to preach, it was for life."

—BILLY GRAHAM

"Billy Graham doesn't give you tactical advice on what to do politically. He talks about the moral dimension of the issues. And the reason world leaders have sought his advice is precisely because he doesn't try to tell them what they should do tomorrow. But he does try to show them a way of thinking about the problem that adds a new dimension to their thinking."
—HENRY KISSINGER, SECRETARY OF STATE

Meetings with World Leaders

Throughout his ministry, Billy has had the opportunity to meet with many of the world's leaders and visionaries. From heads of state to religious leaders, many testify to the effectiveness of his ability to influence their thought processes, noting that he adds a moral dimension to their thinking.

Leaders have long appreciated Billy's respect for their privacy and the fact that he does not approach them with a personal agenda. President Ford said, "Billy made many, many contributions to our society across the board and because of his inspirational abilities, he was able to influence millions and millions of people. . . . His interest was in social justice— Billy Graham spoke from the heart, from the Bible, and from his own conviction on social issues that were on the agenda at the time."

"I saw Mr. Graham and spoke to him for quite a long time. I was very glad he came along to Number 10. His message was absolutely vital. This life is more than about material things."
—MARGARET THATCHER

◄

Billy met with British Prime Minister Margaret Thatcher in 1989.

The MINISTRY

"Everywhere I go I find that people . . . both leaders and individuals . . . are asking one basic question: 'Is there any hope for the future? Is there any hope for peace, justice, and prosperity in our generation?'"
—BILLY GRAHAM

◄

Queen Elizabeth II, Prince Philip, and the Queen Mother welcomed Billy and Ruth to Sandringham, where he preached in the chapel.

◄ China, 1988
Premier Li Peng

◄ United States, 1997
Chinese President
Jiang Zermin. At left
is Ned Graham,
president of East
Gates Ministries
International, which
provides Bibles and
other assistance to
the churches of
China.

▲ North Korea,
1992
President
Kim Il Sung

► Japan, 1980
Prime
Minister
Zenko
Suzuki

▼ Taiwan (China),
1956
Chiang Kai-shek

▼ South Korea,
1951
President
Syngman Rhee

*"The Chinese constitution guarantees
freedom of religious belief. But in the
past we didn't practice it in full. We are
trying to correct the past. China needs
moral power and spiritual forces if it is
to prosper and grow strong."*
—Li Peng,
*as quoted in the Chinese press
after his private meeting with Billy*

◄

The Kremlin,
USSR, 1991
President Boris
Yeltsin

▲

The Kremlin,
USSR, 1991
General Secretary
Mikhail Gorbachev

▶

West Germany,
1970
Chancellor Willy
Brandt

▶

Canada, 1982
Prime Minister
Pierre Trudeau

*"I will always remember the
great interest you have shown in
Israel and the Middle East, and
your readiness to help the cause
of peace with honor in the area."*
—YITZHAK RABIN,
FORMER PRIME MINISTER OF ISRAEL,
EXCERPT FROM LETTER TO BILLY GRAHAM

▶

France, 1986
President François
Mitterand

▶ Israel, 1969
Prime Minister
Golda Meir

"Billy Graham is a great teacher in all the important matters to humanity, and a dear friend of Israel."
—GOLDA MEIR

▲ Israel, 1969
Mayor of
Jerusalem
Teddy Kollek

▲ Germany, 1993
Chancellor
Helmut Kohl

"Mr. Adenauer invited me to come have coffee with him in his office. The first question he asked me was, 'Young man, do you believe in the resurrection of Jesus Christ?' And I said, 'I do sir.' 'So do I', he said. 'If Jesus has not been raised from the dead I don't see one glimmer of hope for the human race. This is the Good News that the world needs to hear.'"
—BILLY GRAHAM

▲ Egypt, 1975
Vice President
Hosni Mubarak

◄ Jordan, 1960
King Hussein

◄ India, 1956
Prime Minister
Jawaharlal Nehru

► Philippines, 1977
President Ferdinand
and Imelda Marcos

► Liberia, 1972
President William
and Mrs. Tolbert,
and Pat Nixon, who
represented the
United States at
President Tolbert's
inauguration

► India, 1973
Prime Minister
Indira Gandhi

◄ Kenya, 1976
President Daniel
Arap-Moi

> *"I think it's the mission of a minister to change people. It is not the mission of a minister to change governments. The people that he changes may change governments."*
> —RICHARD NIXON

► Argentina, 1991
President Carlos Menem

▼ Paraguay, 1962
President Alfredo Stroessner

► Ethiopia, 1966
Emperor Haile Selassie

▲ Brazil, 1974
President Ernesto Geisel

◄ Mexico, 1981
President Jose Lopez Portillo

*The*MESSAGE

> *"During all my years as an evangelist, my message has always been the Gospel of Christ. It is not a western religion, nor is it a message of one culture or political system. . . . It is a message of life and hope for all the world."*
> —BILLY GRAHAM

▲

Los Angeles
Mayor Tom
Bradley, 1985

"Billy, by your own example, you have shown how the humanity and conviction of the citizen can become a force for good in this world—first, in one's own hometown and country, then within the larger community of nations. We all have the God-given ability to better the world in which we live. In our own way, each of us can come to know the special grace that service brings."
—U.S. SECRETARY OF STATE JAMES A. BAKER III

"Billy Graham, a prophet in our time, reaches an amazing range of people. His message crosses all barriers which traditionally separate our societies and nations into the have-nots, the powerful and the weak, the affluent and the poor, the liberal and the conservative, and the religious divisions of denominations and faiths."
—REVEREND ERNEST GIBSON, PASTOR, WASHINGTON, D.C.

◄

Defense Secretary
Dick Cheney and
Joint Chiefs of
Staff Chairman
General Colin
Powell, 1991

▶

Chicago
Mayor
Richard J.
Daley, 1962

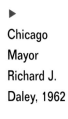

◄

Secretary
of State
Henry
Kissinger,
1973

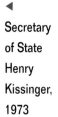

▶

Senate
Majority
Leader
Bob Dole,
1986

"There has never been a more truly international figure in the field of evangelism than Billy Graham. During his crusade in Sydney . . . he gave himself to the crusade with unselfish and unsparing dedication of time and strength. [I came to the conclusion that] the most distinctive note in his preaching . . . is authority. He can preach as he does because he has the moral right to say what he chooses to say, and people recognize by instinct the ring of that strong authority. . . . Behind his voice they hear the call of God."
—MARCUS L. LOANE
ARCHBISHOP, SYDNEY, AUSTRALIA

Chief Rabbi Rosen of Romania hailed Billy as "a bridge-builder between nations and people," 1985.

Cardinal Cushing, Boston, 1964

▲

Archbishop of Canterbury George Carey, 1991

"I had a long talk with the Chief Rabbi in Israel. I asked him if he believed in the coming of Messiah, and he assured me that he did. I told him that I, too, believe in the coming of Messiah, but that when Messiah comes we will all recognize that He is Jesus who was on earth once before. The Chief Rabbi smiled over his cup of coffee and said, 'Of course, that's our difference.'"
—BILLY GRAHAM

"I have never known of a religious crusade that was more effective than Dr. Graham's. I have never heard the slightest criticism of anything he has ever said from any Catholic source. You're preaching Christ and Christ crucified. No one could listen to you without becoming a better Christian."
—CARDINAL CUSHING

▲

Patriarch Alexei, Russia, 1984

▼

Pope John Paul II, 1993

▼

Coretta Scott King, 1987

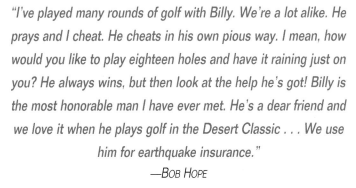

"I've played many rounds of golf with Billy. We're a lot alike. He prays and I cheat. He cheats in his own pious way. I mean, how would you like to play eighteen holes and have it raining just on you? He always wins, but then look at the help he's got! Billy is the most honorable man I have ever met. He's a dear friend and we love it when he plays golf in the Desert Classic . . . We use him for earthquake insurance."
—BOB HOPE

▼
Billy and Ruth with Roy Rogers and Dale Evans

▲
Muhammad "The Greatest" Ali, three-time world heavy-weight boxing champion, visited Billy and Ruth at their mountaintop home in 1979.

"When I arrived at the airport, Mr. Graham himself was waiting for me. I expected to be chauffeured in a Rolls Royce or at least a Mercedes, but we got in his Oldsmobile and he drove it himself. I couldn't believe he came to the airport driving his own car. When we approached his home I thought he would live on a thousand-acre farm and we drove up to this house made of logs. No mansion with crystal chandeliers and gold carpets, it was the kind of a house a man of God would live in. I look up to him."
—MUHAMMAD ALI

◄
In the 1960s Billy discussed the filming of *The Ten Commandments* with Y. Frank Freeman and Cecil B. DeMille.

▲
Filmmaker and theme park designer Walt Disney, 1966

▲
Golfer Arnold Palmer, 1968

◄
Top British solo recording artist Sir Cliff Richard, 1984

▲

Comedian Bob Hope, 1971

◄

NASCAR driver Jeff Gordon and his wife, Brooke, 1999

▼

Alabama coach Paul "Bear" Bryant and his wife, quarterback Joe Namath, and Dallas coach Tom Landry, 1972

The**MAN**

"I often feel like the man in the South who had a mule. He decided to put his mule in the Kentucky Derby. His friends said, 'You don't expect him to win, do you?' 'No, but look at the company he'll be in.' That's the way I feel when I'm with people like you who are so talented."

—BILLY GRAHAM

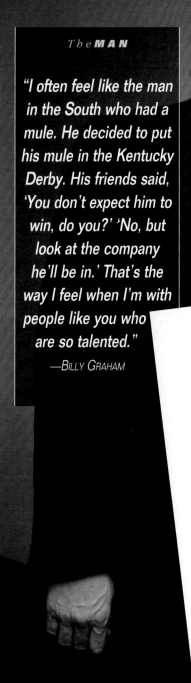

JOHNNY CASH

I have never known a greater man among men. Yet his simplicity, his common touch, his childlike compassion for his fellowman is the source of his greatness.

As a friend of mine, he is one of those in the inner-circle; those four or five friends you will only know in a lifetime of friends that come and go. He is true, He is faithful. He is what he appears to be; a dedicated vessel of Gods earthly endeavors among men. Billy Graham is my friend, and I love him.

Johnny Cash

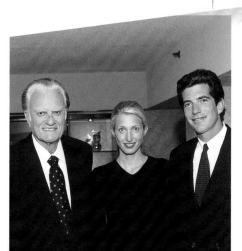

▲

Singer Johnny Cash, 1985

◄

Magazine publisher John F. Kennedy, Jr. and Carolyn Bessette Kennedy, 1996, whose untimely deaths in 1999 touched millions.

Encouraging Special Groups

While Billy may be best known for his crusades, he has also spent countless hours meeting and speaking with special groups around the world. As a result of his public visibility he has received invitations to speak at breakfasts and luncheons, at civic and government meetings, at schools and sporting events, to military and religious organizations, and at conventions such as the National Chamber of Commerce, the American Bar Association, the National Governors Conference, and the International Police Chiefs. Many of the meetings are coordinated with Billy's travels to various cities for crusades, while others are special invitations that he accepts. Billy has spoken to business groups, troops on the battlefield, young people at rock concerts, college students, prison inmates, and a wide variety of other specialized groups.

"I have not taken an honorarium for any speech that I have given since 1951," Billy said. "They offer me huge fees to come to some of these conventions to give an address but I always say, 'You give it to your favorite charity or, if you want, send it to our association, but I will not take any personally.'"

Always looking for opportunities to present the message of God's love to new audiences, Billy said early in his ministry, "I will go anywhere to preach—if there are no strings on what I am to say." That philosophy and his message of encouragement, faith, and integrity remain unchanged to this day.

▲ Billy answered questions from a group of young people at Eurofest, Brussels, Belgium, in 1975.

The **MESSAGE**

> "*People from all walks of life are searching for answers to life's problems. I believe the Bible has the answer to man's deepest needs.*"
> —*BILLY GRAHAM*

▼ Billy spoke and answered questions from students at the John F. Kennedy School of Government, Harvard University 1982.

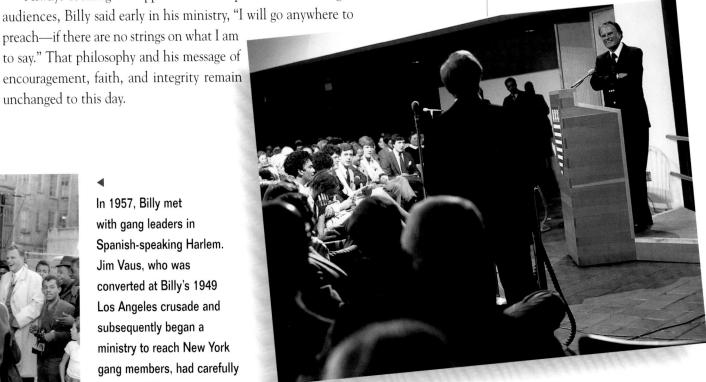

◄ In 1957, Billy met with gang leaders in Spanish-speaking Harlem. Jim Vaus, who was converted at Billy's 1949 Los Angeles crusade and subsequently began a ministry to reach New York gang members, had carefully negotiated the meeting.

Honor America Day, Washington, D.C., 1970

► Honor America Day, Washington, D.C., 1979

◄ Billy has spoken at the Air Force Academy chapel in Colorado Springs as well as at the other service academies at West Point and Annapolis.

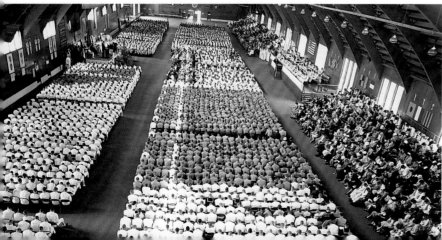

◄ Several thousand trainees turned out to hear Billy at the Great Lakes Naval Training Center.

"Pericles built a civilization upon culture and it failed. Caesar built a civilization upon power and it failed. Our forefathers founded the United States upon faith in God, and our country will survive only as it honors God. . . . Our nation was built on a foundation of moral law, in which a person's rights were also balanced by a person's responsibilities. . . . Why should I, as a citizen of heaven and a Christian minister, join in honoring any secular state? . . .

The Bible says, 'Honor the nation.' As a Christian or a Jew, or as an atheist, we have a responsibility to an America that has always stood for liberty, protection, and opportunity.

There are many reasons why we honor America today. America has opened her heart and her doors to the distressed and persecuted of the world. America has been the most generous nation in history. We have shared our wealth and our faith with a world in need. America has never hidden her problems and faults. With our freedom of the press and open communication system we do not sweep our sins under the rug. America defends the right of her citizens to dissent. Dissent is the hallmark of our priceless freedoms. But when dissent takes violent forms it becomes anarchy.

We may be a vastly different people today than we were two hundred years ago. Our society is far more complex, more pluralistic. But of this we can be sure. God has not changed and His laws have not changed. He is still a God of love and mercy. But He is also a God of righteousness and judgment. Any individual or nation which ignores His moral and spiritual laws will ultimately face His judgment."

—BILLY GRAHAM

▼ Holland, 1983. Billy chatted with young people in an Amsterdam park.

◄ Sheffield, England, 1985. A coal miner had questions for the evangelist.

"Billy comes to Charlotte for a visit whenever he can, and occasionally he'll spend half a day on the farm with me. With a lot of people, what he's done and being so famous would have gone to their heads, but I can truthfully say Billy Frank's just the same when we're alone today as when we were growing up."
—MELVIN GRAHAM,
FARMER AND BILLY'S BROTHER

▶ Cleveland, Ohio, 1972. While visiting the Westside Deli, Billy called the owner's mother—an admirer of his— to say "hello."

▲ After a crusade in 1979, Billy talked with the clean-up crew.

"The evangelist has not permitted his association with presidents and kings to come between his friends in lesser walks of life."
—BRODIE GRIFFITH, BUSINESS LEADER AND
PUBLISHER, CHARLOTTE, NORTH CAROLINA

▲ Northern Ireland, 1972. Billy took the Word of God to a Belfast pub.

◄ Romania, 1985. People greeted Billy on the streets.

"Yes, it has been a privilege to know some of the great men and women of the latter part of this century. However, most of my time has been spent with people who will never be in the public eye and yet who are just as important to God as a Queen or a President. God's forgiveness in Christ is available to all of us, no matter who we are or what we have done."

—BILLY GRAHAM

"I don't remember a great deal about the meeting in Cambridge, but one thing registered deeply. Billy Graham said, 'If you're looking for a depth of peace and a real sense of joy, then find it in Jesus.' When the appeal came at the end, I was in a state of semiconfusion. I felt that I ought to stay. I was duly counseled and prayed for—I took the literature and read it carefully. Back at my lodgings, I went over everything the counselor had said, and I did it with a great deal more understanding. I made a deliberate act of commitment. I had found God, and I had a sense of purpose. There was an immediate change in my life. My drinking stopped, my swearing stopped—just as if someone had dropped a curtain on it. I realized that the Bible had to be my guide, that it was the Word of God.
—BOB DURNETT, STUDENT AT CAMBRIDGE UNIVERSITY, ENGLAND

"What are the problems students face? They're searching for something and if they don't believe in God, they must have a substitute for God. There is a great identity crisis among students today. Who am I? What is the purpose of life? Where did I come from? Where am I going? The Bible has a direct answer to this great big philosophical question and unless God seals the vacuum among youth today, then some other ideology will, because young people must have a faith. They must believe in something to find fulfillment in their lives."
—BILLY GRAHAM

► Billy was invited to speak at Expo '72 in Dallas, Texas, where 80,000 students from all 50 states and 75 foreign countries filled the Cotton Bowl for seven days.

▼ Oxford University, England, 1980. Billy was invited to speak to the Oxford Union debating society.

▼ University of California, Berkeley, 1967. Responding to posters that suggested "investigating" the evangelist, 8,000 students filled the school's outdoor theater.

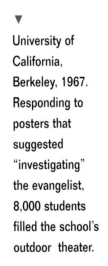

California, 1958. Inmates listened intently when Billy visited San Quentin prison.

Illinois, 1962. Billy brought God's Word to the Statesville penitentiary in Joliet.

Florida, 1969. During a break in the music, rock fans listened to Billy at the Miami Rock Music Festival.

The MAN

"I was thankful for their youthful exuberance; I was also burdened by their spiritual searching and emptiness."

—BILLY GRAHAM

▲

Denver, 1987. Billy addressed the area Civic Clubs.

▼

London, 1989. Billy was invited to address a distinguished gathering at historic Guildhall, the former center of city government that dates back more than 800 years.

THE NEED FOR INTEGRITY

"Many people ask, what is integrity? It means a person is the same on the inside as he or she claims to be on the outside. A man of integrity can be trusted. He is the same person alone in a hotel room a thousand miles from home as he is at work or in his community or with his family.

We have seen the tragic results of moral breakdown and shattered trust in people—from leaders in business and government to well-known sports figures, to husbands, wives, and families and, yes, even the church. The erosion of basic moral and spiritual values seems to be getting more serious at every level of society. We are waking up to the fact that we are paying a terrible price for corruption in government and business—all testify that something is wrong. It's easy to point the finger at prominent people accused of corruption. We can easily see their sins and the results. But a careful look reveals that the same poison of self-gratification and greed exists in our hearts as well.

We all make decisions based on what we truly believe. Many people today wonder if there is absolute truth. They say there is only perspective, that truth is whatever you perceive it to be; whatever works for you. If that is the case, then there is no right or wrong, only differing opinions, and one is as good as another. But God's standard is expressed in the Bible, and the ultimate example of that standard is Jesus Christ. Jesus said, 'You will know the truth and the truth will set you free' (John 8:32). When we live by the truth, we possess integrity.

Unless moral and spiritual values are strengthened, the free way of life we have known in the modern world may be in danger. The problem can be solved if enough people are willing to commit themselves to being part of the process, and taking one step at a time in the right direction. I believe integrity can be restored to a society one person at time. The choice belongs to each of us."

—BILLY GRAHAM

CHAPTER FIVE

REACHING OUT TO A BROKEN WORLD

As a young Christian, Billy was clear about his responsibility to his immediate neighbor, and frequently spoke on the virtues of being a Good Samaritan. But not until he began to travel and see more of the world did he fully understand that the Gospel he preached carried with it a global responsibility linking all humanity. In reflecting on his early years he recalled, "I had no real idea that millions of people throughout the world lived on the knife-edge of starvation and that I personally had a responsibility toward them." Many years later, after witnessing the devastating aftermath of the San Francisco earthquake, he said, "We cannot, and we must not, isolate ourselves from the world in which we live and the problems it faces. . . . The Gospel of Christ has no meaning unless it's applied to our fellow man who hurts and is in need. That's our neighbor, and Jesus said we're to love our neighbor as ourselves."

Billy's status as a world figure, with access to heads of state and political leaders on every continent, has enabled him to initiate a ministry of reconciliation. As part of his crusade structure, Billy encourages the establishment of a Love-in-Action committee in each crusade city, with the specific responsibility of exploring ways to provide assistance to those in need in the local community. Through this effort, tons of food and clothing are provided to the homeless and others with special needs.

◄

When he visited the bombed-out homes of Belfast, Northern Ireland, in 1972, Billy witnessed firsthand the effects of human brutality.

Civil Rights in the United States

The **MAN**

"The race question will not be solved by demonstrations in the streets, but in the hearts of both Negro and white. There must be genuine love to replace prejudice and hate. This love can be supplied by Christ and only by Christ!"

—BILLY GRAHAM

Perhaps it was a part of God's plan that the evangelistic career of Billy Graham should run parallel to the civil rights movement in the United States.

Although he grew up in the American South during a time when racial segregation was generally accepted, as an adult Billy searched the Scriptures and found nothing to support separation of the races. "The ground is level at the foot of the cross," he said, taking a position that he maintained through the entire movement: be a peacemaker and strike at the root of the problem, which is basically spiritual. As a result, he desegregated his crusades, tearing down all racial barriers, even in his meetings in the deep South.

Two years before the landmark Supreme Court decision that banned discrimination on a racial basis (May 17, 1954), Billy struck his first blow for integration when he took down the ropes that separated people by race. At the 1952 crusade in Jackson, Mississippi, 362,300 men, women, and children sat side by side, regardless of the color of their skin.

More than a year before the Court's decision, Billy's Chattanooga, Tennessee, crusade was the first to be integrated from the planning stage. It began March 15, 1953, and was Billy's first crusade in the deep South after Jackson. He told the crusade committee that all participants "must be allowed to sit anywhere," and he overruled protests and ignored forecasts of trouble. Disappointingly, the attendance of blacks was sparse—but those who came had their choice of seats.

Billy worked closely with the Presidents—beginning with Eisenhower, Kennedy, Johnson, and Nixon, who were all involved in the civil rights issue—encouraging them to take steps to end racial segregation.

Billy's commiment was so deep that he cancelled several European engagements in order to visit some of the South's worst trouble spots.

When racial trouble hit Little Rock, Arkansas, in 1957, Billy offered to hold a crusade there, but the local committee thought it would be impossible at that time. When the Little Rock crusade finally did take place two years later, open threats by local segregationists to stage a protest demonstration against Billy for permitting integrated services failed to materialize.

After the crusade, the editor of one of Little Rock's papers wrote Billy saying, "That meeting has done more [to promote racial harmony] than any single thing that has happened in Little Rock."

▲

Billy refused to allow segregated seating at his 1952 Jackson, Mississippi, crusade.

NEWSWEEK, OCTOBER 7, 1957

Among the Southern clergymen who moved forward most resolutely was, characteristically, the Rev. Dr. Billy Graham, the tireless North Carolinian who has preached to more people than any other evangelist in history. Last week he conferred daily with Little Rock ministers, and has since offered to go to Little Rock and conduct a crusade whenever they want him to come. But the ministers there suggested that he wait until a more psychologically appropriate time, possibly about two months from now.

THE ARKANSAS BAPTIST SEPTEMBER 24, 1959

Miracles in Little Rock

God has used Evangelist Billy Graham and his associates to perform miracles in this city, the name of which has become the synonym for racial strife around the world.

"*To base racial segregation on the Bible, I think is ridiculous. Of course, you can make the Bible prove anything. You can twist the Scripture all around and take verses and chapters out of context, but the Bible teaches that we are rightly to divide the Word of Truth, and that we are to do it with spiritual discernment. I just cannot find anything to substantiate racial barriers and difference in the Bible. I think they have to go elsewhere for that.*"

—BILLY GRAHAM

▶ Two years after racial unrest broke out in Little Rock, local officials finally consented to a Billy Graham crusade at War Memorial Stadium.

▼ Total attendance at the March 1953 Chattanooga, Tennessee, crusade reached 283,300.

Little Rock White And Colored Stand Together To Accept Jesus

By PHIL NEWMAN
United Press International

LITTLE ROCK, Ark. (UPI)— Evangelist Billy Graham wound up a two-day whirlwind crusade telling a racially mixed crowd and Gov. Orval Faubus that Little Rock would have no trouble if its people followed Christ.

The Little Rock crusade was Graham's first in three and a half months—since he returned to the United States from Australia. It wasn't the first time he had spoken in an integration hotspot, however, he said.

"I spoke in Clinton, Tenn., too,"

tionists who objected to the evangelist demanding that there be no segregated sections at War Memorial football stadium.

It was filled with 25,000 person Sunday. Some 20,000 persons hear him Saturday night.

"If people lived like Christ a believed in him, there would no problem in Little Rock," G ham said. It was the only dir reference he made to race or tegration during the sermon.

But afterward, when sev hundred persons—both white colored—came forward at his vitation to accept Christ, Gra spread his arms wide and

"*At Billy's 1952 Jackson, Mississippi, crusade, ropes had been put up to keep seating for blacks and whites segregated (as was common practice for public meetings in the South at that time). Billy physically took the ropes down, saying, 'Look, we're all equal before God,' and he refused to let them be put back.*"

—CLIFF BARROWS

"The influence of his message has given us the will and understanding to have greater love for our fellow man. Birmingham will be an improved and better place in which to live because of Billy Graham."
—MAYOR OF BIRMINGHAM, QUOTED IN THE BIRMINGHAM NEWS, MARCH 30, 1964

On a peaceful September morning in 1963, Birmingham, Alabama's, 16th Street Baptist Church was bombed, leaving four black children dead and an entire nation stunned—and making Birmingham the focal point of America's racial upheaval.

Billy offered to bring his team to Birmingham on one condition: "The meeting must be integrated," he told the ministers.

"We would not come otherwise. If we can't meet at the cross of Christ as brothers, we can't make it in other areas."

On Easter Sunday, 1964, his rally in Birmingham's Legion Field drew 35,000, half black, half white—the largest integrated audience in the state's history—and an observer noted that "the races went out of their way to be friendly to one another."

"The most segregated hour of the week in America is the eleven o'clock Sunday morning Christian church service. It is natural for churches to organize and function along ethnic and nationalistic lines. . . . The sin comes when a church becomes exclusive and certain groups are refused admission or fellowship in worship because of race or color."
—BILLY GRAHAM, READERS DIGEST, AUGUST 1960

► As the civil rights struggle deepened, Billy prayerfully canceled engagements in Europe and took his team on a preaching tour of the deep South. The tour ended in June 1965 with an eight-day meeting at the Cramton Bowl in Montgomery, Alabama.

Graham In Alabama Under Tight Guard

BIRMINGHAM, Ala. (UPI) — Evangelist Billy Graham arrived in Birmingham under tight security guard Saturday to address an anticipated 50,000 people at an integrated Easter service.

The evangelist told a news conference shortly after his arrival that Birmingham now is the symbol of "racial discord." He said his appearance would create a new love...

"It has raised questions in the minds of many persons as to why God would allow such a thing to happen," Graham said. He indicated his sermon would help answer the question.

"I have come to Birmingham the gospel, just as I... over the...

Graham Attracts Largest Integrated Audience In Ala.

BIRMINGHAM, Ala. (AP)—Evangelist Billy Graham's Easter appearance before an integrated audience of more than 35,000 was hailed as a tremendous inspirational success by Negroes and white persons.

The gathering at Legion Field, a football stadium in Birmingham, was the largest integrated audience in Alabama's history. It also was the largest religious gathering in...

Turner, said, "After waiting some 15 years for such a visitation as Billy Graham and his team, I am moved almost beyond expression to the outpouring of confidence in our fellow man as seen today."

A Negro minister, Rev. J. L. Ware, said, "It is my candid opinion that this great Ch...

B'ham Refuses Plea To Halt Integrated Easter Ceremony

▶

Blacks, whites, men, women, and children all came forward together at the Cramton Bowl in Montgomery, Alabama.

*The*MINISTRY

"Jesus was not a white man; he was not a black man. He came from that part of the world that touches Africa and Asia and Europe. Christianity is not a white man's religion and don't let anybody ever tell you that it's white or black. Christ belongs to all people; he belongs to the whole world."

—BILLY GRAHAM

▲

Billy and Howard Jones faced tremendous criticism when Jones became the first black associate evangelist to serve on a crusade team.

U.S. NEWS & WORLD REPORT

A wealthy white woman who came forward one evening was counseled by a black woman, and when the white woman's husband mentioned this, his wife answered, "I didn't even notice the color of her skin."

"My association with Billy Graham dates back to 1957 when he invited me to serve as the first black evangelist on his team during the New York crusade in Madison Square Garden. Immediately Billy received many offensive phone calls and letters from white Christians who opposed his position on racial integration and vowed not to continue their moral and financial support of the crusade. Billy, however, courageously stood by his God-given conviction, willing to suffer any repercussion for Christ's sake. Personally, I enjoyed the ten weeks of my ministry there with the team but, at times, I experienced racial harassment in various ways by some whites attending the crusade. The pressure at times was overwhelming. I prayed to God for help. I thought of quitting the team. But Billy was aware of my situation and his love, counsel, and prayers and those of the team gave me the support I needed to continue my ministry. One year later he invited me to join the team full-time as one of his associate evangelists, a ministry that I've cherished from the Lord."

—HOWARD O. JONES

▶

Newspapers and magazines covered Billy's fight against segregation.

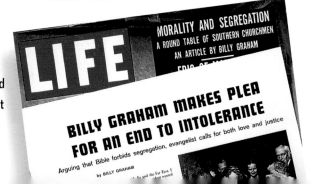

MORALITY AND SEGREGATION
A ROUND TABLE OF SOUTHERN CHURCHMEN
AN ARTICLE BY BILLY GRAHAM

LIFE

BILLY GRAHAM MAKES PLEA FOR AN END TO INTOLERANCE

Arguing that Bible forbids segregation, evangelist calls for both love and justice

by BILLY GRAHAM

The **MAN**

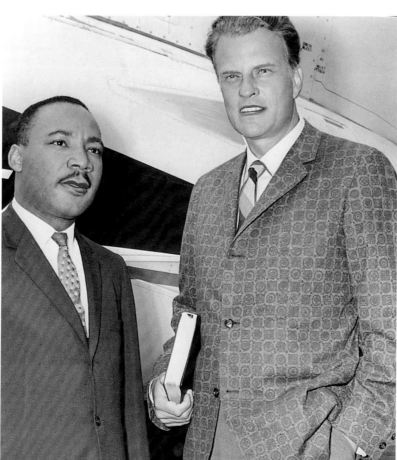

"We arranged some historic meetings in the Oval Office [concerning civil rights] . . . Billy Graham played a major role in that because he knew the black leaders, having had crusades in all of those cities or most of the cities of the South. . . . I give him great credit and I appreciate what he did."
—RICHARD NIXON

"Had it not been for the ministry of my good friend, Dr. Billy Graham, my work in the civil rights movement would not have been as successful as it has been."
—MARTIN LUTHER KING, JR.

▲
Billy (right of fireplace) attended a meeting with President Nixon (left of fireplace) and black ministers in 1969. At left is associate evangelist T.W. Wilson.

"The night the civil rights bill was passed, I had the privilege of being at the White House and Senator Hubert Humphrey (now Vice President) came over to the White House very tired. There were groups of people talking and he came straight over to where I was standing and said, 'Billy, we now have the law on the books, but it will never work unless you and others like you can get people to love from the heart.'"
—BILLY GRAHAM

"When I appointed a Negro— the first—to our school board, the community accepted it as the right thing to do. I don't think that would have happened without the new spirit engendered among your people during the Billy Graham crusade. And save for what happened to me personally in that crusade, I doubt if I would have made such an appointment in the first place."
—MAYOR OF A CITY IN THE DEEP SOUTH

◄
Martin Luther King, Jr. credited Billy with having a major role in lessening tensions between the races.

▼

Alpheus Zulu, bishop of Zululand, attended a crusade with Billy.

"The spirit of reconciliation we today sense in many hearts of South Africans can be traced directly to the Billy Graham meetings held in Durban and Johannesburg in 1973. He was the one who demanded total integration for all of his meetings, and it was done. The Christians then realized that it can be done. From that moment on we were on the road to reconciliation."
—ALPHEUS ZULU,
BISHOP OF ZULULAND,
IN A LETTER, SEPTEMBER 1985

Speaking Out on Human Rights

Billy did not confine his sense of racial justice to the movement in the United States. When he toured Africa for three months in 1960, preaching to thousands of Africans in ten different countries and holding rallies in seventeen cities, he deliberately avoided the Union of South Africa where apartheid ruled.

During his visit, a group of South African clergymen chartered a plane and urged Billy to come to their embattled country. He said he would do so only if multiracial meetings could be arranged. Although the clergymen said his terms could probably be met within two years, it was not until thirteen years later (in 1973) that the South African government relented and permitted an unsegregated Billy Graham crusade.

In the first integrated public meetings ever held in South Africa, Billy preached to overflow crowds, touching more than one hundred thousand people in Durban and Johannesburg. And through a simultaneous live radio broadcast, people across the nation heard Billy's message of brotherly love.

In 1982, Billy was invited to speak at the Moscow Peace Conference. Addressing the participanrs, he took advantage of the opportunity to speak out publicly on the topic of human rights. "We urge all governments," he told them, "to respect the rights of religious believers as outlined in the United Nations' Universal Declaration of Human Rights. We must hope that someday all nations (as all those who signed the Final Act of Helsinki declared) 'will recognize and respect the freedom of the individual to profess and practice, alone or in community with others, religion or belief, acting in accordance with the dictates of his own conscience.'"

In addition, he preached at several churches and met privately with members of the Politburo and the Communist Party's Central Committee, speaking forcefully with them about his concern for human rights and freedom, and particularly about the rights of religious believers. He also raised the issue of imprisoned believers and carried with him a list of 150 names of those believed to be in prison at the time, which he gave to the authorities.

"As a Christian, I believe that we are all created in the image of God. I believe that God loves the whole world. . . . The life of no human being is cheap in the eyes of God, nor can it be in our own eyes."
—BILLY GRAHAM

▶

The first fully integrated public meeting ever held in South Africa was the 1973 Billy Graham crusade in Durban.

▶

Billy's 1982 Moscow visit provided an opportunity to press for the rights of people everywhere.

The MESSAGE

"The deepest problems of the human race are spiritual in nature. They are rooted in man's refusal to seek God's way for his life. The problem is the human heart, which God alone can change."

—BILLY GRAHAM

SUNDAY
MARCH 18
TRIBUNE
BILLY GRAHAM: APARTHEID DOOMED

Concern for World Peace

Unlike any other time in history, today's greatest threat may not come from the so-called superpowers; rather, it may come from the numerous smaller nations in possession of nuclear, biological, and biochemical capabilities that could, at any moment, start a new holocaust.

Billy, like millions of others, realized that with the advent of nuclear weapons humankind had taken its first steps into an ominous new age. Billy said, "Never before has humanity held in its hands such awesome weapons of mass destruction—weapons that could destroy life on this planet within a matter of hours. Man has far exceeded his moral ability to control the results of his technology. Man himself must be changed. I agree with Albert Einstein, who said, 'The unleashed power of the atom has changed everything except our way of thinking.'"

In dealing with this troubling issue, Billy sought assistance from Christians sensitive to the issue of world peace. He also conversed with world leaders in many countries and began to search the Scriptures "in relation to my responsibility as a peacemaker. Should I avoid the issue altogether?" Billy asked. "What should Christians do—throw up their hands in despair, or work to make the world a more peaceable place in which to live?" Christ's words, "Blessed are the peacemakers, for they shall be called sons of God" (Matthew 5:9), took on new meaning for him.

"My visit to Auschwitz will certainly be one of the most unforgettable events of my life. The memory of the incredible horror which took place here will be burned on my mind and heart as long as I live. For Auschwitz is more than a place—it is a blot on the whole human race. It was the invention of minds so depraved and demonic that they defy any rational explanation. It reminds us of the terrible potential man has for violence and inhumanity."
—BILLY GRAHAM

◄

In Poland (1978), Billy spoke at Auschwitz's Wall of Death, where 20,000 people were shot between 1940 and 1945.

МОСКВА 1982

The **MESSAGE**

"I speak to you today as a follower of Jesus Christ. Each of us has our reference point and as a Christian the reference point by which I measure my life and thought is the Bible . . ."

". . . in spite of many fundamental differences we come together in an atmosphere of mutual respect and concern because we share at least two things in common. First, regardless of our background we are all members of the human race, and the problem with which we are dealing is one that affects every human on this planet, no matter what his cultural or political or religious views may be. Second, although we have various religious differences we share a basic conviction about the sacredness of human life and the need for spiritual answers to the problems that confront humanity."

"I call upon the leaders of all nations to work for peace, even when the risks seem high. I call upon Christians to pray and work for peace in whatever constructive ways are open to them. I do not believe this is only a political issue; it is a moral one as well."

—BILLY GRAHAM, SPEAKING TO DELEGATES AT THE "RELIGIOUS WORKERS FOR SAVING THE SACRED GIFT OF LIFE FROM NUCLEAR CATASTROPHE" USSR PEACE CONFERENCE, MAY 11, 1982

Six hundred Buddhist, Shinto, Muslim, and Christian delegates from various parts of the world listened to Billy's message at the peace conference in Moscow.

Times of Tragedy

The worst terrorist attack on American soil in the history of the United States took place on Wednesday, April 19, 1995, when a truck packed with five thousand pounds of explosives blew up in front of the Alfred P. Murrah Federal Building in Oklahoma City. Two Americans were charged with the deed, which killed 168 people, including 19 children who were in a day-care center located in the building, and injured another 400 people.

Billy joined President and Mrs. Clinton in meeting with families who had lost loved ones in the blast and delivered a message of hope and consolation at a memorial prayer service in Oklahoma City.

"No matter how hard we try, words simply cannot express the horror and the shock and the revulsion we all feel over what took place in this city last Wednesday morning," Billy said. "That blast was like a violent explosion ripping at the heart of America.

"But how do we understand something like this? How can things like this happen? Why does God allow this to take place? First, it is a mystery. I have been asked on hundreds of occasions why God allows tragedy and suffering. I have to confess that I can never fully answer this question to satisfy even myself. I have to accept, by faith, that God is a God of love and mercy and compassion even in the midst of suffering. But the Bible . . . tells us that Satan is real, and that 'He was a murderer from the beginning' (John 8:44). And it also tells us that evil is real, and that the human heart is capable of almost limitless evil when it is cut off from God and His moral law.

"The forces of hate and violence must not be allowed to gain their victory, not just in our society, but in our hearts. Nor must we respond to hate with more hate.

"Times like this will do one of two things: They will either make us hard and bitter and angry at God, or they will make us tender and open, and help us reach out in trust and faith. I pray that you will not let bitterness poison your soul, but that you would turn in faith and trust to God, even if we cannot understand. It is far better to face something like this with God's strength than to face it alone and without Him.

"My prayer for you today is that you will feel the loving arms of God wrapped around you, and will know in your heart that He will never forsake you as you trust Him."

Billy spoke at a memorial prayer service attended by city officials, Governor and Mrs. Keating, President and Mrs. Clinton, and many who were in the building or lost loved ones in the explosion.

A Time of Healing

Statewide Prayer Service
Sunday, April 23, 1995
State Fairgrounds Arena
3:00 p.m.

A terrorist attack demolished the Alfred P. Murrah Federal Building in Oklahoma City, Oklahoma.

"These men were daily facing death for the sake of their country and freedom. . . . As I gave invitations for men to accept Jesus Christ as their Lord and Savior, hundreds raised their hands in front of their buddies. Many were weeping unashamedly— men who had faced death just hours before."

—BILLY GRAHAM

▲

Korea, 1952. The war was in its third, bloody winter and more than 21,000 young Americans were dead. Billy wanted to spend Christmas with the troops, so he petitioned Washington and finally received permission. With full military cooperation, Billy visited and preached at the battlefront, where men stood throughout the final service on Christmas Day.

"I wept more in Korea than in all the past several years put together. These experiences changed my life. I could never be quite the same again . . . I felt sadder, older. I felt as though I had gone in a boy and come out a man. . . .

—BILLY GRAHAM

▼

Vietnam, 1966 and 1968. William C. Westmoreland, commanding general of the American forces, invited Billy to the Republic of Vietnam to visit and preach to the troops at Christmas. At a M.A.S.H. unit (mobile army surgical hospital) they spoke and visited the wounded—with the background sights and sounds of choppers thundering overhead, bringing still more wounded wrapped in blood-stained blankets.

▶

In Vietnam, Billy visited aircraft carriers, air bases, hospitals, and jungle outposts, where soldiers, sailors, marines, and airmen stood in the hot sun, pouring rain, and ankle-deep mud to hear about God's love for them.

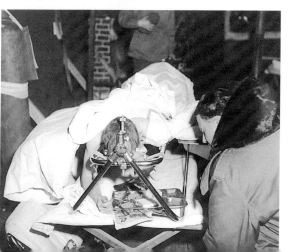

◀

At a M.A.S.H. unit, Billy prayed with a young man who lay face down, able to move only his right arm. Doctors said he would never walk again.

"As Christians we have a responsibility toward the poor, the oppressed, the downtrodden, and the many innocent people around the world who are caught in wars, natural disasters, and situations beyond their control. The Bible has more than a thousand verses related to helping our neighbor in their time of need. Jesus said in Matthew 25:40, 'When you helped these my brothers, you were helping me.'"

—BILLY GRAHAM

Global Relief Efforts

In 1973, at Billy's request, the final offering at his Minnesota crusade was designated for famine relief in drought-stricken Central West Africa, and the $77,000 given that night was the beginning of the World Emergency Relief Fund.

Since then, food and supplies have reached many remote villages, donated and delivered by Christian workers with the desire to satisfy both physical and spiritual hunger. Every dollar donated to the fund goes directly to those in need, through existing Christian ministries and organizations in each disaster area. Funds have provided hospitals, medical supplies and equipment, small planes, food, shelter, and churches (which have served as both community centers for refugees and places to preach the love of God).

Since the fund's inception, more than $10 million has been donated to the World Emergency Relief Fund, with 100 percent of every dollar earmarked specifically to provide assistance. For more than thirty years, the BGEA World Emergency Relief Fund has come to the aid of those in need throughout the world, bringing God's love in a vital and tangible way.

In December 1977, Andhra Pradesh, a place in southeast India that few Americans had ever heard of, was indelibly stamped onto Billy's heart. A cyclone-whipped tidal wave, described as the greatest disaster of the twentieth century, hit India's southeast coast, destroying 200,000 homes and killing 100,000 people.

Billy had just completed a week-long crusade in Manila and was in India preaching. When he heard the horrible news, he flew into the ravaged region with five members of his team to witness one of the most numbing experiences of his life. Billy watched as makeshift work crews of prisoners from local jails feverishly searched for victims in the salt-stained sawgrass and low thorn woods. An occasional shout went up—when a corpse was found—and Billy prayed as the bodies were covered and burned to prevent the spread of disease.

The ride from Vijayawada back to Madras that evening was perhaps the quietest trip Billy ever made. Upon landing, he arranged for all the financing he could muster from the World Emergency Relief Fund—$238,000—to help rebuild 285 homes. At the 1980 dedication ceremonies for the new town, which the Indian people named "Billy Graham Nagar," smiling faces could be seen among the freshly painted white houses.

In 1989, when Hurricane Hugo hit the South Carolina coast with winds up to 135 miles per hour, destroying more than 36,000 homes and claiming eighteen lives, the BGEA quickly responded with a visit from Billy and more than $80,000 for relief efforts. In Southeast Asia, the BGEA turned its attention to the refugees and orphans of Thailand, providing food, medical supplies, and church buildings. Money, equipment, and volunteers have been sent to troubled areas in nearly every corner of the world.

◄

The **BGEA** World Emergency
Relief Fund provided food, shelter,
and churches to the victims of
war-torn Beirut, Lebanon.

The **MINISTRY**

"If we are going to touch the people of our communities, we too must know their sorrows, feel for them in their temptations, stand with them in their heartbreaks."
—BILLY GRAHAM

"This cyclone which struck the coast of Andhra Pradesh in 1977 remains a nightmare experience. It caused immense damage. With the help of the Billy Graham World Relief Committee, 285 houses have been rebuilt, which are being dedicated on 29th June. My good wishes for this function being held in the village named after the well-known preacher."
—INDIRA GANDHI,
PRIME MINISTER OF INDIA

▲

In 1976, an earthquake measuring 7.5 on the Richter scale left 12,000 dead and one million homeless in Guatemala. The Grahams' helicopter tour of the country included the village of San Martin-Jilotepeque (pop. 18,000), where 3,800 were killed and 98 percent of the homes were destroyed. The BGEA chartered ten jets to deliver food and medical supplies.

▲

After the 1989 San Francisco earthquake destroyed homes and collapsed a section of Interstate 880, BGEA donated $100,000 and Billy spent two and a half days in the area, encouraging and praying with victims and rescue volunteers.

◄

Funds were provided to rebuild 285 homes. The town was named by its residents as "Billy Graham Nagar."

"I came here to see people. The damaged buildings you can see on television, but television can't show the damaged hearts and lives. Hopefully I can encourage them to trust in God."
—BILLY GRAHAM, SPEAKING IN SAN FRANCISCO

"My wife found a few dishes that weren't broken, but that's it. Everything else was gone. I thought people would forget about us, but they haven't. We are very grateful."
—LEROY CUMMINGS, A 70-YEAR-OLD RETIREE WHOSE HOME WAS DESTROYED BY A 20-FOOT-HIGH WALL OF WATER FROM HURRICANE HUGO

◄

Billy greeted a family whose home had been destroyed by Hurricane Hugo. With him were South Carolina Governor Carroll Campbell and Franklin Graham (left), president of Samaritan's Purse, which, with the help of BGEA, donated trailers to families left homeless by the disaster.

▼

Shelly Cruz, a young mother, lost her home, car, and all of her possessions in a fire caused by the earthquake. As Billy toured the area, he walked over, took her hand, spoke words of comfort, and prayed with her. Later she said, "I can never tell you how much Billy Graham's visit meant to me."

◄ Food shortages have been a constant problem for the people of North Africa.

► BGEA funds assisted the Annoor Sanatorium, a tuberculosis hospital in Mafraq, Jordan, that helped the Bedouins who roam the deserts of the Middle East.

▲ In 1973, the Fund provided famine relief to drought-stricken West Africa.

► Associate Evangelist Howard Jones (third from right) talked with missionary Don Corbin (left) and Pastor Fulgence N'Dour (center) about the food needed to stave off hunger in tiny Loul Sessene, Senegal.

Through Ned Graham's East Gates Ministries International, the Fund provided a mobile dental care van for North Koreans. Accepting the van was Kim Yong Nam (left), minister of foreign affairs. ◄

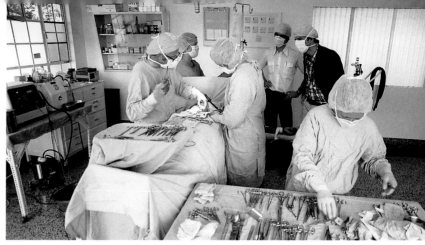

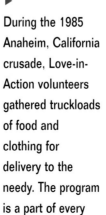

◄ Franklin Graham and Walter Smyth inspected a church in Thailand that the BGEA built to serve as a place to preach the love of God and as a community center for Cambodian refugees.

▼ Funds for small planes were provided to transport food and medical supplies to remote jungle areas in Kenya, Africa.

▲ The World Emergency Relief Fund helped equip this surgical theater in Tenwek, Africa.

◄ After the 1989 San Francisco earthquake, Billy walked through pouring rain and three inches of mud to visit families in Watsonville whose homes had been destroyed and who were temporarily sheltered in tents provided by the Salvation Army.

► During the 1985 Anaheim, California crusade, Love-in-Action volunteers gathered truckloads of food and clothing for delivery to the needy. The program is a part of every American crusade.

◄ Billy gave a food donation to the Washington, D.C., Love-in-Action committee.

CHAPTER SIX

REFLECTIONS FROM HOME

Ruth and I don't have a perfect marriage, but we have a great one. For a married couple to expect perfection in each other is unrealistic, since no one is perfect."

When Ruth came from China to the States to go to college, she met Billy. "I was planning to go back to Tibet as a missionary," she said. "We nearly broke up because he said God was not calling him to Tibet."

Ruth continued, "Finally, he asked me, 'Do you believe that God brought us together?' And I did without question. Instead of the mission field of Asia I have had the mission field of our home, one of the most challenging, difficult, and rewarding jobs in the world. It has been a privilege from God Himself."

"God has given you the gift of an evangelist," Ruth told Billy, "and I'll back you. I'll rear the children and you travel and preach." "Ruth took the major responsibility," Billy said, "which she did magnificently. I have to give her 99 percent of the credit for those children because she's the one who listened to them, wiped their tears when they cried, and helped them through the rough places. I'd come home and she had everything so organized and so calmed down."

Ruth always considered herself a career woman. "My career is being a wife and mother. Bill has the earth for his parish. I have a home and five children for mine. Our household faced all the problems common to most families, from broken bones to police calls."

Billy said, "I tried to let all five children know that I loved them and that I missed them when I was

◄

Ruth and Billy, at home on their front porch, celebrated their fiftieth wedding anniversary in 1993.

"I have been asked the question, 'Who do you go to for counsel, for spiritual guidance?' My answer: My wife, Ruth. She is the only one I completely confide in. She is a great student of the Bible. Her life is ruled by the Bible more than any person I've ever known. That's her rule book, her compass. Her disposition is the same all the time—very sweet and very gracious and very charming. When it comes to spiritual things, my wife has had the greatest influence on my ministry."
—BILLY GRAHAM

"I would rather spend two weeks out of the year with Bill than any other man full time."
—RUTH GRAHAM

away, that I supported their mother's discipline of them, and that I wanted them to discover God's perfect plan for each of them. We did all we could to encourage the children and give them memories of life together as a family that would be warm and happy.

"Without Ruth's partnership and encouragement over the years, my own work would have been impossible. We were called by God as a team."

"Your attitude to God, your husband and your family must create an atmosphere of love, appreciation, and encouragement which every family needs."
—RUTH GRAHAM

▶

Ruth and Billy have always enjoyed spending time at home (above, 1967 and right, 1993). The German inscription above their fireplace is from Luther's hymn, "A Mighty Fortress Is Our God."

▼

Ruth has written several books, including a collection of her own poems.

"I cannot keep up with the man. In fact, taking me on a crusade is rather like a general taking his wife to battle with him. Our happiest times together are at home or on vacation (though he usually takes his vacations like the drivers of the Indianapolis 500 take their pit stops—as seldom and as quickly as possible)."
—RUTH GRAHAM

In 1963 Ruth slipped this humorous photo (inscribed "All My Love—Ruth") into Billy's suitcase before one of his long trips. He carried it for years.

It was Ruth's turn to speak during the 1972 Cleveland, Ohio, campaign.

"I guess one thing that has always impressed me over the years has been the humility of my parents and their deep integrity. They were always careful not to do anything that would hinder the Gospel."
—FRANKLIN GRAHAM

Ruth has always found time to study her Bible.

The MAN

"Ruth likes to say, 'If two people agree on everything, one of them is unnecessary.'"
—BILLY GRAHAM

Billy and Ruth relaxed on the couch in a rare quiet moment.

▲

Franklin, Bunny,
Anne, Gigi, Ruth,
and Ned at home
in Montreat,
1958

"It had been one of those hectic nights, and I had overslept. Without fixing my hair or pausing for makeup, I hurriedly pulled on my bathrobe, lifted Franklin out of his bed without bothering to change him, and set him in the high chair. I proceeded to set the table hurriedly for breakfast so the children would not be late for school. That morning, every time Gigi opened her mouth to say something, Bunny interrupted. Finally, in exasperation, Gigi slammed down her fork. 'Mother!' she exclaimed. 'Between listening to Bunny and smelling Franklin and looking at you, I'm not hungry!' The children taught me much as they were growing up: about themselves, about the world around them, about me, and especially about God."
—RUTH GRAHAM

"A little black lady came to me and she was very sweet. I had spoken in her church. She said, 'I have a little piece of your life. I've got an investment in you.' And I'd never met her before in my life. She said, 'Your father has sent me a Christmas card for years. I've been a supporter of the Billy Graham Association. We used to have these pictures of all of you children sent to us. I have prayed for you ever since you were a little boy. I have a little piece of your life, a little investment.' I would just like to say that I appreciate those prayers— for me and my family—little did she know how much I needed them."
—FRANKLIN GRAHAM

▲

Gigi often helped
Ruth in the
kitchen.

"The Bible stayed open in my kitchen all day. Whenever there was a spare minute, I grabbed that minute and spent it with the Bible. More likely than not, the book was open to Proverbs. If I had a problem I almost always got help there. Proverbs has more practical child help in it than ten books on child psychology."
—RUTH GRAHAM

▼

Ned's wedding
in the front yard,
1979

Billy and Bunny,
1950s

◀

"Franklin's guardian angel
has always had to work
overtime."
—RUTH GRAHAM

▶

Billy and Gigi, 1971

▼

Billy and Ned,
1974

"At the age of twelve or
thirteen I had been very rude,
and Daddy spanked me. I then
asked him in anger what kind
of a father he thought he was
anyway, always being gone.
Tears filled his eyes; it was
the first time I had seen tears
in Daddy's eyes. Afterward
we talked it over, and I
have never forgotten that
experience. It was the first I
began to realize as a young
adult just how much he was
giving up by being gone."
—GIGI GRAHAM TCHIVIDJIAN

"Children are facing temptations
and pressures we never had to
face—instead of
'Thou shalt not . . .' it is
'Why not? . . .
Teach your children the
Word of God as soon
as they can talk . . .
Young people are confused. We
turn our children out in high-pow-
ered cars onto the highway of life
without road rules, road signs,
guardrails, centerlines, and with
faulty brakes and wonder why there
are so many wrecks. . . .
Your children need love,
appreciation, and guidance—love
your children and let them know it."
—RUTH GRAHAM

▼

Ned, Billy, and
Franklin, 1965

▶

Anne and
one of the
many
Graham
dogs, 1961

▲

Billy and
Franklin, 1979

"Knowing how long and how hard God has worked on this particular servant of His, I had to come out here and, like Moses at the burning bush, stand aside and see this great sight. In case there's some mother out there concerned for a son who is away from the Lord—let me say this morning nobody's hopeless. I mean it— NOBODY."

—RUTH GRAHAM,
SPEAKING AT FRANKLIN'S ORDINATION

the MAN

"Ruth sometimes felt like a single parent, with all the problems that that entailed. We tried to discipline the children fairly, but at the same time we tried not to lay down a lot of rules and regulations. When I objected to Franklin's long hair, Ruth reminded me that it wasn't a moral issue—and I kept my mouth shut on that subject thereafter. Actually, as Ruth pointed out with a twinkle in her eye, Franklin was in the tradition of the prophets and apostles."

—BILLY GRAHAM

"For any who might be waiting for the return of a loved prodigal, here is some of the comfort and assurance we found during the years of our waiting. One night when I could not sleep, I started worrying about him. We mothers have great imaginations, and somehow we always imagine the worst. The Lord said to me, 'Get your eyes off the problem and start studying the promises.' So I turned on the light and I opened my Bible. And I began to study the promises. And as I studied I began to thank God for His goodness and His faithfulness. And as I began to thank and worship God, the worries disappeared. I learned that worry and worship cannot live in the same heart. God said to me, 'You take care of the possible and trust me for the impossible.' For years I had been trying to do God's work for Him, while I neglected my own. . . . 'Your department is to love, pray, provide a warm, happy home, provide for the physical needs of your family.' God in His faithfulness brought him back."

—RUTH GRAHAM

▼

Billy and Ruth on their front porch, 1972

▶

The mountaintop house, 1968

▲

Billy prayed with Franklin and his wife, Jane Austin, at Franklin's ordination in 1982.

▶

Right to left, William Franklin Graham II, III, and IV at a 1994 crusade.

The **MAN**

"We have a log-and-frame house perched 3,600 feet above sea level on a 200-acre site, that fits the Appalachian mountain scenery. Ruth filled it with antiques she picked up at auctions, secondhand stores, and junk shops. In the forty years since it was built, the place has seen 'a heap of lovin' and has stood solid through all kinds of storms—internal as well as external. Ruth made it a safe and happy home for the children and a real refuge for me. Our house on the mountain solved the problem of family privacy once and for all. Home was a refuge for me, a place I could truly relax."

—BILLY GRAHAM

"Both my parents had a great influence on me. I never heard my father use a profane or even a slang word. I always respected him because of his complete integrity. In his business dealings his handshake was like a contract. He was as good as his word. Of all the people I have ever known, my mother has had the greatest influence on me. She was seemingly more religious than my father in the earlier years. The last few days before my mother died she said to a friend, 'I'm not going to be satisfied here anymore.'"
—BILLY GRAHAM

▼ Morrow and Frank Graham, Billy's parents, 1960s

"He hasn't changed toward family and friends in spite of his having been with Presidents and dignitaries throughout the world. He and Melvin tell jokes, some of which our Daddy told years ago, and they are still just as funny."
—CATHERINE GRAHAM MCELROY, BILLY'S SISTER

▲ Catherine, Billy, Melvin, Jean, Morrow, and Frank Graham, 1962

"People often ask, How do you feel when you see Billy on TV? My answer is always the same. I feel wonderful, and I sit in awe when I think of the great things the Lord has done."
—MORROW GRAHAM, BILLY'S MOTHER

"The same principles and promises we applied to our children are still true for our grandchildren and great-grandchildren. We pray for each one each day and spend time on weekends talking with them on the phone."
—BILLY GRAHAM

▼ Dr. L. Nelson Bell and family in China. (Ruth is standing on the left)

▲

Billy and Ruth with thirteen of their nineteen grandchildren, 1982

▼

Nelson and Virginia Bell, Ruth's parents, 1972

"One of the great influences on our children when they were young were their grandparents, Dr. and Mrs. Bell, Ruth's parents. They lived just across the street (and later down the hill). Dr. Bell didn't mind telling them exactly what was right, either. They kept them, they loved them, and they taught them. They made it part of their ministry to help Ruth raise our children. They took them in many weeks at a time when we would be gone."
—BILLY GRAHAM

"The Billy Graham the public does not know is the man confronted with thousands of invitations to preach around the world. Invitations press in on him as opportunities [and he] is forced by these and other circumstances to spend hours in prayer. There are sleepless nights and early-morning hours in Bible study."
—DR. L. NELSON BELL, BILLY'S FATHER-IN-LAW

"Billy hasn't changed a bit, he's like he always was. Billy's way of speaking and his personality are an advantage, but the real drawing power is the power of God."
—MELVIN GRAHAM, BILLY'S BROTHER

"Because of their example, I respected them and listened to their advice. I saw Daddy live what he preached. I saw them making Christ their life— not just their religion."
—GIGI GRAHAM TCHIVIDJIAN

"As busy as Daddy was, he spent time with me, he loved me, he prayed with me, he cried with me, that will always be a special memory. And I don't believe Mother has ever been recognized and honored for what she has done; because without her, Daddy's ministry would not have been possible."
—RUTH (BUNNY) GRAHAM MCINTYRE

"They set the tone for our lives by the way they lived theirs. Their depending on God was obvious—Mother's light would be on late at night and early in the morning as she studied her Bible and prayed. And Daddy, even though the world acclaimed him as a great man, and so many sought him for advice, would still get on his knees and humbly ask the Lord for His guidance. Through all of this we learned that seeking God was not a sign of weakness but a sign of strength."
—ANNE GRAHAM LOTZ

◄ When Ruth and Billy celebrated their fiftieth anniversary in 1993, Ruth tried on the dress she was married in— and it still fit!

"I know it was lonely many times for us children not having Daddy at home more, and there were times we would ask questions. But today as I travel around the world with the work of Samaritan's Purse and World Medical Mission, I meet people who tell me they came to Christ through one of Daddy's meetings. Then I think back on those lonely times and say it was worth it all to sacrifice that time with Daddy so they could come to faith in Christ."
—FRANKLIN GRAHAM

"Their love and prayers have guided me all my life, including my own commitment to Christ. What I rebelled against, in hindsight, was God's call in my life to ministry. I didn't want that responsibility . . . [but my parent's] unconditional love eventually became irresistible."
—NED GRAHAM

◄

Gigi, Anne, Ruth (Bunny), Ruth, Billy, Franklin, and Ned celebrated Ruth and Billy's fiftieth wedding anniversary at their home in Montreat.

"Someone asked me recently if I didn't think God was unfair, allowing me to have Parkinson's and other medical problems when I have tried to serve Him faithfully. I replied that I did not see it that way at all. Suffering is part of the human condition, and it comes to us all. The key is how we react to it, either turning away from God in anger and bitterness or growing closer to Him in trust and confidence."

—Billy Graham

"Billy reads long passages of the Bible at a time. It isn't as if it's 'from seven to seven-thirty, I'll have Bible reading'. That's not Bill's nature, but he does read the Bible continually, every day, and large portions of it."
—RUTH GRAHAM

The MAN

"I am in favor of hanging the Ten Commandments in every schoolroom in the country so young people can know the difference between right and wrong. They don't know the difference and we're seeing the evidence of that all around us every day."
—BILLY GRAHAM

◀

Billy, 1978

▼

Ruth, 1987

"I wrote an article for a ladies magazine on the women's liberation movement in the States. I submitted it to my wife, because she's a marvelous critic. She handed it back to me all blue-penciled and said, 'I don't agree with most of this.' So I rewrote it. I said that the liberation Jesus gave was a liberation of the spirit. Ruth said 'I think we're being taken for a ride. It's men's lib because it's relieving them of the responsibility of supporting and caring for their families.'"
—BILLY GRAHAM

"Bill's and my tastes differ (in books, music, style, decor, food, hobbies, and so forth). Even our forms of relaxing differ. I go for a good book. He, immersed in books most of the time as it is, used to play golf, now walks. Our temperaments differ. By nature I am easygoing to the point of laziness, and am basically optimistic. Bill is highly disciplined and drives himself unmercifully."
—RUTH GRAHAM

T.W. Wilson, who often travels with Billy, says: "How can you be in God's will and pray for His leadership if you already have a fixed idea about what you are going to do? The very fact that Billy is willing to change, that he's flexible—is because he always seeks God's guidance. And he does that with his schedule also. God knows Billy better than we do, and has made him the way he is. I've seen again and again where I thought, 'Not another change!' And yet it was the very thing needed."

Billy's answer is: "I want to be flexible so that I can change plans at the last minute if necessary, to go and do what I believe the Holy Spirit would have me to do—like Philip [in Acts 8], who was suddenly whisked away to talk to one man, the Ethiopian nobleman—which was not in his date book!"

▼

Billy, 1987

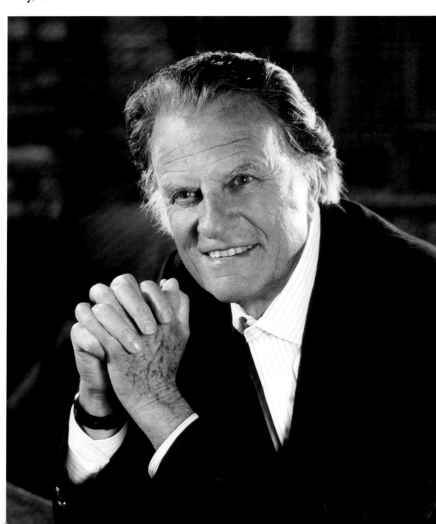

"When I was young, I sometimes wanted to answer all my critics. Now, I just leave them with the Lord. If I tried to answer every critic that's all I would have time to do. But God has called me to preach and be about the business of winning the lost."

—BILLY GRAHAM

▼
Billy often prepared sermons in his office at home, as here in 1965.

"One of the greatest prices I have to pay is the fact that I am instantly recognized by so many Americans and foreigners. I am actually a prisoner in a hotel room or in my home. . . . It is impossible for me to go out for a quiet meal with my wife or family, to stroll down a street, to walk in a park. I used to so terribly resent the invasion of our privacy. Now I have learned to live with it and have dedicated it many times to the Lord."

—BILLY GRAHAM

THREATS ON THE LIFE OF BILLY GRAHAM

The Defiant In Alabama; L.A. 'Fast'?

HERALD EXAMINER

8 STAR LATEST SPORTS

Evangelist's 'Protection' Is His Faith

'I Have Faced Many Dangers . . .'

Kennedy Calls Out 'Barry'

Extra Police at Crusade To Protect Billy Graham

"I can honestly say that I have never been nervous or intimidated by any threat. My life is in God's hands, not those who may oppose His work."

—BILLY GRAHAM

"Many times I have been driven to prayer. When I was in Bible school I didn't know what to do with my life. I used to walk those streets in that little Florida town and pray, sometimes for hours at a time. In His timing, God answered those prayers and since then prayer has been an essential part of my life."
—BILLY GRAHAM

◄

Unfortunately, people in the public eye often have to contend with threats from those who are mentally unstable or, as in Billy's case, those who are violently opposed to what they do. In many crusades, there were threats against Billy, the team, and Billy's family.

▶

Billy, 1972

CHAPTER SEVEN

A Continuing Ministry

Reflecting back on his half-century of ministry, Billy has said, "I realize more than ever that this ministry has been a team effort. Without the help of our prayer partners, our financial supporters, our staff, and our board of directors— this ministry and all of our dreams to spread the Good News of God's love throughout the world would not have been possible."

The central core of Billy's ministry team has been a group of men and women who have been together for more than three decades. "The key has been our team and the faithful and gifted staff that have carried the greatest part of the burden," Billy said. "BGEA is more than one man, and its work will outlive any individual member of the team. I will never be able to repay the debt I owe them for their friendship and their sacrifice over the years. In order to do whatever needed to be done, they have subordinated their personal lives, reordered their priorities, accepted disappointments and endless changes in schedule, stretched their patience, absorbed criticism, and exhausted their energy to do whatever needed to be done. They were the heaven-sent ones who propped me up when I was sagging. They did not back away from correcting me when I needed it or counseling me with their wisdom when I faced decisions. I'm convinced that, without them, burnout would have left me nothing but a charred cinder within five years of the 1949 Los Angeles crusade."

Through his team, board, staff, and others who make his ministry possible, Billy's vision continues to have an impact on our world.

◄

After Billy's visit in 1967, Yugoslavian Christians commissioned a local artist to paint "The Sower," a portrait of Billy in Yugoslav dress.

Billy Graham Evangelistic Association

What is the BGEA? In a nutshell, they are the support team that makes it all possible.

Who could have dreamed what God had in mind when the one-room office with two employees opened in Minneapolis, Minnesota, in 1950? The first *Hour of Decision* radio broadcast on the ABC network was about to begin. At the close of the broadcast Billy said: "Just write me, Billy Graham, Minneapolis, Minnesota. That's all the address you need, and May the Lord bless you real good!"

As a result of the early broadcasts, mail began pouring in from across the United States, and the organization was forced to grow. Then, for three months in 1957, the New York crusade was telecast live on the ABC network across the nation every Saturday night, and literally millions wrote for spiritual help. As those broadcasts were translated into different languages and sent out by shortwave, letters began arriving from every conceivable corner of the globe.

The daily sacks of mail demanded answers, so a Spiritual Guidance Department was formed. It consists of experienced pastors and counselors qualified to answer the many requests for help from people with every imaginable human problem—many in desperate circumstances. The Spiritual Guidance Department points them to the Lord Jesus Christ and offers biblical answers to help with their needs. Many are referred to organizations which can provide for special needs. Each month thousands of pieces of Bible-centered literature are mailed throughout the world from the Minneapolis office. In fact, the BGEA is one of the U.S. Postal Service's largest volume mailers.

The money needed to make this worldwide ministry possible—telling people the Good News, that God loves them—comes from thousands of people who send relatively small gifts on a regular basis.

All finances are handled with integrity and openness. The Internal Revenue Service has audited the BGEA several times, and each time has commended the organization for its carefulness in financial matters. The annual financial report (audited by a national accounting firm) is available to anyone who desires it. Joel Aarsvold, CPA, vice president for finance, and a longtime employee, oversees the day-to-day financial operations realizing, as does everyone, that they are accountable to God for all money entrusted to the BGEA.

> "Billy is a great delegator. He gives you a job and he trusts you to get it done. He doesn't stand over your shoulder and monitor what you are doing, but he expects you to do the job and do it right. He doesn't want you to tell him, 'I can't.' He'll say, 'You keep working at it.' At the same time, he's a good forgiver."
> T.W. WILSON,
> PERSONAL ASSISTANT TO
> BILLY GRAHAM

▶ With a little extra help from the U.S. Postal Service, Billy has received mail with every conceivable address—even "Planet Earth."

▼ In 1950, George M. Wilson opened the first office and for many years was executive vice president and business manager of the Billy Graham Evangelistic Association.

"In the beginning we were just three or four simple people—we still are simple—who didn't know any better than to trust the Lord."
—BILLY GRAHAM

"Our job is to dispense the world's greatest product— with the greatest economy—to the greatest number of people—as fast as possible. Everything we do is directed to winning souls for Christ."
—GEORGE M. WILSON

▲ The BGEA office in Minneapolis, Minnesota, has grown from the original two employees to four hundred, and now occupies nearly a square block. The staff begins each working day with ten minutes of prayer. Calls to the switchboard go unanswered while all employees— from janitors to computer operators— ask for God's guidance for the day ahead.

▲ Joel Aarsvold has been vice president of finance for more than thirty years.

▶ Dr. John Corts became president and chief operating officer in 1987.

▲ Esther LaDow was George Wilson's executive assistant for thirty-seven years.

"During one year there were over 8,500 requests directed to Billy which required an answer. He's only one man and most of them had to be turned down—gracefully. I try to let them know he's regretful."
—T.W. WILSON

The Team and Associate Evangelists

The men and women around Billy are a unique ensemble. Drawn from many different denominational persuasions, races, ages, cultural backgrounds and parts of the world, they constitute a gifted and varied group of men and women of great dedication and effectiveness. Some have retired or passed away, but Billy has always encouraged younger men and women to utilize their gifts for the continuance of BGEA's mission.

In an effort to reach as many parts of the world as possible, Billy has chosen several men over the years to serve as associate evangelists. They have held hundreds of crusades in almost every corner of the world, often in very difficult places. Robert Cunville and Akbar Abdul Haqq, for example, have been especially effective in their native land of India. Oxford-trained John Wesley White has not only spoken on dozens of university campuses, but in cities and towns across the world. Canadian-born Ralph Bell likewise has ministered in a wide variety of situations, including numerous prisons. And during the crusades, they have taken speaking engagements that Billy has been unable to accept.

"Billy remains a simple, honest, gentle man, completely faithful and devoted to his original calling, loyal and sensitive to his co-workers—and blessed with the good sense to have married Ruth Bell Graham."
—TEDD SMITH

▶ Stephanie Wills has served as Billy's secretary for more than twenty-five years.

"Though very forceful in the pulpit, Billy in private is a true gentleman, quiet, always thoughtful of others. I have never heard him give a command to those with whom he works. It is always, 'Would you like to do this?'"
—GEORGE BEVERLY SHEA

▶ Walter H. Smyth served as director of international crusades for many years.

▲ For most of his ministry, Billy has worked closely with T.W. Wilson, his personal assistant and longtime friend.

▶ Together since the beginning, pianist Tedd Smith, choir and program director Cliff Barrows, personal assistant Grady Wilson, Billy Graham, and soloist Bev Shea in Columbia, South Carolina, 1987.

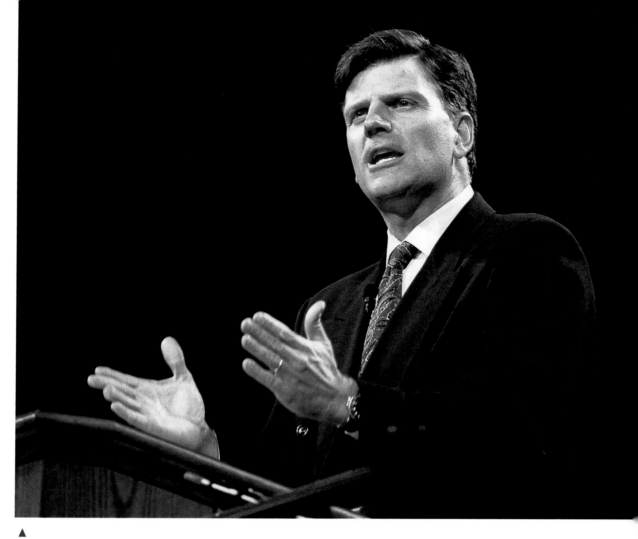

"I get up and preach and that's the easy part. . . . We're just simple, ordinary people that God has chosen to bring together with various gifts and talents. And I count it the greatest possible privilege to have had you around me as a group of men and women devoted and dedicated to the Lord. I love every one of you."

—BILLY GRAHAM,
DURING A TEAM AND STAFF MEETING

◄ Charlie Riggs was a senior crusade director and head of BGEA's Counseling and Follow-up Department.

"Billy Graham has been gifted with the ability to gather around him men and women of great skills who can execute and bring to pass the things he envisions. His vision, leadership, and businesslike gifts come from a man whose blameless life, financial integrity, and loyalty to the Word of God is unequalled."

—DR. HAROLD LINDSELL,
EDITOR OF CHRISTIANITY TODAY

▲

In recent years Franklin Graham, Billy's older son, has been recognized as an effective and gifted evangelist, able to reach a new generation with the unchanging message of Christ. In 2000 the BGEA board unanimously elected Franklin chief executive officer (CEO).

"Although he is known primarily for his ability as an evangelist, Billy Graham is equally gifted as a leader . . . inspiring people to work harmoniously toward visionary goals. The most effective form of leadership is by example. Billy Graham's dedication to Christ motivates all who work with him to a higher standard of commitment."

—STERLING HUSTON, DIRECTOR OF
NORTH AMERICAN CRUSADES

▼

For most of his ministry Billy worked closely with brothers Grady (right) and T.W. (left) Wilson. Both were Billy's closest friends, traveling companions, and personal assistants.

"Billy is an excellent general; he's superb. There are several reasons why he's so good. He has the gift of strategy and of vision. God has given him the idea of what this ministry can be. But I also see him as having one of those rare qualities that the greatest of leaders have—of being able to share the glory. He always shares the reward, publicly."
—ALLAN EMERY,
BOSTON BUSINESSMAN AND LONG-TIME CHAIRMAN OF BGEA'S EXECUTIVE COMMITTEE

▶

The Billy Graham Evangelistic Association Board of Directors gathered for a meeting in 1993.

▶

Billy addressed board members at a directors' meeting in 1997.

Board of Directors

Early on, Billy was urged to get a managing board of directors and an executive committee. They supervise all of the BGEA's finances and meet regularly to oversee the organization and make major decisions. The board consists of distinguished men and women who represent the business and professional world and the clergy. No BGEA employee, including Billy, serves on the executive committee.

Over the years more than seventy men and women have guided the BGEA by serving on its board of directors.

"I have served on many boards but I have never been associated with an organization that has such high standards of business procedure and financial controls as the Billy Graham Evangelistic Association. . . . The word that I think describes Billy Graham best is integrity. It is personal integrity, but more than anything else, biblical integrity. This combination makes the Billy Graham Evangelistic Association unique."
—GEORGE F. BENNETT,
BGEA CHAIRMAN EMERITUS, FORMER HARVARD UNIVERSITY DEPUTY TREASURER (25 YEARS), AND FORMER FORD MOTOR COMPANY BOARD MEMBER (15 YEARS)

Billy Graham Center at Wheaton College

The **MAN**

> *"A building is only a tool, an instrument. This building represents a major investment, but it is more than an investment in bricks and mortar; it is an investment in people around the world for Christ."*
>
> —BILLY GRAHAM

Located on the Wheaton College campus in Wheaton, Illinois, the Billy Graham Center contains the archives of the Billy Graham Evangelistic Association, as well as information about other religious groups. The Center also houses one of the world's largest libraries on evangelism and missions, and hosts conferences and seminars for strategic planning and training for world evangelism. The main floor features a museum on the history of evangelism in America and Billy's fifty years of worldwide ministry.

On behalf of the BGEA Board of Directors, the building was presented as a gift to Wheaton College by Allan Emery, then chairman of the BGEA Board, in honor of Billy and Ruth, who both graduated from Wheaton in 1943. The Center is owned and operated by Wheaton College.

Commenting on the Center, Billy said, "I realized that my ministry would someday come to an end. I am only one in a glorious chain of men and women God has raised up through the centuries to build Christ's church and to take the Gospel everywhere. I asked myself, 'What contribution to world evangelization can I make after I'm gone?' . . . We believe the ministry of this Center is in safe hands at Wheaton College which has, for more than one hundred years, been dedicated to the theological concepts, the world vision, and the academic excellence that we believe in."

Ruth once said to Dr. V. Raymond Edman, former president of Wheaton, "Wheaton trains leaders." Edman replied, "No, Ruth, not leaders but servants."

In his remarks at the Center's dedication ceremony Billy said, "We felt God wanted this project to be more than a place to house things. We wanted it to be an ongoing ministry that would serve the Church, throughout the world, especially in the field of evangelism.

"The important thing is not this building, but what will take place here. Our desire is that this building will not be interpreted as a monument to a man or an organization. Our desire is solely to glorify God. Our concern must always be that this Center be an instrument, which God can use to further His kingdom through the world."

▲
Since its dedication on September 13, 1980, the Billy Graham Center at Wheaton College has become an international center of information, research, and strategic training on evangelism and missions.

Billy Graham Training Center at The Cove

After years of prayer, Billy and Ruth felt they were led by God to develop a Bible training center. Billy described The Cove, which was dedicated May 25, 1993, as "unique—not a school, not a conference center—but a Bible training center. Our only textbook is the Bible. There are no diplomas, no graduations. It is for average, ordinary people who want to know more about the Word of God and to grow in their faith and learn how to share their faith with others."

Nestled in the wooded foothills of the Blue Ridge Mountains, The Cove sits on 1,500 acres near Asheville, North Carolina. Guests enjoy staying at the two inns, worshiping in the inspiring chapel, and learning in the beautiful training center where seminars are conducted by top Bible teachers throughout the year. The Cove also hosts a summer camp with its own campgrounds, mess hall, and Olympic swimming pool for children age nine to fifteen.

▲
Chatlos Memorial Chapel at The Cove offers God's Word in the midst of nature's beauty.

▲
Small group Bible study and discussions are a regular part of the conference center's activitities.

◄
The training center welcomes visitors from across the United States and Canada to The Cove.

HOW TO COMMUNICATE THE GOSPEL

"Now, how do we communicate the Good News of our Lord Jesus Christ to modern scientific man? We communicate through the cross on which He died for our sins, through the resurrection, and the Holy Spirit.

First, preach with authority. The authority for us is the Word of God. Faith comes by hearing the Word of God.

Second, preach with simplicity. I think many times we talk over the heads of our hearers and they don't understand what we are talking about.

Third, preach with repetition. Jesus probably repeated Himself more than five hundred times. And those disciples never forgot what He said.

Fourth, preach with urgency. It is very urgent because eternity is at stake, and heaven and hell are at stake.

Fifth, preach for a decision. There are many methods of people making decisions. You want them to make a decision before God.

I am convinced if the Church went back to the main task of proclaiming the Gospel it would see people being converted to Christ, and it would have a far greater impact on the social, moral, and psychological needs of people than anything else it could possibly do. Some of the greatest social movements of history in this country have come about as a result of people being converted to Christ."

—BILLY GRAHAM, EXCERPT FROM MESSAGES TO MINISTERS

Billy Graham Schools of Evangelism

A deeply concerned San Francisco businessman named Lowell Berry told Billy in 1958 that the best way to strengthen the churches would be to train its pastors in evangelism. From that vision came the Billy Graham Schools of Evangelism—a series of training conferences in evangelism for pastors and other Christian workers.

A typical School of Evangelism brings together approximately a thousand pastors and their spouses representing up to one hundred denominations. For three to four days, they receive intensive training from experienced leaders in the field of evangelism. To date, more than 160 schools have been conducted on six continents, with more than 126,000 people worldwide attending the schools.

▼
At the 1991 Moscow School of Evangelism, Billy addressed almost 5,000 participants from all parts of the Soviet Union.

▲
A Billy Graham School of Evangelism in Chicago, Illinois

International Congresses on Evangelism

Recalling the first international congresses on evangelism, Billy said, "God laid upon my heart the desire of bringing together theologians, educators, mission executives, pastors, and church leaders from around the world. Our goal is nothing short of the evangelization of the human race. . . . To evangelize

is to spread the Good News that Jesus Christ died for our sins and was raised from the dead according to the Scriptures, and . . . now offers the forgiveness of sins and . . . the gift of the Holy Spirit to all who repent and believe."

With a theme of "One [Human] Race, One Gospel, One Task," the Berlin World Congress on Evangelism convened on October 26, 1966, in Berlin's Kongresshalle with 1,200 delegates from 100 countries in attendance. Billy served as honorary chairman and the Billy Graham Evangelistic Association organized it and raised the money. *Christianity Today* acted as sponsor of the Congress. One church leader commented, "No other person could have brought together so varied and esteemed a group."

Eight years later, the International Congress on Evangelism was held in the Palais de Beaulieu in Lausanne, Switzerland. The event was planned by a coalition of international religious leaders whose goal was to study Christ's Great Commission—"to make disciples of all nations"—and to seek ways to fulfill it in our time. Their theme was "Let the Earth Hear His Voice." The Billy Graham Evangelistic Association sponsored the Congress and financed three-fourths of the budget. More than 4,000 delegates from 150 nations attended.

Billy said, "I remember there came a day when I was ready to cancel the Congress because I didn't feel we had the money and I felt we were going over our heads. And I'll never forget, Ruth came to me and said, 'Bill, don't cancel the Congress. This may be the last time we'll ever have a Congress like this. Let's believe God.' And Ruth's statement changed the direction of that conference."

In Billy's closing address, titled "The King Is Coming," he stressed the urgency to evangelize because of the certainty of Christ's return.

▲

"Let the Earth Hear His Voice" was the theme of Lausanne '74.

▶

The 1966 Berlin World Congress included an outdoor rally at the historic Kaiser Wilhelm Memorial Church.

"It has been tremendous meeting people from all over the world and hearing God's men giving us a message that we need."
—ATTENDEE FROM GHANA

"This has been a congress of tears—tears of joy, tears of conviction, tears of hope. This congress is a hope for our world."
—ATTENDEE FROM ECUADOR

"When I preach—no matter where it is in the world—I can always count on five areas of human need that afflict all peoples.

First, emptiness: Man keeps crying for something, and he never quite finds it 'till he finds God. He doesn't know what he's searching for. He doesn't know why this emptiness is in his heart.

Loneliness: the second thing I notice is loneliness, existential loneliness, philosophical loneliness. You can be in a crowd, and for just one moment there's a sense of loneliness, even with friends. What is this loneliness? It's a loneliness for God. We were created for God, and without God there is a sense of loneliness.

Guilt: The third thing I find is guilt. All people have a sense of guilt. It haunts us and hounds us and in the end plays havoc with our peace of mind.

Fear of death: Even for the Christian, death is a mystery which the Bible calls the 'last enemy.'

Deep-seated insecurity: Modern man clamors for security; material things are never enough. The Bible says, 'A man's life consisteth not in the abundance of the things which he possesseth.'

You and I, God's ambassadors, are called to sound the warning, to call sinners to repentance, to point the way to peace with God and the hope that is in Christ."

—BILLY GRAHAM

Amsterdam Conferences

More than 4,000 delegates from 133 countries converged in Holland for "Amsterdam '83"—the International Conference for Itinerant Evangelists. Due to a limited budget and lack of hotel space, more than 8,000 requests had to be denied. But three years later a second and larger conference—"Amsterdam '86"—was held. This time a total of 10,000 participants came from 174 nations and territories of the world, representing more countries than belong to the United Nations. A total of 61 airlines were needed to carry participants to and from their remote homes, and it took 100 buses just to transport people from 85 different hotels and dormitories to the conference center each day.

The Amsterdam conferences were not American conferences teaching Western ideas. Speakers for the daily seminars were 91 percent non-American, emphasizing that God has given every culture things to share.

The average age of participants was thirty-one; many had never traveled outside their own countries before. Some had not even been outside their own provinces. For many, the trip involved their first plane rides. One group from a very poor country had never seen an elevator. They refused to enter, calling it "the disappearing room" because when the door closed the elevator was full but when it opened again the elevator was empty!

Billy described the Amsterdam conferences as "a rainbow of men and women with far greater dedication and gifts than I'll ever have. These itinerant evangelists are the most important ambassadors and messengers on earth. They are a mighty army, spreading out across the world with a vision to reach their own people for Christ."

Plans are underway for a third Amsterdam conference, to be held in summer 2000.

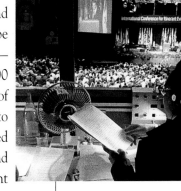

▲

One hundred translators ensured that all participants heard God's Word—in their own languages.

▼

The RAI Center hosted Amsterdam '83 and '86.

The **MINISTRY**

"All that I have been able to do I owe to Jesus Christ. When you honor me you are really honoring Him. Any honors I have received I accept with a sense of inadequacy and humility and I will reserve the right to hand all of these someday to Christ, when I see Him face-to-face."

—BILLY GRAHAM

Honors and Awards

In recognition of his work and ministry, Billy has received hundreds of honors and awards from all parts of the world. In May 1996 he and Ruth were awarded the Congressional Gold Medal, the highest honor the U.S. Congress can bestow upon a citizen. The citation read, "You have touched the hearts of the American family . . . You have touched that part of the American spirit that knows Providence has a greater purpose for our nation."

"I cannot take credit," Billy responded, "for what God has chosen to accomplish through us and our ministry. Only God deserves the glory."

Nigerians named a mountain for Billy because he climbed it when he preached in their area; citizens of South India named a town for him after he came to the aid of thousands who had been devastated by a tidal wave; and Charlotte, North Carolina, Billy's birthplace, named a freeway in his honor.

In fifty years of preaching to the world, Billy Graham has been named Most Admired, Most Photographed, and Man of the Year. He has been inducted into Halls of Fame and given Medals of Honor; he has been named Honorary Sheriff, Honorary Citizen, Grand Marshal, and Salesman of the Year; and he has been awarded doctoral degrees by institutions of higher learning in the United States and several foreign countries. Cities across the United States have proclaimed Billy Graham Days to honor him for coming to their areas to preach the Good News of God's love.

Religious groups of all types have bestowed honors upon Billy. In 1977, he was the first recipient of the American Jewish Committee's National Interreligious Award. The National Conference of Christians and Jews gave him their 1967 Silver Medallion and Brotherhood Award, and in 1969 he received the Torch of Liberty Award from the Anti-Defamation League of B'nai B'rith. Roman Catholic organizations have honored Billy, first with the Celtic Cross Award from the Catholic War Veterans, and later with an honorary Doctor of Humane Letters from Belmont Abbey College.

The 1963 Gold Award of the George Washington Carver Memorial Institute was presented to Billy by New York Senator Jacob Javits in recognition of his contributions to race relations.

"Billy Graham's contribution to the well-being of mankind is literally immeasurable. Millions of lives across the globe have been enriched because of his good work. The world is a better place because of Billy Graham."
—RONALD REAGAN, PRESENTING THE PRESIDENTIAL MEDAL OF FREEDOM, FEBRUARY 23, 1983

▼

The Presidential Medal of Freedom is the United States' highest civil award.

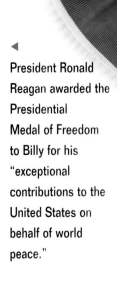

◄

President Ronald Reagan awarded the Presidential Medal of Freedom to Billy for his "exceptional contributions to the United States on behalf of world peace."

▼

On May 2, 1996, Billy and Ruth were honored with the Congressional Gold Medal, the highest honor that Congress can bestow. Billy was the first clergyman to receive the honor for ministry, and the Grahams were the third couple to receive the award.

THE CONGRESSIONAL GOLD MEDAL

"I am especially grateful that my wife, Ruth, and I are both being given this honor. No one has sacrificed more than Ruth has, or been more dedicated to God's calling for the two of us.

Exactly 218 years ago today, on May 2, 1778, the first recipient of this award, George Washington, issued a general order to the American people. He said, 'The . . . instances of Providential goodness which we have experienced and which have now almost crowned our labors with complete success demand from us . . . the warmest returns of gratitude and piety to the Supreme Author of all good.'

Less than four years from now the world will enter a new millennium. What will it hold for us? You know the problems as well as I do—crime and violence of epidemic proportion, children taking weapons to school, broken families, poverty, drugs, teenage pregnancy, corruption. The list is almost endless. Would the first recipients of this award even recognize the society they sacrificed to establish? I fear not. We have confused liberty with license, and we are paying the awful price. We are a society poised on the brink of self-destruction.

What is the problem? The real problem is within ourselves. It is our heart. Why is the human heart this way? The reason is because we are alienated from our Maker. We have lost sight of the moral and spiritual principles on which this nation was established— principles drawn largely from the Judeo-Christian tradition, as found in the Bible.

What is the cure? Is there hope? Ruth and I have devoted our lives to the deep conviction that the answer is yes. There is hope! Our lives can be changed, and our world can be changed. The Scripture says: 'You must be born again.' You can have spiritual rebirth today. First, we must repent. Repentance means to change our thinking and our way of living. It means to turn from our sins, and to commit ourselves to God and His will. Second, we must commit our lives to God. Think how different our nation would be if we sought to follow the simple yet profound injunctions of the Ten Commandments and the Sermon on the Mount. Third, our commitment must be translated into action—in our homes, in our neighborhoods, and in our society.

As we face the new millennium, I believe America has gone a long way down the wrong road. If we ever needed God's help, it is now."

—BILLY GRAHAM,
EXCERPTS FROM HIS MESSAGE UPON RECEIPT OF THE CONGRESSIONAL GOLD MEDAL

TEMPLETON FOUNDATION PRIZE

▶

At a 1982 ceremony in Buckingham Palace, His Royal Highness Prince Philip, Duke of Edinburgh, presented Billy with the Templeton Foundation Prize for Progress in Religion and an award check for $200,000. Billy designated the money to be given for world relief, to train evangelists in developing countries, and to promote evangelism in Britain.

Billy was the second American to receive the award, which was initiated by Sir John M. Templeton to highlight pioneering breakthroughs in religion around the world. The award is equivalent to the Nobel Prize in other fields.

The citation read: "The Reverend Billy Graham has given the church around the world a new hope and has contributed vastly to the wider vision and meaning of evangelism. His cooperation with all denominations of the Christian faith and his determination to involve the statesmen of the world in evangelism has left an indelible mark on Christian history."

◀

In the historic U.S. Capitol rotunda, the Congressional Gold Medal was presented to Billy and Ruth, citing their "outstanding and lasting contributions to morality, racial equality, family, philanthropy, and religion."

"I am honored and humbled to be the recipient of this award today. I thank you from the depth of my heart. You know that I stand before you as an evangelical Christian who is comitted to the beliefs of the New Testament. You do not expect me to be anything other than what I am."
—BILLY GRAHAM,
EXCERPTS FROM MESSAGE AT THE NATIONAL INTERRELIGIOUS AWARD PRESENTATION FROM THE AMERICAN JEWISH COMMITTEE

▲

"I would like to speak of what this nation owes to Billy Graham and how important his ministry is at this time in our history. . . . What Billy Graham has done for millions of Americans is to inspire in individuals religious faith . . . moral strength and character without which a nation . . . cannot be great."
—RICHARD NIXON,
SPEAKING AT BILLY GRAHAM DAY

Commemorating Billy Graham Day in the evangelist's home town, President Nixon and his wife, Pat (left), presented a plaque to the city of Charlotte. When the day was over, Billy confessed to a friend, "It's too much for a country boy. I'm turning it all over to the One to whom it belongs—to the Lord. He's the one who made it possible."

"He has accomplished so many things, inspired so many people, changed so many lives. His message of hope is still ringing, his legacy is everlasting."
—JIM HUNT,
GOVERNOR OF NORTH CAROLINA

▼

Ruth and Billy were welcomed by Governor Jim Hunt, Wayne McDevitt, and Gordon Myers in 1996 when the city of Asheville, North Carolina, named Interstate 240 after Billy.

◄ Father Cuthbert Allen, a Catholic, presented the 1969 Torch of Liberty Award, a Jewish award given by the Anti-Defamation League of B'nai B'rith, to Billy Graham.

"Two thousand years ago Jesus Christ was born. Why is only one percent of Japan Christian?"
—MASURU KISHI,
MAYOR OF OSAKA

. . .

"Perhaps His message has not been made clear. I want to make the teachings of Jesus so clear that every one of you will understand."
—BILLY GRAHAM'S RESPONSE

"We all agree a sense of spirituality is important for us to return to fundamental values, especially for our children. Too often we give honors to athletes who don't deserve them and entertainers who don't need them. It is a great pleasure to give it to someone as deserving as Billy Graham."
—BILL CAMPBELL,
MAYOR OF ATLANTA

▼ Atlanta mayor Bill Campbell conferred honorary citizenship on Billy in 1994.

"To Dr. Billy Graham— In recognition and appreciation of distinguished service and inspiring leadership in preserving liberty, counteracting bigotry, and advancing the cause of human rights, dignity, and equal opportunity. Dr. Graham is one of the greatest friends of the Jewish people and of Israel in the entire Christian world."
—RABBI MARC H. TANENBAUM

► Masuru Kishi, mayor of Osaka, Japan, welcomed Billy and presented him with a key to the city.

Tournament of Roses

Billy has been grand marshal of parades in several cities but one of his biggest thrills came on January 1, 1971, when he fulfilled the role in Pasadena, California's Rose Parade.

Billy Graham has been on numerous lists of important, influential, and most admired people. Americans have ranked him among Gallup's ten most admired men since 1955.

By GEORGE GALL

Gallup Poll

Billy Graham Named to List of Most Admired Men for 41st Time

Evangelist Billy Graham has been the most durable figure in 44 years of polling by The organization, having been by the nation's they ad...

with John Kennedy, who lived for too short a period during those years to have gained a higher position...

When the poll results for the past are combined, Billy Gra... ead of the list. Dw... second... Ronal... l II... cade...

THE EVANGELIST PREACHED LOVE AND SALVATION TO THE MASSES

BILLY GRAHAM

THE LIFE 100 MOST IMPORTANT AMERICANS OF THE 20TH CENTURY

"My primary desire today in having my name inscribed upon this Walk of Fame is that God would receive the glory. I hope someday somebody will come and say, 'Who is Billy Graham? What did he stand for?' Perhaps a child will ask his parents or grandparents, and they will tell him that he was not a celebrity, not a star, but a simple preacher of the Gospel. And they might explain the Gospel to him, and that many might find Christ in that."

—BILLY GRAHAM

▲
Billy received the 1,900th star on Hollywood's Walk of Fame—the first clergyman to be so honored for a radio, television, and film preaching ministry. "I doubt there is anyone in Hollywood who has been seen, heard, or enjoyed by more people than Billy Graham," said Johnny Grant, honorary mayor of Hollywood and chairman of the Walk of Fame committee.

Billy has made two hole-in-one shots while golfing on two different courses— one in 1968 and one in 1969.

▼

"I receive an increasing number of invitations each year to be presented with some award and to speak at a celebration or convention. There must be more than ten thousand awards in America every year, each involving a major speech or response, and sometimes I think I'm invited to all of them! Many open a superb opportunity in a nonreligious setting to present God's Good News, that He loves all of us. And I can only take a handful. . . . I wrote a personal friend this reply: 'The spirit is willing but the calendar is limited and the body is weak. . . . I would appreciate your prayers that the Holy Spirit will teach me how to give priority to the right things and the courage to say no to the rest.'"

—BILLY GRAHAM

Honorary Degrees

Over twenty-five honorary doctoral degrees have been conferred upon Billy by colleges and universities in the United States and five foreign countries, including three degrees from Communist countries in Eastern Europe and one from a Catholic school.

In all, Billy has received doctor's degrees in divinity, humane letters, theology, letters, laws, humanities, literature, Christianity, and sacred oratory. He has been presented with degrees from the countries of South Korea, Hong Kong, Hungary, Poland, Yugoslavia, and the United States.

▶

Billy delivered a commencement address at Florida's Jacksonville University in 1973.

◀

Billy received an honorary doctor of theology degree in 1981 from Debrecen Theological Academy, the oldest Protestant seminary in the world, founded in 1538.

The **MESSAGE**

"To you who are graduating today, it's the beginning of a new stage in life. But what kind of world will you be facing? Today we are putting our hopes in materialism, in technological progress, and in freedom from moral absolutes. They have all failed. They've failed because they've been powerless to change the human heart.

What is the answer? There is hope, if we will turn to God. Saint Augustine declared centuries ago, 'You have created us for Yourself, Oh God, and our hearts are restless until they find rest in You.'"

—BILLY GRAHAM

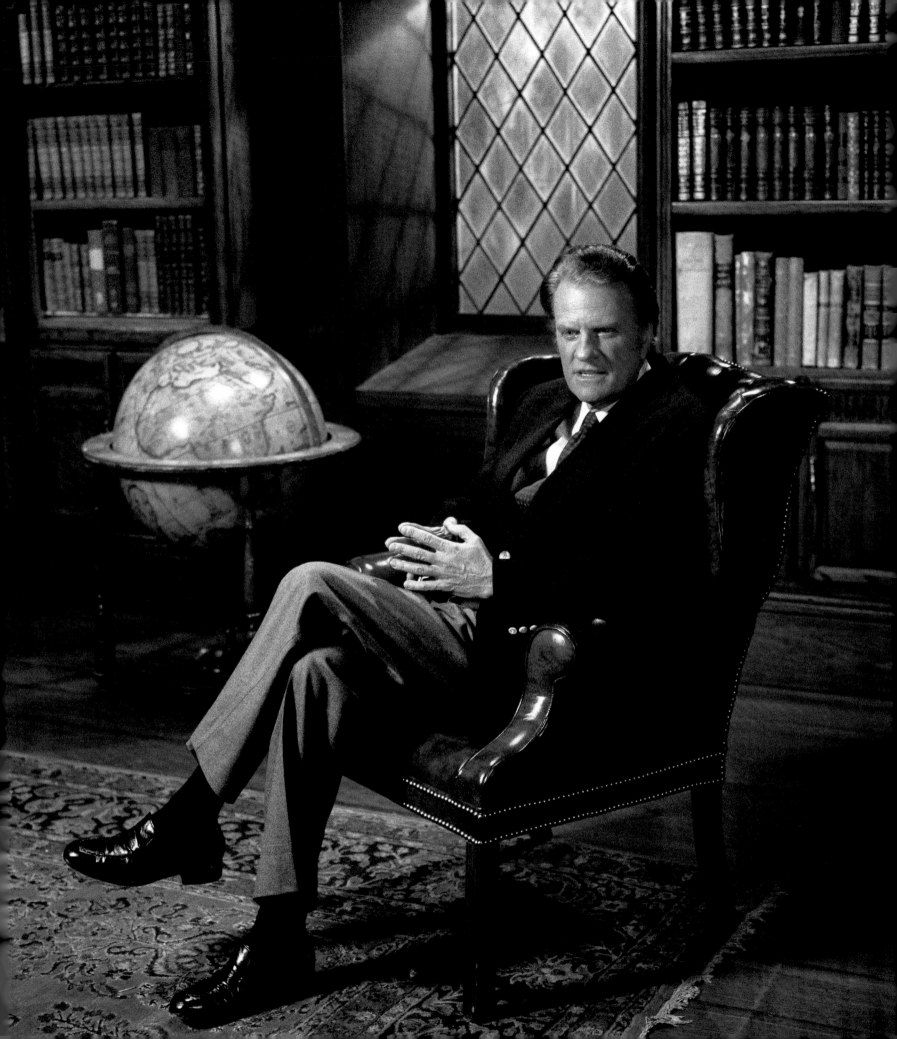

A MESSAGE FROM BILLY GRAHAM

I am often asked, "Do you have any hope for the future of the human race?" Yes, I have hope! I don't think people can live without hope. What oxygen is to the lungs, hope is to our survival in this world. And the Bible is filled with hope.

The United States government has placed a small bronze disk at the Meades Ranch in Osborne County, Kansas, marking the exact geographical center of the United States. From this single scientific reference point, every other position in the United States can be located with precision. I use the Bible as my reference point. I can preach with authority because I believe I am preaching the very Word of God.

I know there is a God. Although I cannot prove it scientifically, the evidence is overwhelming. I look out at the stars, the moon, and the sun (and we now know there are billions of these out in space). I watch the sun come up in the morning and I know our world is moving in perfect precision. The miracle of birth should be proof enough. Something—Someone—beyond ourselves must be behind all this.

But I have another reason why I believe in God—and that is because God has revealed Himself to us! He did this, I believe, in the person of Jesus Christ, whom the Bible calls "God with us" (Matthew 1:23). Do you want to know what God is like? Look at Jesus Christ, as He is revealed in the pages of the Gospels of the New Testament. By His life, death, and resurrection, Jesus demonstrated for all time that God loves us and that there can be hope—hope for new life now, and hope for life after death—as we open ourselves to Him.

But you may say, "What about the millions starving, or all the evil in our world?" To be honest, I don't know the full answer to this puzzle—nor does anyone else. However, the Bible teaches that there is another power at work and it's the power of the devil. Satan is real and is opposed to everything God is doing. Also, we must never overlook the capacity for evil within the human heart.

When a society loses its moral and spiritual moorings, a vacuum is created and it inevitably falls victim to violence, despair, alien ideologies and tyranny. No matter how far we advance scientifically, our hearts are exactly the same. Human nature needs transforming so our hearts won't be controlled by hate and lust and greed. We need new hearts—hearts filled with love and peace and joy. But can this happen?

Suppose I discovered a chemical that, when taken, would make you radiant and happy, give meaning to your life, and assure you of immortal life hereafter. Then suppose I should decide to keep that secret to myself. What would you say about me? Wouldn't you say, "Billy, you're a criminal"?

Well, I have discovered a secret and I'm happy to share it with you. How many times have you wished you could start over again with a clean slate—with a new life? Perhaps you have tried everything else and have not found satisfaction. Resolve right now to allow God to wipe your slate clean, by confessing your sins and asking Christ to give you a brand-new start.

If I didn't know for sure that faith in Christ can transform us, that it gives direction to life and makes life worth living, I'd go back to my little North Carolina farm and spend the rest of my days tilling the soil. But I have seen too many lives untangled and rehabilitated, too many homes reconstructed, too many people who have found peace and joy through simple, humble confession of faith in Christ—ever to doubt that Christ is the answer. May this be your experience as well, as you turn to Christ in humility and faith, and open your life to His love and transforming power.

FINDING GOD'S WILL
FOR YOUR LIFE

"First: The Bible. God will never lead contrary to His word—so get acquainted with the Word of God, the Bible.

Second: Pray. He leads through the illumination of the Holy Spirit in our hearts. I think you can sense God leading by the Holy Spirit, so pray.

Third: Use your talents, money, or whatever you have and be faithful and loyal to the Lord. Not everybody is called into full-time Christian service. But we are called to serve Christ where we are in our community or sphere of influence."

—BILLY GRAHAM

MY HOPE FOR YOU

If you and I could sit together for a few minutes to talk about the future,
I would very much want to share with you the following thought.
The Bible has much to say about the brevity of life and the necessity of preparing for eternity.
I am convinced that only when a man is prepared to die is he also prepared to live. If you want to
know what God is like, then take a look at Jesus Christ. To His disciples Jesus said, 'I am the way
and the truth and the life. No one comes to the Father except through me' (John 14:6).
Surrender your life to the Lord Jesus Christ. Let Him come into your heart and change you.
He can give you a new dimension of living. He will help you achieve your goals as you seek
His guidance. God knows what is best for us. The Bible says, 'Whoever believes in the Son
has eternal life' (John 3:36). I pray that you will make this important decision today.

God Bless You

Billy Graham

BRINGING THE GOOD NEWS

For over fifty years the Billy Graham Evangelistic Association has been at the forefront of proclaiming the Good News of God's love around the world. And for over twenty years, Samaritan's Purse has aided in that effort through international relief.

In this new millennium, it is our desire to continue to use every means available to preach the Good News that God loves sinners and has provided a way for each one of us to be with Him in heaven. By confessing our sins, repenting, and receiving Christ into our hearts and lives by faith we can have eternal life.

Please pray with me that God will continue to guide and direct our every step at the Billy Graham Evangelistic Association and Samaritan's Purse so that the Word of God can be faithfully proclaimed to a lost and dying world.

Our generation is looking for hope, and the only hope for the world is Jesus Christ and Him alone.

With heartfelt thanks,

FRANKLIN GRAHAM

◄

Billy and Franklin both enjoy sharing God's love through Crusade ministries. The two have shared many special moments together during their travels throughout the world.

Samaritan's Purse

For over twenty years, Franklin Graham has served as president of Samaritan's Purse, an international relief and evangelism organization. Samaritan's Purse responds to human suffering in all parts of the world, whether due to war, poverty, disease, or natural disasters. Demonstrating God's love for hurting people, the organization provides food, shelter, medical attention, and other assistance quickly, efficiently, and compassionately.

Samaritan's Purse has cared for millions of suffering people in over 140 countries, while sharing the Good News of God's love. During one year alone, its medical ministry, World Medical Mission, placed 286 doctors and other medical personnel in 21 countries on five continents. The ministry's Operation Christmas Child project brings joy and hope to millions of children in the darkest corners of the world. With simple shoe boxes packed by millions of families and individuals with toys, candy, and other small gifts, Samaritan's Purse provides children with relief from their daily suffering and dreary surroundings. In the year 2000, the ministry delivered more than four million boxes, along with booklets explaining the true meaning of Christmas, to children in 86 countries around the world.

▼

Lui, Sudan, 1998

▲

Nicaragua, 1998

▼

Homestead, Florida, 1992

▲

Honduras, 1999

SAMARITAN'S PURSE®

◄ Beruit, Lebanon,
1982

► Honduras,
1998

"Samaritan's Purse works with local churches and missionaries in strategic locations throughout the world to meet critical needs while sharing the Good News of Jesus Christ."
—FRANKLIN GRAHAM

► Bosnia, 1995

◄ Hanoi, Vietnam,
2000

► Bihac, Bosnia,
1995

Franklin Graham Festivals

As an Associate Evangelist for the Billy Graham Evangelistic Association, Franklin Graham held his first Crusade in March of 1989 in Juneau, Alaska. Since that time, Franklin has held over 80 Crusades on five continents. In the early 90s he changed the name of his meetings from Crusades to Festivals in order to attract a younger generation. "My generation," says Franklin, "is very familiar with 'festivals.' They attend music festivals, art festivals, balloon festivals, and so on. Therefore, in order to effectively reach these people, we offer a familiar setting with music from many top Christian artists and Grammy Award winners where people can hear about and respond to God's love for them."

◄ More than 132,000 persons attended the three-day Festival in Lima, Peru, in 1998.

▲ 54,000 attended the Festival in Raleigh, North Carolina, 1994.

◄ Franklin called for decisions in the rain at the Festival in Sydney, Australia, 1996.

▲ An integrated crowd of 45,000 filled the stadium in Cape Town, South Africa, 1997.

"O Lord, as we come together on this historic and solemn occasion to inaugurate once again a President and Vice President, teach us afresh that power, wisdom, and salvation come only from Your hand. We pray, O Lord, for President-elect George W. Bush and Vice President-elect Richard B. Cheney, to whom You have entrusted leadership of this nation at this moment in history. Give our new President and all who advise him CALMNESS in the face of storms, ENCOURAGEMENT in the face of frustration, and HUMILITY in the face of success."

—FRANKLIN GRAHAM

EXCERPTS FROM THE INVOCATION AT THE 54TH PRESIDENTIAL INAUGURATION, JANUARY 20, 2001, WASHINGTON, D.C.

PROCLAIMING
Jesus Christ until He comes.

FOR HALF A CENTURY,

THE BILLY GRAHAM EVANGELISTIC ASSOCIATION

HAS WORKED TO PREACH THE GOSPEL OF

OUR LORD JESUS CHRIST FROM ONE END OF THIS

EARTH TO THE OTHER IN ORDER TO WIN AS MANY

PEOPLE AS POSSIBLE TO CHRIST BEFORE HE RETURNS.

We invite you to partner with us in taking the

Good News into the new millennium.

If you would like to know more about how

you can be involved, contact us today.

Phone: 877-2GRAHAM (1-877-247-2426)

Mail: P.O. Box 779, Minneapolis, MN 55440

Internet: www.billygraham.org